# REBUILDING ROMANIA

*Research by the Energy and Environmental Programme is supported by generous contributions of finance and professional advice from the following organizations:*

*AEA Technology • Amerada Hess • Arthur D Little*
*Ashland Oil • British Coal • British Nuclear Fuels*
*British Petroleum • European Commission*
*Department of Trade and Industry • Eastern Electricity*
*Enterprise Oil • ENRON Europe • Exxon • LASMO*
*Mobil • National Grid • National Power • Nuclear Electric*
*Overseas Development Administration • PowerGen*
*Saudi Aramco • Shell • Statoil • St Clements Services*
*Texaco • Total • Tokyo Electric Power Company*

# REBUILDING ROMANIA

## Energy, Efficiency and the Economic Transition

**Walt Patterson**

THE ROYAL INSTITUTE OF
INTERNATIONAL AFFAIRS
**Energy and Environmental Programme**

EARTHSCAN
**Earthscan Publications Ltd, London**

First published in Great Britain in 1994 by
Royal Institute of International Affairs, 10 St James's Square, London SW1Y 4LE and
Earthscan Publications Ltd, 120 Pentonville Road, London N1 9JN

Distributed in North America by
The Brookings Institution, 1775 Massachusetts Avenue NW,
Washington DC 20036-2188

A catalogue record for this book is available from the British Library.

Paperback: ISBN 1 85383 207 3

The Royal Institute of International Affairs is an independent body which promotes the rigorous study of international questions and does not express opinions of its own. The opinions expressed in this publication are the responsibility of the author.

Earthscan Publications Limited is an editorially independent subsidary of Kogan Page Limited and publishes in association with the International Institute of Environment and Development and the World Wide Fund for Nature.

Printed and bound in Great Britain by
Biddles Limited, Guildford and King's Lynn
Cover by Visible Edge
Map source: original artwork by Pete Sonderskov, *The Economist*
Cover illustration by Harry Brockway

# Contents

**Tables**

# Figures

# Box

# Preface

Romania, notes Walt Patterson in this book, is a country worth knowing better. The same could be said of many of the countries of central and east Europe, but Romania has some features of unique interest to those concerned with the energy and environmental transition in the region. Romania had the world's first oil industries, and it remains the only country in the region with significant reserves of all three fossil fuels and hydro power. It has a long tradition of engineering excellence, including in the energy field, eclipsed but not extinguished during the Ceaușescu era. And its emergence from that era was uniquely abrupt, with none of the loosening and opening up that preceded the fall of communism elsewhere in Europe. Partly because of this, perhaps, the Romanian energy transition has not received the same degree of study and interaction with western Europe. Studies of energy supply have only recently been published, and this is the first which concentrates upon energy use.

The study was initiated, led and brought together through the personal enthusiasm and dedication of Walt Patterson, and we are grateful to the UK Overseas Development Administration for providing the financial support required. But as well as being indebted to the ODA for their backing and encouragement, Walt is at pains to point out that it is not just his study, nor a UK view. He has sought to stimulate, translate and present the views of a number of Romanian experts – learning Romanian and forging close friendships with the Romanians involved in the process. The resulting book, published simultaneously in Romanian, is intended as much for Romania and other east European countries as it is for the west, and for all audiences it carries important messages about the strategies required to deliver the gains that engineering studies of energy efficiency promise. In pursuing the project to completion, Walt Patterson has broken new ground not only in aspects of the subject matter, but perhaps more widely concerning approaches to energy policy research in the region.

*September 1994*                                   Dr Michael Grubb
                              Head, Energy and Environmental Programme

# Author's Foreword

The fall of the Ceauşescu regime in December 1989 plunged Romania into a transition more abrupt than in any other country of eastern Europe. A crucial dimension of this transition has been its interaction with Romania's energy systems. The ensuing five years have seen a number of reports on energy issues in Romania. This study, however, differs from earlier studies in two important respects: first, it focuses not on supplying fuels and electricity, but on using them; and second, the analyses and commentary here presented are based in the main not on the views of visiting foreign specialists but on those of Romanian energy specialists themselves.

The study was carried out under the aegis of the Energy and Environmental Programme of the Royal Institute of International Affairs, an independent non-governmental policy research institute in London, UK, between April 1993 and August 1994, with the support of the Overseas Development Administration of the UK government. Walt Patterson, Senior Research Fellow in the Energy and Environmental Programme, drafted the text here presented, and bears final responsibility for its content. The text, however, endeavours to represent the data, commentary and opinions of a team of seven senior Romanian energy specialists, who worked on the study together with the author for sixteen months: Dr Jean Constantinescu, Magdalena Cuciureanu, Alexandru Florescu, Professor Calin Mihaileanu, Gabriel Poenaru, and Vasile Rugina, all of the Energy Research and Modernizing Institute (ICEMENERG), and Violeta Kogalniceanu of the Romanian Energy Conservation Agency (ARCE). Where no another source is cited, the Romanian data and information in this report have been provided by ICEMENERG and ARCE. In the course of the study the author visited Romania on five occasions, and six members of the Romanian team visited the UK in September 1993, for meetings at the Royal Institute of International Affairs and at the Energy Technology Support Unit of the UK Department of Trade and Industry. Between visits, study participants in the UK and Romania maintained close contact by telephone, fax, courier and post.

One aim of the study was for Romanian energy specialists to acquire more experience of recent innovations in energy thinking, including environmental concerns and end-use aspects, especially energy efficiency, and to explore how such innovations might be applied to Romanian energy, in the context of the economic transition. Another aim was to analyze the Romanian energy situation through Romanian eyes. Accordingly, meetings and discussions were conducted largely in Romanian, and much of the material prepared by the Romanian team members was drafted in Romanian. Initial discussions, to be sure, were somewhat tentative; the Romanian team members tended to defer to the foreigner in their midst, and were perhaps too polite to express conflicting views or to disagree among themselves. As the work progressed, however, at least in part because everyone was speaking Romanian, discussions grew progressively more animated, on occasion even heated, an unambiguously healthy and encouraging evolution. At length, in the closing stages of the study, the Romanian team stressed that opinions as to the most appropriate ways to deal with energy issues in Romania differ within Romania and even among team members themselves. Moreover, as the study itself makes clear, ICEMENERG and ARCE, although important participants, are only two out of many organizations actively involved in Romanian energy issues; and every such organization, whether Romanian or foreign, has its own interests and its own agenda. What follows does not, therefore, strive to represent a consensus or a final judgement on Romanian energy, much less a comprehensive analysis, but rather a range of significant considerations and an array of possible policy options that Romanians themselves, and their elected representatives, may wish to explore and – if the options appear feasible and desirable – to implement, perhaps in cooperation with foreign colleagues.

Although Romania in the 1990s is one of the lesser-known countries of central Europe, its rich resources, pivotal location and long history of culture and achievement deserve wider recognition. Despite the problems it now faces, Romania has the potential to become again, as it was between the 1860s and the 1930s, a locus of democratic political stability in a volatile region, and an important trading partner on the international scene. Moreover, energy issues in Romania have a great deal in common with those in other economies in transition; and the Romanian example may be instructive. This study is therefore addressed to both specialist and non-specialist readers, and endeavours to set Romanian energy issues in a broader context. Chapters 1-4 describe Romania and the current energy scene there. Chapter 1 offers a brief historical overview. Chapter 2 considers today's Romania, and the present and projected structure of Romanian energy supply and use. Chapter 3 describes key energy institutions for this study, and their activities. Chapter 4 surveys the financial dimension. Chapters 5-7 consider important areas of energy activity and policy, and identify opportunities for improvement. Chapter 5 discusses the concept of energy efficiency in the context of Romania, and how it might be promoted. Chapter 6 considers investments in efficiency, including technical opportunities, especially those arising in end-uses of energy. Chapter 7 reviews current international cooperative activities in the energy field, and how they might be extended. Chapter 8 sums up, reviewing possible policy measures to foster improvements. Appendix 1 lists concise policy proposals from Romanian energy specialists; Appendices 2 and 3 list relevant Romanian organizations with their contact details.

Published in both English and Romanian, this study aims to involve more non-Romanians in Romania, and to involve more Romanians in energy issues – especially energy efficiency, in which every citizen can participate. It aims to stimulate interest in the potential for improvements, and to encourage both Romanians and non-Romanians to take advantage of the opportunities.

# Acknowledgements

To all my Romanian colleagues, and especially to my team members Dr Jean Constantinescu, Magdalena Cuciureanu, Alexandru Florescu, Professor Calin Mihaileanu, Gabriel Poenaru, Vasile Rugina and Violeta Kogalniceanu, I would like to extend my warmest thanks for their cordial and enthusiastic participation in this study, and for their unstinting hospitality. I also want to thank Romanian friends Adrian and Christina Maraşescu, Catalin and Lily Baetoniu, Monica Maraşescu and Liana and Eugen Pop, and their families, for their kindness, generosity and absolute reliability; they made me look forward eagerly to every trip to Romania.

I am grateful to the Overseas Development Administration of the UK government for its unobtrusive, reliable backing and finance for my work with my Romanian colleagues. In the final stages of preparing this text I also had the benefit of comments from a study group at the Royal Institute of International Affairs, and from specialist readers including Professor Aureliu Leca of the Polytechnic University of Bucureşti, Tudor Constantinescu and Mark Velody of the Ministry of Industries in Bucureşti, François Jonquières of Electricité de France on secondment to RENEL, and Ian Brown of the Hungary-EC Energy Centre. I would like to thank all the study group participants and readers for their help; their critiques and suggestions have been invaluable. Michael Grubb, Head of the Energy and Environmental Programme, Programme Manager Matthew Tickle and Programme Administrator Nicole Dando have given me unfailing support and encouragement during the long gestation of this study; to them, too, my warmest thanks. Jonathan Stern first proposed that I undertake the study, and invited me to do so under the aegis of the Royal Institute of International Affairs. Neither of us could have foreseen how far the proposal would lead; my gratitude to him for his vote of confidence and his steadying presence. At Christmas 1989, watching the first television reports from Bucureşti, my wife Cleone insisted that I find her some Romanian friends. At her urging, I did even better; I found us an entire country. As our Romanian friends would say, 'Mulţumesc foarte mult!' – 'Thank you very much!'

*August 1994*                                                                 Walt Patterson

# Executive Summary

Since the fall of the Ceauşescu dictatorship in December 1989, Romania's international image has done the country no favours. But Romania's situation in the 1990s is by no means as black as it has been painted. Its location, its resources, its history and its technical and cultural achievements give Romania the potential to become a valuable political and commercial partner at a strategic crossroads of the world. One important key to this potential is Romania's energy.

Historically, Romania has been a major producer of oil and natural gas; it also has its own coal, lignite and hydroelectricity. Romanian engineering long had an international reputation for excellence, eclipsed only in the 1980s; and Romania still has many highly skilled scientists and engineers, notably energy specialists. But Romania's energy systems suffered badly at the hands of the communist central planners. After 1982, Ceauşescu determined to make the country self-sufficient in everything, including energy. To pay off Romania's foreign debt, everything with export value had to be exported; almost nothing could be imported. As a result, oil- and gas-fields were run down; equipment could not be maintained; and the entire infrastructure of the country deteriorated. Prices for fuels, electricity and heat were set arbitrarily low and supplies allocated centrally, mostly to heavy industry. The efficiency of energy use plummeted; households were left shivering in the dark. Under central planning and enforced isolation, the Romanian currency, the leu, became almost meaningless.

After the fall of Ceauşescu, Romania, like other former communist countries, set in train the transition to a democratic society with a market economy. Unlike most of its neighbours, however, Romania had not begun gradual liberalization in the late 1980s – on the contrary. Romania had no prior preparation for the transition; and it proved slower and more arduous than many initially expected. Nevertheless it got under way, with the new Romanian parliament passing laws to establish the necessary framework. The old communist ministries for fuel and electricity were turned into state-owned bodies with some independence, under an overall Ministry for Industries. The government also set up the Romanian Energy Conservation Agency, ARCE, with a brief to promote energy efficiency.

As Romania began to rebuild its international links, other national governments and international organizations undertook studies of Romania's energy sector; and major firms began to participate. But these activities focused on fuel and electricity supply, paying little attention to the potential for using them more efficiently. When energy efficiency did enter the picture, it appeared to be considered primarily in terms of investment, rather than of energy services and energy management.

By 1994 the Romanian government had increased energy prices, eliminating most subsidies; but the government, not the market, still fixed prices. Realistic energy prices based on the cost of supply are a prerequisite for improving energy efficiency, by making energy waste expensive. But prices alone are not a sufficient stimulus, especially in a country with a recent history like that of Romania. The very concept of 'energy conservation' has been deeply tainted by its usage under Ceauşescu, as propaganda seeking to justify depriving people of basic necessities like warmth and light for the sake of industrial output. The potential to improve Romania's energy efficiency is substantial. If this potential is to be realized, a programme of measures appropriate to Romania will need to be developed and implemented. International cooperation will be valuable; but Romanians themselves must make the essential decisions.

The first requirement is to awaken public awareness of the possibilities – not 'for the good of the country', as under Ceauşescu, but to benefit individual Romanians personally, to better their living and working conditions. Accurate and accessible information must be provided: about what can be done, who can do it and how, how much it will cost and how much it will save – not just energy but money. Properly developed, a national Romanian strategy for energy efficiency could involve Romanians all over the country, at home and at work, in the factory and on the farm, acting on their own initiative to improve their own lives. The initial stages would not entail investment, or major expenditure, but concentrate on so-called 'no-cost, low-cost' measures. They would emphasize 'good housekeeping', like turning off lights and equipment when not in use, repairing faults, and so on – helping to recreate the sense of personal responsibility and initiative so long suppressed under Ceauşescu. Information, education and publicity, carefully shaped to avoid the pitfalls of the old communist propaganda, would be essential.

A preliminary examination of particular end-use sectors suggests a wealth of opportunities for more specific measures, and for targeted investments. Buildings, district heating, lighting and industrial motors all offer major potential for improving efficiency. So do many industries. Each of these sectors needs to be studied separately, to establish the costs and benefits of possible measures, and the priorities for action. Industry still dominates total energy use, but the pattern is changing rapidly. Targeting must also reflect probable rapid growth in energy use in households and for transport. The true status of and prospects for different industrial facilities, for instance, can be established only through on-site audits, within the context of market reforms – including realistic assessment of whether a facility has a long-term future under market competition, and how much improving energy efficiency could improve its overall prospects. In the absence of such specific assessments, investment, however well intentioned, may be premature and misguided.

A programme to promote energy efficiency in Romania could be a valuable accompaniment to government action in pursuit of economic reform and to energy and environmental legislation. It could also influence the evolution of the fuel and electricity supply sectors in a beneficial direction. Both ARCE and the electricity authority RENEL, which also supplies heat through extensive district heating networks, could play important roles in fostering higher efficiency, by preparing and disseminating information, providing training and – under suitable groundrules – supporting investment.

Some international cooperation with Romania on energy is already under way. Energy efficiency offers many opportunities for its expansion, not only at government level but also between companies and other non-governmental organizations; not only nationally but also regionally and locally, embracing also other former Comecon countries. At this initial stage the most important coin of exchange is not money but ideas. Sharing experience and comparing notes could benefit both Romanians and non-Romanians. Romania has the resources and the skills to become again a stable and prosperous member of the international community. Promoting energy efficiency could accelerate the process.

# Chapter 1

## Introduction: A Country Worth Knowing Better

### 1.1 Romania for beginners

Romanians delight in telling sardonic jokes against themselves. One they often recount to foreign friends goes like this: 'When God made Romania, He looked at all the riches He had bestowed, and decided He had overdone it. So He populated the country with Romanians'. The rueful humour is typically Romanian; and it conveys, to be sure, more than a germ of truth. Over the centuries, Romania's miseries have often been at least partly self-inflicted. But the same can be said of many other countries; and Romania has had more than its share of maladministration from outside its borders.

Romania is one of the crossroads of the world. It lies at the southeast corner of Europe, the southwest corner of Asia, the northwest corner of the Middle East and the northeast corner of the Mediterranean. Throughout its long history it has experienced heavy traffic from all four directions, usually to its disadvantage. In the course of two millennia the rich terrain on the west coast of the Black Sea has found itself under the Roman empire, barbarian hordes, the Ottoman empire and its Greek phanariots, and the Austro-Hungarian empire. During the Second World War it was invaded by Nazi Germany. In the last decade of the twentieth century Romania is emerging yet again from darkness – from more than four decades of communism, originally imposed by Moscow under Stalin, that became the brutal dictatorship of Nicolae Ceauşescu. In December 1989, in the startling culmination of a remarkable year, Ceauşescu was overthrown; and Romania once more began the painful struggle to rebuild. In the 1990s, as it shakes off the shackles of isolation and misrule, it is eager for international contact, cooperation and participation. Its abundant resources, its strategic location and its people – tough and tenacious, as might be expected, but also hospitable, generous and disconcertingly funny – make Romania a country worth knowing better.

Romania, with a land area of 238,000 square kilometres, is the largest country in central Europe. It is bordered on the southeast by the Black Sea, on the south by Bulgaria, on the southwest by Serbia, on the northwest by Hungary, on the north and northeast by Ukraine and on the east by Moldova. The Danube River flows south between Romania and Serbia, then curves east between Romania and Bulgaria before swinging north and east through Romania and spreading across a sprawling delta as it reaches the Black Sea. The Carpathian Mountains rise in a majestic arc that separates the historic provinces of Moldavia in the east and Wallachia in the south from Transilvania in the northwest. As well as the spectacular scenery of the Carpathians and the endless beaches of the Black Sea, Romania includes some of the richest agricultural land in Europe, whose black soil can be 10 metres deep. According to the census of January 1992, some 22.8 million people now live within Romania's borders, including 89.4% ethnic Romanian, 7.1% ethnic Hungarian, 1.8% Gipsy and 0.5% German. The capital city of Romania is known in English as Bucharest, but its correct Romanian spelling is Bucureşti. Some 2.1 million people – almost 10% of the population – live in the municipality of Bucureşti, much the largest urban area in Romania. The port city of Constanţa on the Black Sea has 350,000 inhabitants, and six other cities – Iaşi, Cluj, Timişoara, Craiova, Braşov and Galaţi – each have upwards of 300,000. The remaining Romanians – most of the population – live in smaller cities and towns, and in the thousands of villages scattered across the countryside.

Romania abounds in natural resources. As well as its lush agricultural land and sea coast it has forests, a wide range of minerals and the most complete portfolio of energy resources in central Europe – coal and lignite, petroleum, natural gas and hydroelectricity, as well as a nuclear power station still under construction. Romania's climate is as varied as its topography, ranging from the mid-continental in Transilvania, with cold, snowy winters and long hot summers, to alpine in the mountains, to milder and less extreme along the Danube and the Black Sea. Although Bucureşti is in the southeast it can have heavy snow in the winter and scorching sun in the summer. These climatic conditions, with their implications for building design and energy use, have an important bearing on Romanian energy, as will be discussed below.

**Figure 1.1 Map of Romania and surrounding area**

Source: Original map drawn by Pete Sonderskov, *The Economist*.

To outsiders, the Romanian language may come as a surprise. Although Romania is bordered entirely by Slavic and Magyar countries, Romanian is a Romance language closely akin to Italian, Spanish, Portuguese and French. Indeed, Romanian scholars have argued that Romanian most closely resembles the language spoken by the ancient Romans, when Roman legions controlled the province on the Danube they called Dacia. To anyone acquainted with other Romance languages, Romanian will present few difficulties; even a monoglot anglophone looking at a list of words in Romanian will probably be able to guess the meaning of half of them. Even more surprising to a visitor in the 1990s is the number of Romanians who speak English. In the nineteenth and early twentieth century, the second language of educated Romanians tended to be French, and Romanian culture was closely allied to that of France. After the communist takeover in 1947, Russian became compulsory in schools; but in the early 1960s, when Romania's governing communists began to take a political line at odds with that of the Soviet Union, one consequence was to encourage the teaching of English in Romanian schools. In the 1980s Ceauşescu's mounting paranoia and obsession with national self-sufficiency led him to decree the virtual closure of Romania's borders; only a favoured few could travel beyond them, and ordinary Romanians were cut off almost completely from the world outside. But foreign radio and television could still penetrate, and became regular if illicit listening and viewing – often in English. The advent of video further fostered the process. American films were much in demand; one Romanian colleague has described how all the flats in an entire block would be connected by cable to a single video in the building, so that all the tenants could watch the same bootleg cassette copy of an American film simultaneously. In the 1990s, in Romania as in any other country, familiarity with the local language is a considerable asset to a foreign visitor; but in almost any commercial or professional context the visitor will also encounter Romanians eager to practise their English.

At the same time, any visitor to Romania who shows an interest will find Romanians proud of their own language and culture, despite the bleakness of their recent past. Invited to a Romanian home, a visitor may find the building itself a grim, shabby concrete monstrosity, unprepossessing in the extreme; but when the flat door opens the interior is lined with books and *objets d'art*, cherished in the family for generations; the furnishings will be old-fashioned but immaculately clean and cared for, and among the books will be dozens if not hundreds by Romanian writers, in Romanian – fiction, drama, poetry, history, art, science, philosophy, a profusion of which the world beyond Romania is largely unaware. Among Romanian writers perhaps only the national poet, Mihai Eminescu, and the playwright Eugen Ionescu are familiar to non-Romanians, and Ionescu changed the spelling of his name to Ionesco when he moved to Paris. The same is true for Romanian artists and composers – perhaps only the sculptor Constantin Brancuşi and the composer George Enescu are familiar to non-Romanians. Romania is a cultural treasure-trove waiting to be discovered.

## 1.2 Romanian history in brief

Romanians trace their history to pre-Roman times. The ancient Greeks had colonies in towns in the southeast region known as Dobrogea, among them Tomiş (now Constanţa), Callatis (now Mangalia) and Istria. In Constanţa and elsewhere Roman artefacts and structures are still preserved. Curiously enough, although speaking a Romance language and with a culture heavily influenced by Italy and France, Romania is not a Roman Catholic country but an Orthodox Christian country, like Russia, Ukraine and Greece: another consequence of its pivotal geographical location between east and west. Much of its most striking architecture, including that of cathedrals and monasteries, bears obvious evidence of eastern origins, especially Byzantine – but often with distinctively Romanian features, notably the painted monasteries in northern Moldavia. Among the great leaders of Romania's history, two in particular are still commemorated in statues and street-names: Stefan Cel Mare or Stephen the Great, who ruled Moldavia from 1457 to 1504, and Mihai Viteazul or Michael the Brave, prince of Wallachia from 1593 to 1601. Non-Romanians may, however, be nonplussed to learn the identity of another historical leader revered by most Romanians. This is Vlad Ţepeş, who ruled Wallachia intermittently between 1448 and 1476. Ţepeş was called Vlad the Impaler – better known around the world as Dracula. The image of Dracula, the vampire, the undead personification of evil, was created by the British writer Bram Stoker, on the basis of research in the British Museum Reading Room. Stoker never visited Transilvania, and his creation has very little to do with the historical figure of Vlad Ţepeş. To be sure, Vlad Ţepeş acquired his nickname of Vlad the Impaler as a result of his fondness for impaling wrongdoers on spikes. The practice was, however, not uncommon in that part of the world at that time; and the wrongdoers whom Ţepeş impaled were usually unfaithful landowners and thieves. Romanian historians consider Ţepeş to be a comparatively enlightened leader and ruler, strong but just. In the 1990s, nevertheless, Romanians recognize that the fictional figure of Dracula is world-famous, if for somewhat unsavoury reasons. Although Vlad Ţepeş never in fact lived there, Romanians are now promoting Castle Bran, a gloomily impressive stronghold in the Carpathian Mountains, as 'Dracula's castle', for tourist purposes. If the Dracula connection persuades foreign travellers to visit the Carpathians, they may find that the scenery repays the visit even without vampires.

Modern Romania can be said to date from 1866. In 1859 the principalities of Wallachia and Moldavia had agreed to unite. In 1866 the politicians of the united principalities, seeking to bypass domestic factional disputes, invited the young German Prince Carol of Hohenzollern to assume the monarchy. In 1881 he was proclaimed King Carol I of Romania. From the 1860s until the 1930s Romania enjoyed a long period of relative political calm and increasing prosperity, as a democratic country with an elected parliament under a succession of prime ministers drawn from the two main political parties, the liberals and the conservatives. Carol I died in October 1914, shortly after the outbreak of the First World War, and his nephew Ferdinand assumed the throne. Romania strove to remain neutral; but after being invaded by Germany and Bulgaria, Romanian forces eventually fought back. As a result, in 1920, in the aftermath of the war and the break-up of the Austro-Hungarian empire, the Treaty of Trianon joined to Romania the province of Transilvania and the territories northwest of the Carpathians, whose population had long been predominantly Romanian, giving the country almost the geographical shape it has in the 1990s. Basarabia and Bucovina in the northeast, part of the old Romanian province of Moldavia, were also rejoined to Romania in 1919-20, but were to undergo further changes of borders and political control. In the 1920s, Romania united all the Romanian provinces in a unitary state whose population was 88% Romanian.

In the 1920s the thriving cultural life of Bucureşti, its theatres, concert halls, parks, coffee-shops and restaurants, won it the name of 'Little Paris'. Political storm clouds, however, were gathering. King Ferdinand died in 1927. In 1926 his son Carol, caught up in controversy over his mistress, had been forced to renounce the throne, leaving it to his young son Mihai, guided by a regency. But, following the world economic crisis of 1929-30 and because of the indecision of the political leadership, Carol returned in 1930, repealed the law of 1926 and took the throne as Carol II. Beginning in the 1920s a movement called the Iron Guard, with ideology, behaviour and uniforms akin to those of the National Socialists in Germany and the Fascists in Italy, had risen to prominence in Romania. At first suppressed, it gained in power, backed by the Nazis in Germany. Political and diplomatic tensions increased until, in 1938, Carol II dissolved parliament in what came to be called a 'palace coup' and set up a 'royal dictatorship'. As the Romanian historian Vlad Georgescu observed in his superb study *Istoria Romanilor (The Romanians: A History)*, first published in 1985, 'The democracy, imperfect as it had been, was replaced by an authoritarian regime for the first time in the country's modern history'.[1] The point is worth stressing. Despite Romania's difficulties in the 1990s, many older Romanians still remember a time when the country was a thriving and prosperous modern society. Romania needs to restore such conditions; but it does not need to create them for the first time.

Carol II found himself in a power struggle with the Iron Guard. When the Second World War broke out, Romania again tried to remain neutral. However, in 1940, after the fall of France, Hitler made a covert agreement with Stalin, ceding to the Soviet Union control over Basarabia and northern Bucovina, subsequently incorporated into the Soviet Union as the Soviet Socialist Republic of Moldavia. As Nazi forces pressed south and east, Romania had to yield northern Transilvania, giving Germany easy access to the Ploieşti oilfields. Hostile political forces led by the Iron Guard forced Carol to give General Ion Antonescu dictatorial power; and Antonescu at once forced Carol to abdicate and leave Romania. His nineteen-year-old son Mihai resumed the throne he had held as a child between 1927 and 1930; but Antonescu held the power. One of his first moves was to crush the Iron Guard.

Antonescu ruled until 1944, as Romania was buffeted by the war. Romanian forces kept German forces from occupying Bucureşti and other Romanian cities. At length, on 23 August 1944, with the support of the leaders of the democratic political parties, King Mihai commanded that Romanian arms join the side of the allies, after arresting Antonescu who had refused to issue the command. The next day German forces attacked Bucureşti; but Romanian and allied forces – especially the Red Army – counterattacked. Romanian forces liberated Bucureşti; on 31 August the Red Army entered the city. It was to be there for many years. According to Georgescu,[2] in October 1944 Winston Churchill proposed to Stalin a division of the region into spheres of influence: the Soviet Union would get 90% of Romania, 50% of Yugoslavia

---

[1] Vlad Georgescu, *Istoria Romanilor*, Humanitas, Bucuresti 1992; English edition *The Romanians: A History*, I. B. Tauris, 1992. Much of the historical background in this chapter is drawn from Georgescu.

[2] Ibid.

and 10% of Greece, the remainder being for Britain and 'the others'. The Yalta peace conference in 1945 sealed this arrangement; but the Soviet Union soon transformed its 90% of Romania into total control.

Since its inception in the 1920s, the Romanian Communist Party had been a small fringe organization. However, the failure of the old mainstream political parties to accept Mihai's invitation to form a government left the way open for the communists to move in. Party membership expanded from less than 1000 in 1944 to more than 800,000 by December 1947. Moscow favoured the leadership of Gheorghe Gheorghiu-Dej; and after a period of political confusion and turmoil, and heavy pressure from Moscow and Soviet troops in Romania, an election in November 1946 – its results widely declared to be falsified – put the communists into power. By the end of 1947 they had swept away their erstwhile political allies. On 30 December 1947 they forced the young King Mihai to abdicate, and declared the country the 'People's Republic of Romania'. On 3 January 1948 Mihai left Romania for exile in London. The communists under Gheorghiu-Dej at once set about destroying their opponents, executing many and imprisoning many more, including the former leaders of Romania's democratic political parties. They confiscated land, and embarked on a programme of 'collectivization' of farms like that carried out by Stalin in the Soviet Union; in the process the party itself claimed to have arrested 80,000 peasants, and the true number was probably much higher. Collectivization of agriculture was gradual but inexorable, and it was completed by 1962. From 1948 through the 1950s the communists took over banks, industries, shops, restaurants, medical practices and private houses – indeed, essentially the whole economy of Romania. Objections were met with immediate and sweeping repression. Through the 1950s, under the Stalinist Gheorghiu-Dej, the cultural life of the country was submerged in what Vlad Georgescu called 'pure Marxist orthodoxy', with Soviet Russia as the model and ideal. But an unexpected change was in the offing.

Moscow under Khrushchev wanted to keep Romania an essentially agrarian country within the Council for Mutual Economic Assistance (CMEA or Comecon). In 1958, however, after Soviet troops were withdrawn from Romania, the Romanian leadership embarked on liberalization of trade with western countries, and also sought to establish heavy industry. Moreover, from 1960 onwards, Romania's foreign policy began to deviate more and more from the Moscow line, opening steadily towards the west. In the early 1960s Gheorghiu-Dej reversed the earlier policy of stressing the Russian connection; Russian cultural institutions were closed, Russian street-names removed and street demonstrations against Moscow fomented. Gheorghiu-Dej was taking Romania in a new direction, towards autonomy.

In March 1965, however, Gheorghiu-Dej died suddenly. As his successor he had designated Nicolae Ceauşescu. At first Ceauşescu was only one of a collective leadership; by 1967, however, Ceauşescu, who was already secretary-general of the Romanian Communist Party, had bypassed a ban on holding multiple offices, and had become also president of the State Council. Under Ceauşescu the Council gradually took over the functions of government. In the late 1960s liberalization was the prevailing trend: the government allowed private restaurants to open and private homes to be built, reduced police surveillance and lifted restrictions on foreign travel. Russian in schools was replaced by English, French and German. Romanian cultural activities took on fresh vitality.

In foreign policy, Romania adopted an independent stance that was hailed by the west. Romania maintained relations with Israel after the 1967 Arab-Israeli war, established diplomatic links with Federal Germany and refused to send troops to quell the 1968 uprising in Czechoslovakia; it did not take part in Warsaw Pact manoeuvres or allow them on Romanian territory. Visitors to Bucureşti included Charles de Gaulle and Richard Nixon. On the other hand, despite the liberal indications, Ceauşescu was tightening central control. In 1970, at his behest, the government revised the five-year plan already promulgated, transferred investment away from agriculture into heavy industry and launched major projects of doubtful value, notably a canal linking the Danube to the Black Sea. Steel, oil-refining and petrochemical industries were expanded, although Romania had no iron ore, its oil output was declining and the price of imports was rising. After 1970, Ceauşescu fell out with his colleagues in the leadership, in part over the question of the pace and direction of industrialization; and Ceauşescu emerged the winner. In 1973 his wife Elena came into the picture, amid the first signs of a growing 'cult of personality', centred on Ceauşescu, that was to become all-pervasive. Nevertheless, in the late 1960s and early 1970s, Ceauşescu's posture of independence from the Soviet Union won him enthusiastic support from western Europe and the US, who were keen to encourage any split in the communist bloc of the Cold War. In their eagerness to do business with the 'maverick' Ceauşescu, western countries turned a blind eye to his own ruthless brand of repression, capricious and brutal, inflicted by the state security police, the Securitate.

From 1974 onwards, Ceauşescu's ambitions for industrialization caused progressively more severe dislocation of the Romanian economy. But western credits continued to be available for industrial investment, and Romania drew on them ever more heavily. By 1982, the burden of debt to the west had reached US$13 billion; and Ceauşescu reacted with a drastic shift of policy that made the daily lives of Romanians yet more arduous. He decided that Romania would stand alone in the world; to defend Romania's national independence the country must pay off all its foreign debts. The result was disastrous for the country, its people and its economy. Agriculture continued to decline, creating chronic food shortages. Steep price rises and rationing were imposed, 'making the citizens of socialist Romania worse off in the eighties than they were in the sixties – and with far less hope that the situation would be remedied', according to Vlad Georgescu.[3] Imports were summarily cut to the bone. Suddenly industries could no longer purchase spare parts for the western technology they had imported in the 1960s and 1970s, nor even journals and technical books. Anything whatever with export value had to be exported, no matter how urgent the need within Romania. Romanian specialists somehow managed to stay abreast of technical developments, and even undertook energy efficiency measures akin to those under way in western Europe and elsewhere. But the quality of Romanian industrial production, already deteriorating, plummeted further as a consequence of inadequate maintenance of plant and shortages of the imported materials required. Most western export markets faded away.

The problems were compounded by Ceauşescu's burgeoning megalomania. In southwest Bucureşti, one of the most colourful and appealing quarters of the city was obliterated to make way for a garish monument to this obsession, called with callous irony the 'Casa Poporului' or 'House of the People'. It was an unimaginably huge architectural aberration, set on a rise of ground in the middle of a vast clearing, with a grandiose avenue leading up to it, fountains

---

[3] Ibid.

along the central boulevard and looming blocks to either side – all grotesquely out of keeping with that of the old Bucureşti which remained. Diverting already scarce resources to overblown extravaganzas like the Casa Poporului and its surroundings – projects estimated to have devoured as much as 10% of Romania's gross national product in the 1980s[4] – placed intolerable pressure on the country's crumbling economy. Although the boulevard was lined with elaborate lamp standards, here as elsewhere throughout Romania the darkness was growing ever deeper, not only metaphorically but literally. Basic services were collapsing, including street lighting; every nightfall left Romanian cities in eerie gloom. Protest was not only futile but perilous. The Securitate, Ceauşescu's dreaded state security police, permeated every facet of Romanian society, alert for any glimmer of dissent and ruthless in extinguishing it.

In the latter half of the 1980s Ceauşescu undertook measures unspeakably brutal even by his debased standards. Feeling that he could not maintain adequate surveillance on the lives of those who lived in Romanian villages, he decreed that a series of villages be destroyed, and their hapless inhabitants rehoused in the bleak urban housing estates, or moved to new 'agro-industrial' towns. This process, called 'systematization', was launched with merciless efficiency. Villagers were notified that their homes were to be demolished; and they were, sometimes within a day of the notification, bulldozers crashing through walls and crushing any possessions that had not been frantically salvaged. The dispossessed then often found that no provision had been made to rehouse them; they were left homeless, squatting with their remaining belongings amid the ruins of their villages. The process stirred bitter anger outside Romania as well as within the country; many Romanian villages were 'twinned' with villages in western Europe to express solidarity against Ceauşescu's oppression, and the rhythm of 'systematization' slowed down. But Ceauşescu was storing up a legacy of loathing and detestation that was to have a grisly denouement. As the world knows, when the end came in December 1989 it was abrupt, violent and ugly.[5]

---

[4] 'Romania', *Financial Times* Survey, 3 May 1994.
[5] See for example John Simpson, *Despatches from the Barricades*, Hutchinson, 1990; Edward Behr, *Kiss the Hand You Cannot Bite*, Penguin, 1991; and John Sweeney, *The Life and Evil Times of Nicolae Ceausescu*, Hutchinson, 1991. The differing accounts given by these respected reporters indicate the confusion that prevailed.

It started quietly enough, in Timişoara, near Romania's western border. A dissident priest, Laszlo Tokeş, offended the authorities once too often; the church decided to send him to a different post, but Tokeş refused to leave. His bishop asked the local police to evict him from his home, which belonged to the church. When the police arrived on 17 November, they were met by a small crowd that wanted Tokeş to stay; and his supporters then mounted a vigil outside his house, to prevent his eviction. On the evening of 16 December the vigil turned into a demonstration that spread into the centre of Timişoara, with crowds of mainly young people shouting anti-communist, anti-Ceauşescu slogans. The protestors attacked the town hall and Communist Party headquarters, ransacking files and burning them in the street. Police and armoured vehicles then opened fire, killing many men, women and children. The exact number killed has never been verified; Securitate agents collected the bodies and disposed of them. News of the events in Timişoara echoed across Romania, the death toll amplified by rumour and radio broadcasts from Hungary and East Germany, whose communist regimes had already fallen. Before the evening ended, rioting had broken out in Arad and other cities in Transilvania, fuelled by wildly exaggerated reports of up to 40,000 dead in Timişoara.

According to later reports, Ceauşescu ordered his senior military officers to issue a command to shoot to kill; but the command was not given. On the morning of 21 December Ceauşescu took to the balcony of party headquarters in the centre of Bucureşti to address one of his usual rallies, facing the customary enormous crowd bussed in for the purpose, standing in the wide *piaţa* – then named after Gheorghiu-Dej – between party headquarters and the royal palace. He began his harangue, and the rally organizers incited the crowd to shout the usual adulatory slogans. Within a few minutes, however, voices at the back of the crowd began a rising chant of 'Ti-mi-şoa-ra! Ti-mi-şoa-ra!' As the electrifying vocal dissent rapidly spread through the crowd, Ceauşescu broke off his speech; the television cameras, broadcasting live, relayed the pictures of his sudden uncertainty, and the booing of the crowd, all over the country. Television screens throughout Romania went abruptly blank. When nothing happened immediately, the television pictures came back, and Ceauşescu continued his harangue, announcing pay rises and other sweeteners. But the mood of the crowd had changed.

Alerted by the live broadcast, people all over Bucureşti poured into the streets, heading for the city centre. The word was passed urgently along: 'Don't leave the streets!' At nightfall the Securitate moved in and the shooting started, from armoured vehicles and from snipers in buildings in the city centre, killing indiscriminately. Despite the terror, the crowds did not disperse. Soon the whole centre of Bucureşti seemed to be a raging gun-battle. Throughout the night and into the following day the city echoed with the roar of artillery and automatic weapons. The western news media began to arrive, and soon live television pictures of the battle were bouncing from satellites all over the world. Then something remarkable happened. The army joined the uprising – on the side of the people. In the late morning of 22 December a helicopter took off from the roof of party headquarters, carrying the Ceauşescus. Their flight became a grisly black farce, culminating in their capture, interrogation, summary trial and immediate execution – on Christmas Day.

The initial euphoria faded, and the doubts remained. How did it happen, and why? Five years later, the questions still linger. The scars of Romania's recent past will not be rapidly effaced. The damage inflicted, both physical and psychological, is too deep to be swept away overnight, or even in a few years. Nevertheless, despite its problems, Romania as a whole does not deserve the harsh judgements that many in the West have passed upon it since December 1989; nor should it have to linger indefinitely at the back of the queue for its share of international support and recognition. Romania is a country with a long and vivid history, a democratic period lasting many decades, memorable accomplishments in culture and technology, and enormous potential, not only for its own people but as a political and trading partner for other democracies. After its long isolation, Romania is eager to be accepted again into the community of nations. A stable, prosperous Romania would be a valuable linchpin in a part of the world all too often shaken by turmoil. The world has an interest in helping Romania rebuild.

## 1.3 Energy in Romania: historical background

In rebuilding Romania, one key focus must be Romania's energy, not only because energy is always a key factor in modern industrial society but also because Romania has been and is singularly endowed both with a profusion of energy resources and with long experience in their development. The world tends to date the petroleum era from 1859, and the oil strike of Drake at Titusville in Pennsylvania that year; but international oil statistics record that in 1857, two years earlier, Romania was the only country in the world producing petroleum commercially – 271 tonnes of petroleum, extracted from wells dug by hand in the oil province of Ploieşti northwest of Bucureşti. Ploieşti was to become the centre of one of the world's major oil industries.

Again, the world knows that the first electricity generating stations for public supply started up in London and New York in 1882. In that same year the first power station in Bucureşti also started up, a demonstration plant supplying external electric lighting to the National Theatre and the Cotroceni Palace, with an overhead cable more than a kilometre long linking the two sites. The power station was supplied by the English-Austrian Brush Electric Company Ltd, based in Vienna, a subsidiary of the International Electric Company of London. The demonstration plant operated for two years. In 1884 a hydroelectric station on the Peleş River began supplying electric light to the Royal Palace at Sinaia, north of Bucureşti. In the same year the first thermal power station started up in Timişoara – known as Temesvar in Hungarian, while it was part of the Austro-Hungarian empire – supplying the largest network of public lighting in Europe, with 731 50 watt lamps. The first permanent power station in Bucureşti came on stream in 1885. Four years later a hydroelectric station, called 'the water factory', was operating on the bank of the Dambovița River on what was then the western outskirts of Bucureşti at a site called Groszavești. The power station supplied street lighting and, after 1894, electric tramways and cars. In 1906 Bucureşti municipality granted the Bucureşti Gas Company, set up in 1870 to produce gas for lighting, a new forty-year lease, as it took over generation and distribution of electricity to become the General Company for Gas and Electricity – SGGE Bucureşti.

Romanian engineering was developing an international reputation. In 1895 the railway bridge over the Danube near Cernavoda, on the line between Bucureşti and Constanța, came into service. At the time it was the longest bridge in Europe. A century later it is still in use, an elegant structure crossing the Danube floodplain on tall pillars either side of the central span over the river itself. In 1909 a leading Romanian engineer, Dimitrie Leonida, founded the country's first museum of technology; the museum now bears his name. Leonida also designed and built the Groszaveşti III thermal power station, near the cogeneration station of the same name that now serves the west of Bucureşti; and in 1920 Leonida established Romania's first school for electricians and power mechanics.

By the time of the First World War Romania's oil industry was already of major strategic interest, not only producing oil, especially from the oilfields around Ploieşti, but also refining it to produce fuel for motor vehicles and other commercial fractions, for use both within Romania and for export, as well as heavy oil for domestic thermal power stations like Groszaveşti. The Romanian oil industry was by this time a major source of foreign exchange, although less important than agriculture, which was Romania's major economic activity until after the Second World War. In the 1920s and 1930s Romania also developed production and distribution of natural gas. Until the discovery of the Groningen gasfield in the Netherlands in 1959, Romania was the second largest producer of natural gas in Europe; only the Soviet Union was larger. Romania was also developing deposits of lignite, especially in the southwest of the country, and of hard coal, especially in the Jiu River valley. The solid fossil fuels were used for power generation and for steam-raising in industry.

Romania has cold winters, particularly in the mountains and Transilvania. The capital, in the southeast of the country, has a milder climate; but even in Bucureşti winters often bring heavy snow and sub-zero temperatures for weeks at a time. Historically most domestic heating was wood-fired; even today, and even in many homes in large cities, pride of place in the main room is given over to a massive wood-stove reaching to the ceiling, covered in elaborately figured glazed ceramic tiles. In the cities and towns, however, many of these stoves, some more than a century old, have been converted and fitted with burners for natural gas. As power generation became more widespread, an increasing number of generating units were designed and built to cogenerate electricity and heat for district heating. District heating grids were laid in more than sixty urban centres, mostly after the communist takeover in 1947. As will be described later, the advantages of district heating are sometimes overtaken by its disadvantages.

By 1924 the Romanian government had become so aware of the crucial role of energy in the country's economy that it passed an Energy Act, establishing an overall official framework for energy developments (see Chapter 2). A further Energy Act followed in 1930, and a Law of Mines later in the 1930s. In 1938 came the Law for Organizing Communal Utilities; but it was overtaken by political upheavals, and proposed projects for hydroelectricity, railway electrification, and national electricity and gas transmission systems were postponed. By the time they came back on to the agenda, after the communist takeover of 1947, these and other energy developments had become components of a series of long-range plans, directed by the central planners in the new ministries set up under Gheorghiu-Dej. In 1950 Romania had 740 MW of installed electric generating capacity, with an output of 2.1 TWh, and 2,000 km of transmission lines. The plan, to run from 1950 to 1960, aimed to add 1,860 MW of new capacity; it managed only 1,039 MW, but electricity output in 1960 reached 7.7 TWh.

When the Soviet Union enveloped Romania in its sphere of influence, especially after similar communist takeovers in the other countries of central Europe, its initial intention, as noted above, was to keep Romania as an agricultural supplier, with other countries in the communist bloc providing the industrial raw materials and manufacturing capability. The Romanian communists, however, had other ideas, possibly even harking back to Lenin's dictum that 'Communism equals soviet power plus electrification of the whole country'. In Romania the 'soviets', in particular the collective farms, were not fully established until the early 1960s, after more than a decade of ruthless measures against private farmers. One consequence of agricultural collectivization, in Romania as in the Soviet Union before it, was the steady decline of productivity. Output from animal husbandry fell, and that of cereals, vineyards and orchards slowed behind that in the west. But the Romanian communists had no desire to be relegated to what they saw as a pastoral role in the new communist future, and embarked on a programme of forced industrialization of Romania, also modelled on the Soviet Union. Electrification, of course, was essential; thermal and hydroelectric power stations were constructed, including the Porţile de Fier (Iron Gates) 1 and 2 stations across the Danube, and transmission and distribution networks established. Even under the communist regime, Romanian engineering continued in its strong tradition; but many of the basic premises of the central planning under which it evolved were far from optimal. Heavy industries were created, giant complexes – chemical plants, steel mills, cement plants and so on – distributed throughout the entire country on the basis of some perceived principle of geographical equity that proved to have little or no regard for access to necessary raw materials, component suppliers or markets – or, indeed, the requisite skilled labour. New towns were built near these complexes to house workforces moved to the site. These heavy industries dramatically increased the demand for Romania's indigenous energy resources – not only electricity but petroleum, natural gas, coal and lignite.

After Ceauşescu took power in 1965, Romania moved ever further away from Moscow. The west granted generous credits and transferred many categories of technology to Romania. After 1982, however, because of the crisis caused by debts to the west, Ceauşescu was determined to make Romania completely self-sufficient in everything. The effect on the energy industries, as on the whole Romanian economy, was catastrophic. Romanian oil engineers were directed to increase output from the oilfields, disregarding basis principles of reservoir management; even so, Romania's domestic oil production fell far short of its refinery capacity. (By this time, of course, refinery capacity in west European countries likewise substantially exceeded indigenous production.) Romanian crude is sweet and of good quality, and its refineries were set up to process this standard of material. But Ceauşescu, determined to expand exports of petroleum products, arranged to import sour lower-quality crude, particularly from Iraq; and the imported crude rapidly fouled the refineries and polluted their surroundings. Romania, once a major energy exporter, became an energy importer.

The energy infrastructure began to deteriorate; but process plant engineers and other plant operators, including those in the electricity and heat supply systems and the coal mines, were refused permission to import spares for their foreign-designed equipment. Spares produced in Romania were introduced into factories almost as prototypes, and were often unreliable. Adequate maintenance became impossible. As mines, oilwells, refineries, chemical plants and other industries struggled with deteriorating machinery to meet production quotas set by the central planners in Ceauşescu's ministries, the increasingly limited supplies of fuel were diverted ever more disproportionately to industry. Natural gas was burned as a boiler fuel in power stations and industrial plant; gasfields, too, were ordered to increase output, degrading the fields as the reservoir pressure fell. Homes that had depended on gas for heating and cooking had their supplies cut off. Even when gas supplies to domestic users were nominally available, pressure in the distribution system sometimes fell so low that burners went out; if supply pressure then increased, explosions and fires resulted.

At the same time the Ceauşescu government was destroying many neighbourhoods in Romanian cities, replacing the existing buildings, often elegant and comfortable dwellings dating back a hundred years or more, with new apartment blocks of crass ugliness, poorly constructed with inadequate materials. In his passion to export everything marketable, Ceauşescu even decreed that petroleum was not to be used to manufacture thermal insulation material for new buildings in Romania. The actual design of buildings probably improved after 1985, as indeed did building technology; but the construction work itself was of very poor quality, because the builders lacked the necessary technical discipline. As a result, blocks of flats erected in the 1980s were cold, damp, draughty concrete boxes with ill-fitting windows and doors and unreliable plumbing: miserable and cramped quarters for the unfortunate Romanians compelled to live there. As the new concrete housing estates sprang up in city suburbs, the district heating networks were extended, overstretching the capacity of the power stations serving them. The temperature of the water in the district heating grids fell steadily. The grid extensions were laid with substandard materials, and district heating engineers were unable to obtain supplies to carry out necessary maintenance on pipework and heat exchangers. Leaks proliferated, further overloading the power stations. So much make-up water was needed to replace the losses that the water-treatment facilities, too, were overloaded; and untreated make-up water accelerated corrosion and deterioration of pipework and heat exchangers. By the late 1980s a grim Romanian joke summed up the situation all too succinctly: 'Oh yes – the temperature in our two-room apartment is 24 degrees – 12 degrees in each room'. Nor could rooms be heated by gas or electricity. Electricity and gas supplies to domestic premises had become sporadic at best. Almost all available energy resources were allocated to industry, leaving Romanian households shivering in the dark. Romanian television transmitted for only two hours a day; however, since the broadcasts consisted exclusively of meticulous reportage on the latest activities, accomplishments and pronouncements of the Conducator – the leader – and his wife Elena, most Romanians found two hours of television more than enough.

In the energy field as in every aspect of Romanian society, the Ceauşescu era left a legacy of destruction. In certain respects, nevertheless, the damage inflicted may not perhaps have been quite so devastating as some reports have suggested. Despite the isolation of the 1980s and the lingering deprivations of the 1990s, Romanian engineers continue to maintain a high level of technical ability. Moreover, Romanian energy specialists can still look back not only to the years between the 1860s and the 1930s, but also to the brief flowering of the 1960s and 1970s, to recall that Romania has known better times and, in particular, that Romania has been among world leaders in energy and energy technology. As later sections of this study will discuss, the many opportunities to improve energy use and supply and to increase energy efficiency now offer an important key to rebuilding Romania.

# Chapter 2

# Starting to Rebuild

## 2.1 Picking up the pieces

Outside Romania, what happened in December 1989 is often called the Romanian revolution. Inside Romania the term 'revolution', when it is used at all, tends to have a sceptical undertone, whether implicit or explicit. Romanians usually just refer to the 'events' of December 1989. Too many unanswered – and possibly unanswerable – questions linger about what actually happened and why.[6] That said, however, December 1989 marked an abrupt and dramatic transformation in Romania, in its politics, its society, its economy and its international relations – a revolution by any criterion. Unlike other countries of central Europe, Romania was utterly unprepared for this upheaval. Poland, Hungary, the then Czechoslovakia and even Bulgaria had already begun to liberalize their economic and political life; the collapse of their communist regimes in 1989 just accelerated processes already under way. Such was not the case in Romania. In the final years of the Ceauşescu era, far from relaxing controls, Ceauşescu and his adherents were relentlessly tightening them. Living in a brutal and arbitrary police state, Romanians had come to expect capricious and irrational dictates from above. Personal initiative or responsibility could be actively dangerous; distrusting everything and everyone was safer. For most Romanians daily life was frustrating and arduous. Light, heat and hot water were sporadic; food tended to be basic, scarce and unappetizing. Individual Romanians somehow managed to keep their balance; a sense of humour helped. But below the surface the

---

[6] As noted in n. 5, Ch. 1 above, see for example John Simpson, *Despatches from the Barricades*, Hutchinson, 1990; Edward Behr, *Kiss the Hand You Cannot Bite*, Penguin, 1991; and John Sweeney, *The Life and Evil Times of Nicolae Ceauşescu*, Hutchinson, 1991.

paramount objective was simply survival, a tenacious determination to get through the day. The 'events' of December 1989 exploded almost without warning, astonishing the world and Romanians alike. After the overnight collapse of the Ceauşescu regime, Romania started cold. In the circumstances, the confusion and uncertainty that ensued are not surprising. Much remains to be done; but in the five years since that bleak, tumultuous Christmas Romania has come a long way.

The startling, chaotic broadcasts from the central television studio in Bucureşti on 22-3 December 1989 brought together an incohesive cluster of Romanians opposed to the old regime. Out of this cluster emerged the so-called 'National Salvation Front' (FSN), a de facto governing group headed by Ion Iliescu, a one-time minister in Ceauşescu's government who had fallen out with his leader in the late 1970s. Another prominent figure in the FSN was Petre Roman, an engineer and technocrat. At first the FSN disclaimed any intention of becoming more than an ad hoc interim body formed to guide the country towards free elections. By the spring of 1990, however, the FSN had reconstituted itself as a political party. Political dispute, suppressed for two generations, was soon vigorous and vehement. When the first elections were held, in May 1990, FSN candidates took most of the seats in both houses of the new Romanian parliament, the senate and the chamber of deputies. Iliescu was elected president, and Petre Roman was appointed prime minister. Other political parties were also represented in parliament, among them the old National Liberal Party and National Christian Democrat Peasants' Party dating back a century, a party representing the Hungarian-speaking minority in Romania, and parties with a nationalistic and ultimately extreme agenda. The democratic process faced many problems; but it was clearly under way.

Almost immediately after it took power the FSN decreed measures with obvious popular appeal, easing the burden of daily life for Romanians. Restrictions on electricity and gas supply to households were lifted. 'Systematization', the demolition of villages and neighbourhoods, was halted. Forced labour in mines and elsewhere was stopped, and working hours shortened. The press, hitherto a mouthpiece for the Ceauşescu regime, was freed, and burst into life with bylined polemics that could have cost reporters and editors their lives only months earlier. The new government did, to be sure, have one lever available with which to apply indirect pressure on the press. The national daily *Romania Libera*, for instance, outspoken in its opposition to the new government and deeply sceptical about the 'events' of December 1989, began to have problems obtaining newsprint, and claimed that the government was using its control of the import and allocation of newsprint to obstruct critical reporting. Be that as it may, however, new periodicals were soon crowding on to the impromptu pavement newsstands in Bucureşti and other Romanian cities. None more vividly personified the break with Romania's repressive immediate past than the fortnightly *Academia Caţavencu*. Named after a character in a classic nineteenth-century farce by Romania's master playwright Ion Luca Caragiale, *Caţavencu* was filled with scabrous, viciously hilarious satires, parodies and cartoons, attacking Romania's ruling elite with gusto and glee. Interspersed with the ferocious humour was incisive investigative reporting on the underside of the new Romania. For politically aware Romanians – and they were surprisingly numerous – *Caţavencu* quickly became required reading. One gesture symbolized the startling change that had taken place. A sprawling monolith in the northwest of Bucureşti, bearing a striking resemblance to Moscow University, had been the home of the government-controlled press. It faced on to a square called Piaţa Scinteia, named after Lenin's communist newspaper; and a statue of Lenin on a plinth stood at the front of the building looking on to the square. After December 1989 the statue was pulled from the plinth; the building was given over to *Romania Libera* and other newspapers and periodicals; and the square was renamed Piaţa Presei Libere – Free Press Square. Throughout the five years since December 1989, whatever other setbacks Romania has suffered, the press is undoubtedly free – impressively so.

The Romanian press quickly began to uncover some of the ugly legacy of the Ceauşescu era; and so did the foreign press. Worldwide coverage of the events of December 1989 awakened international media interest in Romania; but after the initial euphoria came the horror stories. As early as 1967 Ceauşescu had become determined to increase Romania's population. By the 1980s his determination had become obsessive. He banned contraception and abortion; but in the desperate conditions of Romania in the 1980s many children were born to families utterly unable to provide for them. Some of these children were placed in orphanages; but the orphanages, too, were starved of resources. Throughout 1990 foreign newspapers and television were filled

with distressing images of Romanian orphans; and at the bar of world opinion the whole of Romania was blamed for their plight. In June 1990 another
ugly manifestation put a further blot on Romania's already dubious international image. Coalminers from the Jiu Valley in southwestern Romania invaded Bucureşti, rampaging through city streets and raiding the offices of
opposition politicians and newspapers; and President Iliescu was accused of
inciting the onslaught.

Troubling developments like these seriously jeopardized Romania's efforts
to demonstrate its commitment to reforms, and to win international support.
International funding agencies and potential foreign investors feared continuing political instability in Romania, or even a reversion to the old totalitarian-
ism; and they had a plethora of other options open to them. The fall of the
Berlin Wall on 9 November 1989 and the collapse of the communist regimes
in Poland, Hungary, the then Czechoslovakia and Bulgaria had launched intense competition between the fledgling democracies of central and eastern
Europe for international recognition and investment. Romania found itself at
the back of the queue. Nevertheless, Romania had recreated an elective parliamentary system, flawed though it might be; and the Romanian parliament
addressed itself immediately to many of the issues of concern not only to the
recently enfranchised Romanian electorate but also to the world beyond Romania's borders. Throughout 1990 and 1991 the Romanian parliament passed
a series of laws that probably deserved wider acknowledgement, as an attempt to rectify previous injustices and re-establish a legal framework for
Romanian society itself, for the Romanian economy and for Romania's international relations. Romanian laws are identified briskly and easily by chrono-
logical number and year. Law 15/1990, of 8 August, for instance, the 'Law
on Restructuring State-owned Enterprises', redefined the nature and structure of the enterprises previously under the direct control of government ministries; some were to be kept under state control but given more managerial
autonomy, and others were to be privatized (see Chapter 2). Law 31/1990, of
17 November, the 'Company Law', laid out the groundrules for commercial
activities, including the various kinds of organizations now to be legally recognized, from partnerships through joint stock companies to limited liability
companies, including private banks. Law 12/1991, of 30 January, laid the
basis for 'Tax on Profit'. Law 35/1991, of 3 April, the 'Foreign Investment

Law', provided incentives and guarantees for foreign investors in Romania. Law 58/1991, of 14 August, the 'Law on Privatizing Commercial Companies', set out the programme for privatization (see Chapter 2). One law of particular significance was Law 18/1991, the 'Land Law', which set in motion the process of returning land seized by the communists, including farm land, to private ownership.[7]

To be sure, passing a law did not guarantee that its provisions would be effectively implemented. A law is designed to be an expression of policy; and the very concept of a law in a post-communist country may still suffer from a hangover of habits of mind acquired from central planning. A law can become a matter for negotiation between those attempting to apply it and those to whom it is to apply. Implementation and enforcement of laws may be hampered by bureaucratic obstructiveness carried over from the former regime, leaving an awkward gap between words and deeds. Laws alone do not suffice; the context within which they can operate effectively must also emerge, and that may take longer than drafting and passing the laws. Romania, like other post-communist countries, is still experiencing this uncomfortable evolution. On the other hand, the nature of the legal regime is by no means a crucial determinant for foreign investors. Laws can change; and many long-term investors, notably international oil and gas companies, have long experience of putting major investment into localities with legal regimes much shakier than that of Romania in the 1990s. Expressions of alarm about local laws may be no more than a negotiating stance on the part of potential foreign investors, as they weigh risks and rewards compared to other opportunities. What really troubles such potential long-term investors is political instability; and Romania in the 1990s may have suffered more from an international perception of such instability – justified or not – than from any shortcomings of Romanian law.

With the high expectations common to all the emerging democracies of central and eastern Europe, Romania embarked on discussions with international bodies like the World Bank and the International Monetary Fund (IMF), the newly established European Bank for Reconstruction and Development (EBRD), the European Investment Bank and the PHARE programme of the

---

[7] *Law Digest for Foreign Investors*, Romanian Development Agency, September 1993.

European Commission, as well as national agencies like the US Agency for International Development (USAID), the 'Know-How Fund' set up by the UK government, and similar agencies in other European countries. But Romania was to be disappointed. International financial backing was wary and tentative. Other countries in central and eastern Europe had started their reforms earlier, and were much further advanced, making them considerably more attractive to foreign investors. Moreover, foreign funding sources remained doubtful about Romania's commitment to reform, in part because Romania's president was a one-time senior figure in Ceauşescu's government and because the old institutional structure was being altered only slowly. In some ways, however, this latter circumstance was all too understandable. By the late years of the Ceauşescu era, almost anyone with any competence or experience had been compelled to come to terms with the regime in some way. Dismissing everyone associated with the old regime would have left Romania stripped of leadership. Moreover, ordinary Romanians had been short of basic everyday necessities for years. The reforms advocated by OECD countries appeared likely to cause further hardship, by creating unemployment, disruption and social unrest. Wisely or unwisely, against this background, the Romanian government opted to make the reform process gradual. By so doing, however, it aggravated international concerns, and Romania fell further behind most of its central European neighbours. In 1991 the breakup of the Soviet Union added an additional distraction. International concern shifted away from the old Comecon satellite countries to the turmoil further east. The international media withdrew their reporters from Romania, and Romanian coverage in the world press almost evaporated. Considering, however, that most of the coverage in 1990-91 had concentrated on horror stories, for Romania no news was effectively good news.

## 2.2 Into transition

Until 1989 no one had ever tried to convert a communist, centrally planned regime into a democratic society with a market economy. Doing so proved to be more difficult inside the countries in question than most foreign commentators and consultants expected. OECD countries, their governments, banks and management consultants, were all very free with advice: privatize industry, close down inefficient operations, lay off surplus workers, throw the economy open to the free market nationally and internationally and let the market pick winners and losers. However theoretically appropriate such measures looked from the outside, from inside a fragile emerging democracy that had to live with its newly enfranchised electorate they looked distinctly less appealing. Even in OECD countries, the early 1990s were evidence that the confident assumptions of the 1980s about how best to run an economy left a lot to be desired. Stubborn economic recession gripped many member countries of the OECD; factories closed, bankruptcies multiplied, unemployment reached into the most stable job sectors. Despite these intractable problems in their own economies, advisors from the OECD countries had no doubt what the countries of central and eastern Europe ought to do, and told them so repeatedly. When Romania was reluctant to adopt these prescriptions wholeheartedly, it was castigated as being uncommitted to reform. The implication was that the old *nomenklatura* of the communist era was clinging to power and privilege, reluctant to surrender its perquisites. From a less ideological viewpoint, however, the 'losers' in a headlong plunge into a privatized free-market economy would not be confined to the old *nomenklatura*. On the contrary, those most at risk would be workers in industries whose output could not compete on price and quality in a free market. Restructuring industry to make it competitive, and providing retraining and a social 'safety net' for workers whose jobs would vanish, could not be done overnight. Habits of mind carried over from an authoritarian regime – bureaucratic obstruction, refusal to take initiatives or accept personal responsibility, and simple institutional inertia, a resistance to change – can combine with genuine concern about social side-effects to place persistent stumbling-blocks in the way of reform. In Romania, where no glimmer of reform had prefigured the fall of Ceauşescu, the task was yet more challenging.

The phrase that rapidly came to encapsulate the situation, in Romania as in other formerly communist countries, was 'the economic transition': the transition from a centrally planned to a market economy. In practical terms, however, the 'transition' in question involved much more than purely economic issues. In a centrally planned economy, all economic power – hiring, firing and paying employees, from shop floor to senior management; investing in buildings, plant and equipment; purchasing raw materials, energy and other requirements; deciding product lines and outputs; pricing goods and services; and so on – lay in the hands of the central planners. They laid down 'norms' and 'quotas' that workers were directed to meet, and allocated resources by diktat from the centre. In the old Comecon countries these central planners were in turn responsible to the Communist Party bosses. To make this system function, however, required much more than purely economic authority. The whole apparatus of government had to be authoritarian and ultimately re-pressive, to suppress dissent and crush opposition, especially when the mecha-nisms of central planning failed to deliver the prosperity they promised and proclaimed. In Romania, in the 1980s, the planners were responsible to Ceauşescu and his immediate circle; as Ceauşescu became ever more para-noid, this circle shrank until it was centred mainly on members of his family. As the system progressively crumbled, leaving more and more Romanians shivering in the dark, the repression grew steadily more arbitrary, brutal and ruthless. What was collapsing was not the economic system alone, but the whole structure of Romanian society.

To refer, therefore, to Romania in the 1990s as a country in the process of 'economic transition' seriously understates the scope and depth of the 'tran-sition' involved. The transition is not merely from a centrally planned to a market economy. In the Romania of the late 1980s – only five years ago – people were subject to arbitrary arrest, imprisonment and even murder by the agents of a tyrant. The climate of fear casts a long shadow. For two genera-tions of Romanians, communism and dictatorship systematically stifled indi-vidual initiative and responsibility. Rebuilding Romania therefore involves much more than restructuring the economy. It involves reawakening indi-vidual and communal purpose, and re-establishing a social consensus based on the rule of law – that is, government with the consent of the governed. The real challenge for Romania, and for Romania's international partners, is to recreate a sense of community and a framework within which people can hope to satisfy their aspirations by their own efforts. A market economy is an important aspect of this framework, but much more is needed: not just an economic transition but a social transition.

Fortunately for Romania and its people, this transition appears to be well under way, as any visiting observer can testify. The streets of Bucureşti, so recently grey, sombre and forbidding, now bustle with activity, as well-dressed

Bucuresteans with briefcases go about their business, stop to chat animatedly on the pavement or enjoy a drink under a sunshade on the terrace of an out-door restaurant. Passersby browse through oddly assorted publications on pavement tables – from differential calculus to TV magazines to pornography. The biggest-selling daily newspaper is now *Evenimentul Zilei (The Daily Event)*, founded in June 1992. Whereas other dailies tended to fill their pages with party politics, the new broadsheet burst on the scene with tabloid gusto, reporting murders, rapes and sex scandals, human-interest stories, celebrity doings and other topics that would win mass sales on any west European news-stand; but its editor, Ion Cristoiu, writes a signed column of comment on the front page that is often a scathing critique of official policy and office-holders. The open-air markets are overflowing with produce; peasant farm-ers now working their own land in the surrounding countryside bring fresh fruit, vegetables and flowers into the city to sell, amid vigorous haggling – a free market in full cry. The city's many parks throng with families, children, dogs, young couples and pensioners. Many fountains are once again playing. In June the fragrance of the lime trees that line the boulevards is overpower-ing; but their fragrance now has to compete with exhaust fumes, as the streets fill with private cars. The ubiquitous Romanian-built Dacias and newer Oltcits, and the most successful new model, the four-wheel-drive ARO, combine with imported foreign models to generate traffic jams already sometimes resem-bling London's West End; Romanians are finding – a lesson already learned in western Europe – that their new freedom to drive does not necessarily mean the freedom to move. In the evening the city centre, where darkness ruled, is now sparkling with lights. In the National Theatre the chandeliers glow. The marble lobby of the Ateneu, the city's magnificent concert hall, once dingy with grime, has been polished until it gleams. Pride is returning. Bucureşti feels like a city emerging from a bad dream. Much the same can be said about other Romanian cities – Cluj, Braşov, Timişoara, Constanţa – and about the thousands of villages scattered across the countryside. The anecdo-tal evidence of change is striking, especially in a mere five years from such a grim beginning.

In general, this visible change appears to be the result not so much of posi-tive government action as of the removal of constraints on individual enter-prise. Recreating a functioning democratic political system has proved challenging, and so far only partially successful. In the rush of euphoria after the fall of Ceauşescu, new political parties sprang up with abandon; in the first elections, in May 1990, some 100 parties participated. Of these only a few survived.[8] The National Salvation Front of Iliescu and Roman took 355 seats out of the 506 in the senate and the chamber of deputies. The old National Liberal Party and National Christian Democrat Peasants' Party, banned under the communists, took 38 and 13 seats respectively, and the ethnically based Hungarian Democratic Alliance of Romania 41 seats, with a scattering of seats for other parties. The opposition was thus diffuse and incohesive, and the electorate found them unpersuasive. Despite opposition protests, in December 1990 some 60% of those Romanians who bothered to vote approved the proposed new constitution.

In 1991 the parliamentary process began to bog down in bickering. At length, in September 1991, the Jiu Valley miners once again invaded Bucureşti, attacking the government's austerity programme and proclaiming that Iliescu had failed to fulfil his undertakings. In response, Iliescu dismissed Roman as prime minister, replacing him with Theodor Stolojan, a caretaker prime minister with no party affiliation, and promised a new general election. Stolojan attempted to continue the gradual reforms; but progress was slow. Although he issued dire warnings about the deleterious effects of delaying the election, parliament stalled and hesitated. Meanwhile, the initial ineffectiveness of the opposition at length impelled fourteen of the leading opposition groups to pull together, to form a coalition called the Democratic Convention. The advent of the Convention transformed the political picture; in the local elections in February 1992 Convention candidates were elected mayors of Bucureşti and Timişoara, and polled well throughout the forty-one county towns. The conservative rural vote, wary of the changes that reform would bring, bailed out the National Salvation Front, which took 38% of the run-off vote against 29.6% for the Convention. But the Front was now beset by internal dissension, notably disagreement between Iliescu and Roman about the speed of reforms. At the Front's Congress in March 1992 Roman split with Iliescu and refused to endorse him for the coming presidential election; 154 FSN senators and deputies lined up with Roman, while another 120 formed a new

---

[8] Adrian Foreman, 'Romania: An Ability to Surprise', *The World Today*, Aug.-Sept. 1992.

party calling itself the Democratic National Salvation Front, loyal to Iliescu.

After protracted delays, presidential and parliamentary elections, on a system akin to that of France, took place on 27 September 1992, with Iliescu running for president against the Convention's candidate Emil Constantinescu, a leading academic and reformer. The campaign was closely fought; and once again the rural vote came to Iliescu's rescue. He regained the presidency, and his Democratic National Salvation Front, soon to rename itself the Social Democratic Party of Romania, took 34% of the seats in parliament. Efforts to form a government of national unity with the Democratic Convention failed; and Iliescu's new prime minister, Nicolae Vacaroiu, an economist, instead formed a government by winning informal support from four small parties, including former communists and extreme nationalists.

In February 1993 the Romanian parliament approved the Vacaroiu government's programme of economic reform.[9] The government reaffirmed its commitment to tight monetary and fiscal policies, and to restructuring industry, in terms that international observers welcomed. Putting these undertakings into practice, however, took longer than anticipated. Vacaroiu's government nevertheless survived four votes of no confidence in 1993, and implemented at least two potentially unpopular major measures without significant incident. On 1 May 1993, in line with moves towards market pricing, the government abolished direct subsidies on most goods and services, including electricity and gas; that on heat was phased out through the remainder of 1993. Prices jumped immediately; that of electricity for domestic users, for instance, quadrupled. In July 1993 prices rose further; as a step towards fundamental reorganization of government revenue-raising in a market economy, the government imposed value-added tax (VAT) at a standard rate of 18% on most transactions. Both the May and July measures were preceded by massive national publicity and media campaigns; fears that they might meet with social disturbance proved groundless. But the reform process remained sluggish. Some foreign observers expressed concern that the pressure for reform now seemed to be coming more from outside Romania than from within the country itself. Early 1994 was punctuated with street demonstrations and labour unrest,

[9] *Romania: The Economic Reform Programme*, Government of Romania, March 1993. See also *Romania: An Economic Assessment*, published by the OECD the preceding month, which gives a foreign analysis of the macroeconomic issues facing Romania at the time.

demanding more rapid reforms. On 29 June 1994 the Vacaroiu government survived yet another vote of no confidence, amid promises of more vigorous reform measures. Meanwhile the Romanian parliament continued to grapple with its basic responsibilities, as draft legislation, including several proposed laws important for Romanian energy, queued up for its attention. The progress of industrial restructuring and privatization remained hesitant.

## 2.3 Awakening enterprise

Despite protracted discussions with the World Bank and the IMF, international financial support was slow in coming. The Gulf war of 1990-91 and the war in the former Yugoslavia further aggravated Romania's international financial position. Iraq owed Romania some $600 million for petroleum services, particularly refining; as a result of the Gulf war, in which Romania aligned itself with the western allies, this debt remained unpaid. Romania had long maintained close economic relations with Yugoslavia, its neighbour across the Danube. The 2,100 MW Iron Gates 1 hydroelectric power station was operated jointly by the two countries; Romania supplied large quantities of steel, petrochemicals, salt and other products to Yugoslavia; a chemical complex on the Romanian side of the Danube was linked by a direct pipeline to another on what became the Serbian side; barge traffic on the Danube was overseen jointly by the two countries; and so on. The break-up of Yugoslavia and the consequent interruption of traffic on the Danube drastically reduced Romania's income from the Danube ports, the Danube-Black Sea Canal and the port of Constanţa. Nevertheless, after the imposition of UN economic sanctions on Serbia, Romania took on the task of policing the Danube, to apprehend sanction-breakers, and the Romania government participated fully in the international measures against Serbia, once again at considerable cost to Romania's own coffers.

The government did, however, receive a major and long-awaited boost in autumn 1993, when the US at last restored Romania to the trade status of Most Favoured Nation (MFN). In April 1994, again after much delay and a nationwide strike in February calling for accelerated reforms, parliament at last agreed a budget, on terms acceptable to the IMF, clearing the way for a promised IMF loan of US$700 million. Meanwhile, the trickle of foreign direct investment began to swell. Among the earliest firms to establish a foothold in Romania were international oil companies including Shell, Amoco, Canadian Occidental and Enterprise Oil, and the world's largest engineering firm, ASEA Brown Boveri (ABB), all interested in Romania's energy sector. Lufthansa linked up with the Romanian national airline TAROM to undertake comprehensive refurbishment of Romania's main international gateway, Otopeni airport north of Bucureşti. Under Ceauşescu the terminal at Otopeni had been a grim, threatening introduction for travellers to Romania; five years later it is newly painted and brightly lit, with trim booths, a businesslike luggage carousel and a well-stocked duty-free shop. Coca-Cola set up bottling plants in Romania, and nationwide distribution. Colgate-Palmolive's joint venture in Romania launched more than twenty-five new products in eighteen months; in 1993 Romania was the fastest-growing market out of 175 countries covered by the company. The food and confectionery company Kraft Suchard Jacob set up a joint venture in early 1994, producing chocolates and other goods in Romania to sell to Romanian consumers. Foreign managers are often full of praise for their Romanian employees, and confident about the growth opportunities for sales in Romania.[10]

Meanwhile, since December 1989 some 500,000 private enterprises have been established, accounting for more than 50% of trade and services, including 30% of foreign trade in 1993. At least 80% of land is now privately owned, and the private agricultural sector is booming.[11] Successes like these, however, have to be set against a thus far unimpressive record of privatizing the old state-owned Romanian industry. Law 15/1990 and Law 58/1991 established the basis for restructuring enterprises previously state-owned, and selling them off either through management buy-out or through offer of shares to the public. According to Law 15/1990, state enterprises were grouped into two new categories. Under Romanian law a private enterprise is called a *societate comerciala* (SC). An SC can be, for instance, a *societate cu responsibilitate limitate* (SRL), that is, a limited liability company, like most of the new private enterprises set up in Romania since 1990, or a *societate anonime* or *societate pe actiuni* (SA), that is, a company owned by share-

---

[10] See for example *Central European*, April 1994.
[11] 'Romania', *Financial Times Survey*, 3 May 1994.

holders. State enterprises to be privatized became SAs; some 6,320 SAs were designated. Certain enterprises, including defence industries, mines, oilfields, and electricity and gas production and supply, were considered strategic. Each became a *regia autonoma*, or autonomous administration (RA); some 800 RAs were designated. RAs were to remain under government control, but with comparative freedom for day-to-day management. Law 58/1991 then set up a national State Ownership Fund (SOF), to hold 70% of the shares in the SAs, and five regionally based Private Ownership Funds, to hold the remaining 30%, until the shares were offered for sale. In 1992 ownership certificates with a total value of 30% of the capital of the SAs were issued to all Romanian adults, to be exchanged for shares in state companies as they were sold off. By mid-1994, however, the number of ownership certificates exchanged remained insignificant. Only a few small and medium-sized SAs had been sold to the public, for example the Ursus brewery in Cluj. A number of others had been sold to their management and employees; but this some-times led to accusations that the old *nomenklatura* were enriching themselves by buying Romania's assets cheaply. Until 1994 the SOF was headed by Emil Dima, a conservative senator from the Social Democratic Party, whose lack of enthusiasm for reform seriously impeded the privatization programme and attracted much unfavourable comment. In February 1994, however, Constantin Dumitru, a former communist minister, was appointed to the SOF; and his expressed commitment to privatization may give the programme new momentum. Under his direction the SOF is working closely with the five regional funds towards an arrangement under which the regional funds will be able to sell 100% of enterprises being privatized.[12] In mid-1994 Prime Minister Vacaroiu announced that 3,000 SAs would be privatized in the fol-lowing twelve months; and plans were under way to launch a Romanian stock exchange in the autumn of 1994.[13] By the late summer of 1994 a selection of the most profitable 3,000 state-owned enterprises was being prepared; and new privatization vouchers were to be issued, with a well-defined value, to give the entire population fair access to the shares of these enterprises. The programme was to be put before the Romanian parliament in September 1994.

---

[12] Ibid.
[13] Virginia Marsh, *Financial Times*, 27 June 1994.

Privatization will be crucial to rebuilding much of Romania's economy, in imposing market disciplines, in giving shareholders, managers and employees a stake in the success of their enterprises, and in attracting new sources of finance. For Romania's energy systems, however, on which this study focuses, privatization is likely to play a smaller role, at least in the foreseeable future. For Romania's energy, an essential key to the country's economic and social transition, other policy issues are more immediately important – in particular, pricing and restructuring, both for industry and for the energy suppliers themselves, and seizing the opportunities to improve the efficiency of energy use throughout Romania's economy.

## 2.4 Reshaping energy

### 2.4.1 The old regime

Energy has long figured prominently in Romania's public policy. The country's first Energy Law was passed in 1924. It specified explicitly that the installations for production, transmission and distribution of energy were de jure state property. The state could offer concessions lasting from thirty-five to ninety years, according to type, for construction and exploitation for energy purposes. The law described in detail how concessions were to be granted, and the rights and obligations of the state and the concessionaries. The Ministry of Industry and Commerce was to resolve all problems relating to production, transmission and distribution of energy; it could commission energy studies and initiate programmes, and it kept track of energy use. In addition to the minister, a superior council on energy gave advice on problems brought before it. A special national fund called the 'energy fund' was set up to pay for studies and designs, to grant subsidies, to participate on behalf of the state in some concessions and to carry out the direct work of the government in using energy resources. The money in the fund came from budget allocations, taxes, fines, donations and other sources. The Energy Law of 1924 was amended and extended in 1930 and 1934, but not fundamentally altered.

After the Second World War, Romania entered the Soviet sphere of influence, and its political, economic and social regime changed dramatically. The energy industries, like other industries, were nationalized in 1948. The legal framework in the country became that of a centralized economy. Annual and five-year plans with legal force stipulated exactly how much electricity had to be generated and used, and where; what financial resources the state would allocate to develop the energy sector, and for what purpose; and what volume of products and services had to be delivered, and with what specific use of energy – that is, the amount of energy per unit of product or service. As Romania's communist planners forced the country to industrialize, they allocated substantial initial funds to energy investments, to boost indigenous production of primary energy – petroleum, natural gas and coal – as well as electricity and heat. As a rule, however, both production and use developed according to political will, not economic efficiency. This created serious difficulties in supplying energy to users – difficulties that intensified after 1973 and became very severe after 1980. In 1973, in an effort to overcome these difficulties, the government passed a new law to promote development of energy resources and more efficient use of fuels and energy. The law aimed to intensify geological prospecting; to extend the use of indigenous solid fuels; to restrict the burning of hydrocarbons; and to evaluate new and renewable sources of energy. It also aimed to promote more efficient end-use of energy. The measures proposed included redirecting economic development, replacing old and energy-intensive technologies, operating industrial installations more effectively and recovering so-called 'secondary energy resources', notably waste heat in industry.

Many of the provisions of the law, however, remained declarations of good intent with no discernible effect. Without adequate financial support or normal relations with the external market, Romanian specialists often could not implement the technical measures they proposed. The authorities then resorted to measures typical of a centralized economy. They reinforced the energy-planning laws. Energy could be used only on the basis of quotas allocated by the government. Energy suppliers – in particular electricity suppliers – could contract only to supply a given user the quantity of energy stipulated by this quota, and had to observe a daily supply graph; indeed, for electricity the supply graph was divided into periods of each day. The number of products and services for which the law stipulated specific energy use increased substantially. If an enterprise used more energy than the quota stipulated, the employees' salaries were cut. Allocating quotas, working out norms for specific energy use that consumers had to meet, and periodic verifying and reporting kept a large-scale bureaucratic apparatus busy, both within the government and within energy suppliers and users.

The same distribution regime also applied to energy used by the public: upper limits were set on the amount that could be used at a given location or delivered by the supplier in a given period of time. To assure energy supply for industry, the authorities gradually reduced energy supply to the public to derisory levels, and banned the sale of electrothermal space and water heaters. A relentless publicity campaign in the mass media hammered home the demand for 'energy saving' with heavy-handed slogans: 'If you turn off a lightbulb for two hours you assure the operation of a lathe for ten minutes'. The authorities reduced television broadcasting to two hours a day, Monday to Saturday. In the winter they banned the use of private cars; in other seasons they rationed petrol.

Despite such draconian measures, Romania's energy situation continued to deteriorate. Energy supplies were disrupted increasingly often, not only in households but also in industry. From 1985 to 1989 the national electricity system operated in isolation, disconnected from neighbouring countries; the system frequency dropped from 50 Hz to 47 Hz. The pressure of natural gas in the distribution networks often fell below normal, particularly in the cold Romanian winters. These disturbances also aggravated the inefficiency of energy use, as industrial plants operated below their design capacities. As Romania's economy foundered, shortages became endemic; factories no longer worked at full capacity because they did not have enough orders, raw materials, imported spares or materials for maintenance. In the final years of the communist regime, Romania was corseted by laws and regulations imposing centralized planning and control; but this legal framework could not even make the economy function properly, much less enhance the efficiency of energy use.

## 2.4.2 Getting the picture

By December 1989 the pattern of energy use in Romania was severely skewed compared to those of west European countries. The central planners who decreed quota allocations reserved more than 80% of fuels and electricity for use in industry, especially heavy and energy-intensive industry. As a result, the residential sector suffered acute deprivation; transport and agriculture were undersupplied; basic services like public lighting were minimal; and the commercial sector was effectively non-existent. Since 1990 the picture has altered substantially, as later sections of this study will describe. Residential use of fuels and electricity has increased markedly; Romania's commercial sector has sprung to life; public lighting is both more widespread and brighter; and – above all – private car traffic has exploded, as anyone familiar with Bucureşti through the past five years can testify.

However, detailed analysis of the changing structure of energy use in Romania is handicapped by the fundamental problem of Romania's system of energy statistics, both historical and current. Central planning in Romania emphasized output, and was therefore preoccupied with fuel and electricity supply rather than use. Moreover, all the energy-using activities of an enterprise, including the motor fuel used in its transport and often the fuel and electricity used by its workers in homes and recreational facilities, were subsumed in the same aggregates, and recorded as industrial energy use. All heat produced, whether used inside an enterprise or supplied to outside users, was measured and recorded in the national figures. In the final years of the Ceauşescu era, moreover, another factor became increasingly important. Failure to meet targets could have serious consequences for those who could be blamed. In 1991 Romanian specialists were demonstrating for a foreign visitor their new computer graphics, with charts of Romania's electricity system. One display showed a graph of electricity output peaking in the mid-1980s; the next showed emissions from the system at their lowest while electricity output was highest. When the foreign visitor queried the consistency of these two graphs, the Romanian specialists laughed ruefully; and one responded, in English, 'It's a lie. We were told what numbers we had to report'. One foreign observer has described seeing the notes of a speech delivered by Ceauşescu to the party congress in November 1989. The left-hand column listed the figures to be communicated to the congress; the right-hand column listed the true figures.[14] Energy statistics from the Ceauşescu era, like other historical records of those years, have to be viewed with caution.

Since December 1989, collection of statistics has been put on a much firmer factual basis; but the structure of the data gathered still harks back to the

---

[14] Dennis Deletant, private communication.

communist regime. Comparing Romanian energy activities with those of OECD market economies is accordingly constrained by the very different structure of the available data; and even within Romania disaggregated data about end-use for particular activities is still acutely limited, further complicating efforts to enhance energy efficiency. Similar problems also arise with energy forecasting and planning; the nature and structure of existing data make extrapolation for the purposes of market-based planning even more difficult than usual. Romanian specialists are already engaged in reorganizing the collection and analysis of energy statistics, to provide the types and qualities of information required in a market economy, and to promote energy efficiency; they would welcome international cooperation in this process. In the meantime, however, throughout this study, the overall reservation about comparability and the nature of historical Romanian data should be kept in mind. In some respects – for example as to the specific energy use attributed to industrial production – glancing too casually at the apparent numbers may make the Romanian situation look worse than in fact it is.

The question of Romanian energy statistics is one of the key problems underlined in the most comprehensive analysis of Romanian energy issues to date. In January 1994 the OECD International Energy Agency published a report entitled *Energy Policies of Romania*, prepared by a team of IEA specialists from OECD countries, after extensive consultations with Romanian colleagues.[15] For anyone actively involved in energy in Romania, the IEA report should be required reading. Romanian specialists themselves now frequently refer to it, even when disagreeing with some of the viewpoints it presents. Accordingly, the commentaries presented in the present study draw on and have been significantly influenced by the work of the IEA team, particularly as concerns the supply side of the Romanian energy scene, on which the IEA work focused.[16] The present study therefore endeavours to act as a complement to the IEA report, focusing more on end-use and efficiency, and presenting as much as possible a view from within Romania – not 'the' view

---

[15] *Energy Policies of Romania*, International Energy Agency, 1993.
[16] The author would like to record his thanks to the IEA team, and in particular to Stephen Perkins of the Non-Member Countries Division of the IEA, for the detailed information and thoughtful analysis the IEA report presents, and for valuable comments on the present study.

but 'a' view; as Romanian specialists themselves stress, Romanians are now free to differ among themselves explicitly and vigorously about matters of policy, and do so with enthusiasm.

With the reservations noted above about the nature of existing Romanian energy statistics, the IEA report provides the basis for a snapshot overview of the Romanian energy sector. Romania, as already noted, has its own indigenous oil, natural gas, coal, lignite and hydroelectricity. A central feature of Ceauşescu's drive to make Romania stand alone in the 1980s was an attempt to make the country self-sufficient in energy. The attempt failed; indeed, ironically, by depleting reserves precipitously it left Romania not less but more dependent on fuel imports. In 1989 Romania's total primary energy supply reached a peak of 68 million tonnes of oil equivalent (mtoe), some 50 mtoe from indigenous production. After December 1989 it fell rapidly to only 44 mtoe in 1992, of which only 33 mtoe, or 75%, was from indigenous production; the remaining 11 mtoe or 25% had to be imported. Of the total of 44 mtoe used in 1992, 20.1 mtoe or about 45% was natural gas – 18 mtoe from indigenous production, the remainder imported from Russia. Coal and lignite made up another 25% or 11 mtoe, of which indigenous production amounted to 8 mtoe. Oil represented 27% or 11.8 mtoe, of which about 6.5 mtoe was from Romanian wells. Hydroelectricity supplied 1 mtoe. In 1991 natural gas supplied 41% of final energy use, oil 26%, heat 14%, electricity 12% and coal 7% (see Figure 2.1). The IEA report notes that oil, at 26%, has an anomalously small share of energy end-use; in OECD member countries its share is always higher than 35%. As road transport, and especially private car traffic, expands in Romania the share of oil in the energy mix will undoubtedly increase. The electricity supply system has a nominal capacity of some 22 GW; but peak demand has fallen to less than 10 GW. The first 600 MW unit of the Cernavoda nuclear power station is expected to start up by mid-1995.

Each indigenous fuel now has an RA (see Section 2.3 above) responsible for it, as does electricity; all these RAs are at the moment under the control of the government. Romanian organizations involved in fuel and electricity supply and use include government ministries – in particular the Ministry of Industries, the Ministry of Finance and the Ministry of Research and Technology; the RAs for each fuel, and RENEL, the RA for electricity and heat

**Figure 2.1: Energy supply and use – shares by fuel, 1991**

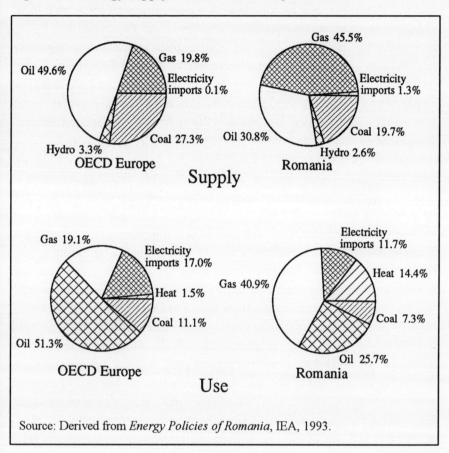

Source: Derived from *Energy Policies of Romania*, IEA, 1993.

supply; the energy research institutes; the Romanian Energy Conservation Agency, ARCE; the Romanian Development Agency, ARD; the banks; the manufacturers of energy supply and end-use equipment; and various other interested parties. Key organizations and their activities will be described in more detail in Chapter 3; but IEA specialists note one general point of obvious importance. The interactions between the different Romanian organizations in the energy field still suffer from inadequate communications; perhaps because of an administrative culture carried over from the old regime, they do not share information or talk to each other enough. More dialogue and closer coordination would benefit all participants. Accurate information, adequately disseminated and understood, is a prerequisite for effective policy.

Many Romanian energy specialists are convinced, moreover, that Romania's emerging energy policy should make explicit provision for improving the efficiency of energy use. Since December 1989, most domestic and international interest in the energy sector in Romania has been concentrated on supply of fuels and electricity, and a number of significant and useful studies have already been carried out, notably the IEA report mentioned above.[17] Box 2.1 lists others of importance. Comparatively little attention, however, has been directed to the actual use of fuels and electricity in Romania, the topic on which this study focuses. Romania offers abundant opportunities to improve the efficiency not only of energy supply but also of energy use; and the process is already under way.

Why is energy efficiency of such interest and importance in a country like Romania, when fuel and electricity use are falling and the electricity supply system already has a massive surplus of nominal capacity? A good case can be made that improving energy efficiency is more important in such a country than almost any measure on the supply side. Even though fuel and electricity use are falling, Romania is still having to import fuel supplies, and these must be paid for in scarce hard currency. Although the nominal capacity of the electricity system is three times the present peak demand, many power stations are operating well below specifications because of their age, inadequate maintenance in the 1980s, shortage of spare parts and other problems; and this poor performance is also contributing to environmental pollution. Heating systems still cannot meet peak demands. Upgrading the electricity, natural gas and heat supply systems will be costly and time-consuming; such expense and effort will make little sense if the electricity, natural gas and heat supplied continue to be wasted by inefficient end-use hardware – buildings, lighting, motors and so on. Improving energy efficiency, on the other hand, starts with measures that may involve little or no investment, directed to 'good housekeeping' – turning off lights and shutting down equipment when it is not required, stopping steam leaks and otherwise maintaining equipment, and many similar activities in industry and households. At a more organized level

---

[17] *Energy Policies of Romania.*

**Box 2.1 Energy supply sector studies**

*For RENEL (electricity authority)*

- Corporate Restructuring Study, 1992: Bossard in association with Electricite de France
- Least Cost Capacity Development (LCCD) Study, Phase 2, Draft Final Report, November 1993: Ewbank Preece in association with Coopers & Lybrand
- Rehabilitation Surveys of Thermal Power Plants: Merz & MacLellan in association with PowerGen plc
- Environmental Impact Assessment Study for Power and Lignite Subsectors: Rehabilitation and Modernization Project, 1993: RH & H Denmark in association with E & EN Netherlands
- Bucureşti District Heating System (Supply Side); Feasibility Study, August 1993: Bechtel
- Bucureşti District Heating System (Distribution and End-use Installations): Danish Power Consult, begun August 1994
- Refurbishment Programmes A1-A3 Rovinari and Turceni; Feasibility Study: Deutsche Babcock and ABB
- Study on Modern EMS/SCADA for the Romanian Power System (financed through a US grant): ECC consultants

*For RAL and RAH (lignite and hard coal authorities)*

- Studies for restructuring the Hard Coal and Open-pit Mining Industries

*General*

- Energy Survey – Romania 1993, Black Sea Economic Cooperation First International Energy Congress, Ankara, Turkey, November 1993 is 'energy management', in which designated individuals take explicit responsibility for energy use at a site, cutting out wasteful practices and otherwise improving performance. Educating and training specialists, and informing the general public, politicians and the media about good practice in energy use must also play a key role. Then come the efficiency measures that do entail investment – rehabilitating or replacing inefficient plant, insulating buildings and so on. Even these measures, which may require substantial investment, have often proved to be less expensive than supply-side investments; many studies have shown that saving a kilowatt-hour, even in a comparatively efficient economy like those of most OECD countries, is almost always cheaper than generating a new kilowatt-hour.[18] Many efficiency investments pay back their costs in only a year or two by reducing consequent fuel and electricity bills; and some, like building insulation, may then go on saving money for years or indeed decades thereafter. Moreover, more efficient buildings, lighting, heating and so on offer better energy services – more comfort, better illumination and other amenities. In a country like Romania, so long deprived of these amenities, improved energy services will be at least as welcome as lower costs.

In most OECD countries, for many reasons, an 'energy efficiency culture' has grown up in the past two decades; even so, many opportunities are still being missed. In a country like Romania no such 'efficiency culture' has yet emerged: on the contrary, 'energy saving' has come to be associated with cutoffs of electricity and gas supplies. The implications of this point will be discussed in Chapter 5. Energy costs have been artificially low and subsidised, both to industry and to households. Fuel, electricity and heat supplies have been allocated centrally; in the past, anyone who failed to use the whole quota, far from being congratulated, might find subsequent allocations reduced. Institutional and cultural barriers like these – and many more can be identified – are a more immediate problem than the problem of financing efficiency; they will be discussed further in Chapter 5. Financing efficiency is itself a complex issue, especially in a country such as Romania where fi-

---

[18] See for instance Jose Goldemberg *et al.*, *Energy for a Sustainable World*, Wiley Eastern, New Delhi, 1987. This classic study by senior energy experts from four continents was a profoundly influential landmark in the development of energy efficiency policy worldwide.

nances, including capital, are scarce, and their sources inexperienced in a market context. In a number of OECD countries, for instance, governments offer financial incentives – grants, low-interest loans or tax breaks – for efficiency investments. In some OECD countries, electricity and natural gas suppliers have embarked on so-called 'demand-side management', or DSM.[19] Instead of investing in new generating plant, they invest in their customers' premises, to install more efficient lighting, heating, ventilation, motors or even insulation. The regulatory authorities who oversee their tariffs allow them to recover the cost of such investments and may also allow them to recoup the cost of lost sales, and indeed to make an appropriate return on the investments. The practice of DSM, and its embodiment in so-called 'integrated resource planning' (IRP), is evolving rapidly, and not without controversy; but many Romanian energy specialists are already studying it, to see how it might be applied in their country (DSM and IRP will be discussed in more detail in Chapter 6). Many Romanian specialists are eager to foster the growth of an 'energy efficiency culture' in Romania, drawing on foreign ideas and experience but adapting them to suit Romania's own circumstances. The opportunities, both for Romania itself and for its potential foreign partners in such a process, are substantial.

---

[19] See for instance *Energy Efficiency and the Environment: Forging the Link*, ed. Edward Vine *et al.*, and *State of the Art of Energy Efficiency: Future Directions*, ed. Edward Vine and Drury Crawley, both published by American Council for an Energy-Efficient Economy, 1991.

# Chapter 3

## Romania's Energy Framework

### 3.1 Key players

Romania inherited from the former regime a sprawling bureaucratic apparatus covering the entire economy, including the energy sector. Reordering, restructuring and dismantling this bureaucracy has proved a daunting task. A good start has been made, but much remains to be done. The IEA report offers a detailed analysis of the existing organizations in the energy sector, their problems and their prospects, viewed from an OECD perspective.[20] Viewed from within Romania the problems and prospects inevitably look slightly different. Romanian specialists are acutely conscious of the political and social difficulties that stand in the way of efforts to restructure Romania's energy sector. In OECD countries managers are used to sacking staff. In Romania, however, as in other former communist countries, a worker might lose a job for political reasons, but not for reasons of economy; communism prided itself on 'full employment', however meaningless this was in practical terms. That, too, is changing. In mid-1994 a foreign visitor watched a senior Romanian energy specialist standing grim-faced by his desk late on a Friday afternoon, working his way through a sheaf of identical letters, signing them one after the other – letters dismissing perhaps a hundred of his employees, adding them to the mounting toll of Romania's newly unemployed. As the stack of signed letters grew he muttered, 'This is the worst job I have to do'. Abstract policy recommendations, however well founded and well intentioned, may have a human dimension that is brutally painful for those who lose out. If Romania is hesitant about implementing measures to restructure, the reasons may not be entirely discreditable.

---

[20] *Energy Policies of Romania*, International Energy Agency, 1993.

Even those who still retain their jobs face acute difficulties. Foreign specialists point out that the primary concern of government employees is not their work but simply trying to make ends meet. A graduate engineer working as a middle-level civil servant earns the equivalent of £10-15 or perhaps US$25 per week. Many therefore also drive taxis or do other jobs to augment their meagre income. The low salaries also lead to a 'brain drain' from the government ministries.

Accordingly, dismantling the old framework is not enough; erecting a new framework to take its place is equally necessary. To do so takes time – more time, perhaps, than was recognized when the old regime collapsed. Nevertheless, the process is clearly under way. Major changes have already taken place and others are in train, often with international assistance. Romania's energy sector is still closely attached to the Romanian government; but its structure and legal status are gradually evolving towards a system more appropriate for a modern market economy. The IEA report, as already noted, focuses mainly on the supply sector, analyzing it in great detail. This study will pay closer attention to energy use and energy efficiency; but the supply sector also of course has a major influence on end-use and efficiency, and relevant aspects will be outlined in this and later chapters.

Among the organizations of particular interest to this study are the Ministry of Industries, the Romanian Energy Conservation Agency (ARCE) and the Romanian electricity authority (RENEL) whose activities already explicitly encompass energy efficiency and even a version of DSM. Other Romanian energy organizations include the RAs for coal, lignite, natural gas and petroleum, and the energy research institutes. Other government ministries with an involvement in energy include the Ministry of Finance, which has to agree prices and tariffs, approve investments and budgets for the energy RAs, and set taxes, and the Ministry of Research and Technology, which oversees the activities and funding of the energy research institutes. The Romanian Development Agency ARD acts as a intermediary between Romanian and foreign firms in the energy field. The National Privatization Agency (ANP) may become increasingly involved in the energy sector as restructuring continues, as some RA activities are reconstituted as SAs and then privatized. Romania's many enterprises manufacturing energy equipment for both supply and use must also figure prominently in efforts to improve overall efficiency.

## 3.2 Ministry of Industries

In its present form, the Ministry of Industries was established in 1990, shortly after the events of December 1989 that overthrew the communist dictatorship. The provisional government that took power wanted to give Romanian industries more freedom. In the old communist system each major industry had its own ministry; the new government replaced this array of industrial ministries with a single Ministry of Industries (MoI). This large ministry now includes a specialized Directorate General for Petroleum and Gas, a Mining Department and a separate Directorate General for Energy, headed by a director general. Within the MoI the section of particular interest for the present study is the Directorate General for Energy. Despite its all-embracing name the Directorate General for Energy is actually responsible primarily for electricity and heat supply. It is also supposed to have overall responsibility for energy policy, but as noted earlier some problems of communication and coordination with other parts of the MoI continue to hamper its activities.[21]

The Directorate General for Energy is responsible for legislation on and regulation of electricity and heat supply. It carries out strategic studies for energy development, correlated with other branches of industry and with the whole national economy. It represents the interests of the Romanian government concerning electricity and heat supply in internal and international relations. It exercises state control, within the limits allowed by law, over RAs and over SAs in the electricity and heat sectors, in which the majority of capital is state-owned. The Directorate has also been responsible for securing the energy resources the government itself requires, but over time this role has been much reduced.

Its other responsibilities in the energy sector, however, remain extensive. The Directorate is an institution for identifying directions and making decisions; it does not administer energy resources directly. On the other hand, it is very much involved in solving problems and implementing decisions about them. It proposes development strategies and takes part in the process of privatization

---

[21] As this study was going to press, Government Decree 451 of August 1994 modified the structure of the MoI. The General Directorate of Energy is to merge with the General Directorate for Oil and Gas and the General Directorate for Correlation of Material Resources. The merged directorate is to be called the General Directorate for Strategies of Energy, Oil and Gas Industries, and it is to be established by 15 September 1994.

in the energy sector, according to the legislation in force. For energy conservation, the Directorate pursues and analyzes trends in specific consumption of fuel and energy in technologies, proposes measures to reduce it, and – together with ARCE – approves the 'National Programme for Energy Conservation, for Recovering and Utilizing Renewable Energy Resources and for Using Unconventional Energy'. It also coordinates activities in Romania's nuclear power programme, including the Cernavoda nuclear power station, uranium mining and processing, and manufacture of nuclear fuel and heavy water.

Throughout the fuel and electricity supply sector the MoI negotiates with the Ministry of Finance and the supply RAs to set prices and tariffs. This arrangement has come in for criticism by the IEA and others, as will be discussed below. The Directorate General for Energy oversees the budgets of RENEL and certain other state-owned energy enterprises, analyzing and giving guidance on income and expenditure. As restructuring progresses, in the event of disputes about share-outs of assets and capital between these RAs and newly formed SAs with state capital the Directorate acts as a mediator. It commissions or makes its own forecasts, studies and analyses of energy use, at national level and in correlation with world trends. It sees that scientific research on energy financed by state funds is turned to good account. It draws up or analyzes draft legislation affecting technologies and standards; it follows the application of regulations already in force, and devises methodologies to set new energy standards.

Concerning capital and financial resources in the energy sector, the Directorate gives advice about documentation for allocations from the government budget and for credit. It initiates proposals and provides advice and specialized assistance to attract foreign capital, and also to establish enterprises with foreign or mixed capital. It analyzes and gives advice about energy investments, and about industrial refitting financed by the government budget; and it advises on and presents technical and economic documentation for approval for investment, including obtaining the necessary credit. It exercises specialized government oversight over energy enterprises within its sphere of responsibility, and analyzes their economic results. On behalf of the Romanian government, the Directorate helps to initiate and sustain international cooperation on energy, and promotes and encourages collaboration between Romanian energy enterprises and foreign firms.

As the Directorate studies the restructuring of Romania's energy sector, it also analyzes management and human resources, and proposes improvements. It maintains government relations with employers in the sector, and assists state-owned enterprises to set up programmes for professional retraining of the graduate workforce.

### 3.3 Romanian Energy Conservation Agency – ARCE

Romania was the first of the emerging democracies in central and eastern Europe to designate a government body explicitly dedicated to energy conservation. The Romanian Energy Conservation Agency, ARCE, was created in April 1991, by Government Decree No. 327. It is a public body within the MoI, with its own headquarters and administration. ARCE is led by an administrative council appointed by the MoI. The council president is the Director General of the agency.[22] ARCE's headquarters is in Bucureşti; the sixteen regional branches are located in large towns, and each branch covers two or three counties. ARCE was created out of the Energy Inspectorate, a government agency dating back to the 1960s. This has proved to have both advantages and disadvantages (see Chapter 3).

ARCE's current role is to assist industrial enterprises, both technically and financially, in their energy conservation and energy efficiency activities, and to set up programmes for energy efficiency in industry. It hopes to expand its activities into the agricultural, residential and commercial sectors. ARCE's main aim is to persuade energy users to take appropriate measures to increase energy efficiency and thus decrease energy intensity. ARCE provides financial support from the government budget, within allocated funds, for energy efficiency projects. It supports the modernization of equipment and the installation of energy-saving devices. Its objectives are to promote renewable energy sources and the replacement of hydrocarbons by other energy sources, to demonstrate new technologies and to disseminate the latest concepts. Within the limits set by its present budget and staff it offers enterprises technical assistance, such as energy audits and evaluation of proposed solu-

---

[22] ARCE's organization and operating regulations were approved by Order No. 1539/ 29.06.1991 of the ministry, and updated by two government decrees, nos 754/1990 and 327/1991.

tions to problems, and provides technical information on energy efficiency. It drafts legislative proposals for rational use of energy. It arranges international cooperation on energy efficiency, and manages external grants for technical assistance projects. It organizes and takes part in workshops, conferences and educational programmes on energy efficiency, and collaborates with research and design institutes, universities, professional organizations and non-governmental bodies for staff training, energy efficiency policy and related activities.

ARCE has three divisions: strategy, planning and projects; programme implementation and monitoring; and financial and economic. Its sixteen regional branches act as ARCE's field agents, specifically responsible for technical and financial assistance. With grants from the government budget, ARCE supports from 10% to 30% of the total amount of investments in energy efficiency. The share that ARCE provides is meant to be an incentive for industries and other energy users to invest specifically in energy efficiency, although the payback period for some of the investments is less than a year. What is even more important for Romania, a major fuel importer, is that energy saved also means hard currency saved, easing the burden on the government budget.

The financial incentives offered by ARCE aim to stimulate energy users not only to use energy more rationally, but also to develop competence in applying for funding from sources other than their own – for example bank loans, grants and external financing. The expectation is that once the investment capital is paid back, the finances will become a sort of revolving fund for other similar investments. Thus far the activity has been encouragingly successful, despite the difficulties arising from inflation, price changes, the high rate of interest for bank loans, the scarcity of enterprises' own capital for investment and so on (see Chapter 4). The number, complexity and value of projects seeking ARCE assistance has grown significantly in each successive year. A technical and financial commission of ARCE experts selects the projects, and forwards the proposals to the MoI.

ARCE is striving to enlarge the field of technical and financial assistance, and to concentrate more on the residential and 'tertiary' sector – public buildings, offices and so on. At the same time, it is promoting energy efficiency research projects, with funds from the Ministry of Research and Technology.

In 1992, the first year of this activity, ARCE launched research projects on energy demand analysis and forecasting, measurement systems for energy parameters, informatics networks for energy indicators, and ways to improve the thermal insulation of communal housing.

Within Romania, ARCE has working relationships with the MoI and the Ministry of Economy and Finances; the Romanian Development Bank; research and design institutes; universities and technological institutes; nongovernmental bodies; and state-owned and private enterprises, including manufacturers of energy equipment. Outside Romania, ARCE has working relationships with other agencies of a similar kind, for instance the Agence de l'Environnement et de la Maitrise d'Energie (ADEME) of France; with international organizations promoting energy efficiency; with the European Commission; and with the World Bank and EBRD.

ARCE specialists say that ARCE's immediate and longer-term aims are: to identify priorities for improvements in energy efficiency; to set up a programme to train energy managers, another for research and development and a third to reduce losses in heat networks and buildings; and to cooperate with international assistance programmes. Later chapters of this study will discuss ARCE's role, strategy and activities in more detail.

## 3.4 Regia Autonoma de Electricitate (RENEL): electricity authority

Until the fall of Ceauşescu, Romania's energy systems were part of the central planning apparatus of government; each had a ministry responsible for it. In 1990 this structure was reorganized. At present, as noted earlier, fuel and electricity supply are still owned by the state, but in the form of a group of so-called *regies autonomes* or 'autonomous administrations' (abbreviated to RA) each of which has a degree of independence in its day-to-day operation. Among the RAs set up after December 1989, the Romanian electricity authority RENEL has already established a high profile, not least in its promotion of energy efficiency. It is one of the most powerful industrial enterprises in Romania, a major employer, a major contractor and a significant part of the Romanian economy in its own right. It is still, however, closely connected to the Romanian state. Although RENEL is a legal entity and operates with its own economic administration and financial autonomy, the MoI, which represents government interests on its administrative council, appoints the president of RENEL, who is also the president of the administrative council. At the moment RENEL is a vertically integrated national company. The strategy for restructuring RENEL up to the year 2000, based on consulting studies by Electricité de France and Bossard, foresees maintaining a natural monopoly for transmission and distribution, but creating conditions for competition in electricity generation, including independent generation.

RENEL contains units with limited autonomy, called 'subsidiaries', made up of power stations or electricity grids. It also has research and design institutes; units without separate legal status, including plants, factories, sections, workshops, centres and offices; and services for occupational health, administration and social protection. RENEL produces and transmits electricity, and dispatches it through the so-called 'national energy system'. RENEL, however, differs from most integrated utilities in OECD countries in that it also produces, transports and delivers heat for industry and for district heating, on contract terms with customers. When Romanian specialists refer to the 'national energy system' they mean not only the electricity networks but also the heat distribution networks; the two systems function together, bringing some advantages but also some disadvantages, as will be discussed in later chapters. (The term 'national energy system' does not, however, encompass either the natural gas grid or the elaborate networks of pipelines for petroleum and petroleum products that criss-cross the Romanian countryside.) RENEL refits and repairs energy installations, seeing to spare parts and equipment; more and more of this work, however, is done by contractors under RENEL control. RENEL carries out applied research to find technological solutions for problems, and to develop new materials and products to generate, transmit and distribute electricity and heat more efficiently. It is endeavouring to optimize the operation of existing energy installations, modernizing them, extending automation and introducing new energy conversion technologies. It is also seeking ways to reduce the environmental impact of energy installations.

RENEL trains professional personnel, both within its own educational network and in the public education system. It draws up and implements its own programmes for investments, repairs and refitting on the national energy system; and it imports and exports electricity, and imports fuel, spare parts and materials for operation and maintenance. It produces electricity and heat in its own plants, using enough capacity to meet the load curve. Together with partners, it administers the water used in the Danube hydroelectricity stations. It ensures that the system of electricity stations and grids operates normally and safely, and that heat is delivered according to the conditions of contracts with industrial end-users and district heating operators. It also manages the national dispatching systems. It designs, implements and commissions capital investment, according to programmes approved by the government. Through its station and grid subsidiaries it oversees the energy activities of users, and sees that its subsidiaries comply with contracts with customers. It reviews and validates production costs; and it negotiates with the MoI and the Ministry of Finance to set tariffs for electricity and heat supplies.

RENEL sees that the provisions of the technical standards and regulations for producing, transmitting and distributing electricity are applied and observed. It establishes, applies and responds to measures for environmental protection and worker safety. It does research to increase technical and economic performance, to develop the national energy system and to refit its installations. It establishes development strategies for production, transmission, distribution and use of electricity and heat; and it has begun to promote and apply so-called 'demand-side management' or DSM in relations with its customers (see Chapter 6). It imports fuel, equipment, technologies and licences; it exports energy and performs services; and it cooperates with foreign firms in the field.

Within its component units, RENEL organizes management activities. It prepares documentation to obtain credit and other sources of finance, from within Romania and abroad, for its own activities and those of its subsidiaries. It programmes and carries out economic and financial activities, drafts budgets, analyzes the execution of the approved budget and directs the income and development funds, observing legal provisions; and it does international business directly, through its own departments. On the basis of the 'RENEL Personnel Statute', RENEL sees that worker discipline and working conditions are observed, and organizes training at all levels for RENEL personnel.

In May 1993 the government approved the Regulation for Supply and Use of Electrical Energy. This regulation contains provisions about contracting for electrical energy, erecting or installing electrical plant for supply and use, technical and organizational conditions for operating installations for supply and use, and so on. RENEL is also drawing up a Regulation for Supply and Use of Thermal Energy, now being approved.

As a public utility, RENEL does not seek to increase its profits, but only to cover the costs of supplying electricity and heat, with a minimum profit of 1% plus a percentage for a 'development fund' as decreed by the government – formerly 1.5% but now significantly higher and different for electricity and heat. The development fund was set up to compensate for the very low rate of depreciation included in costs, and accordingly in tariffs. With this fund, RENEL is creating its own finances for investment and refitting; but RENEL's budget is inadequate to meet all requirements. It has to be augmented with funds from the government budget, for the Cernavoda nuclear station for expenditure in Romanian currency, and from international financial institutions for refitting and for Cernavoda, for expenditure in hard currency.

Some parts of RENEL have already been split off from the RA and reconstituted as SAs to be privatized. A much more fundamental restructuring of RENEL is still under debate. Although no official statements had been made by August 1994, the World Bank is understood to be advocating the separation of RENEL into generation, transmission and distribution companies, privatizing the generation company or companies and introducing competition in generation, along the lines of recent restructuring of electricity supply in the UK and elsewhere. The Bank has also made splitting all nuclear activities off from RENEL a condition for granting a loan to rehabilitate RENEL power plants. Some Romanian specialists broadly favour this approach; others see it as at least premature, and perhaps fundamentally inappropriate, not least because of RENEL's status as a locus of stability in Romania's still fragile economy. The issue is deeply controversial both within and outside Romania; some foreign advisors, notably Electricité de France, are also believed to be opposed to such fundamental restructuring of RENEL.[23]

In any case, compared to utilities in OECD countries, RENEL has been experiencing unusual conditions, presenting both problems and opportuni-

---

[23] Similar controversies have also emerged elsewhere, notably in western Europe; see for instance Francis McGowan, *The Struggle for Power in Europe: Competition and Regulation in the EC Electricity Industry*, Royal Institute of International Affairs, 1993.

ties. After December 1989, industrial electricity use and industrial heat use in Romania fell dramatically. The evolution of electricity use is shown in Table 3.1. At the end of 1992 the nominal installed capacity in Romania was 22,225 MW, of which 92.3% belonged to RENEL. Of this capacity about 16,000-17,000 MW was said to be available, compared to the peak winter demand of about 9,000 MW; some commentators, however, have indicated that the capacity really available might have been closer to 11,000-12,000 MW. Of the total nominal capacity, some 14,500 MW were thermal stations, including 8,500 MW burning coal and lignite; another 5,700 MW were hydro stations, and 5,600 MW were cogeneration stations burning mainly hydrocarbons.

Table 3.2 shows the structure of the thermal capacity of RENEL, according to age, as it was in 1992. As the table indicates, all the thermal power stations in use in 1992 have equipment installed according to technical and design concepts of the years 1960-85, mostly between 1960 and 1980. Of these stations, with an installed capacity of 14,828 MW, about 65% have advanced steam cycles, with intermediate superheating, with a steam pressure of at least 13.6 MPa. About 35% have a simple steam cycle with steam pressure of at most 13.6 MPa; most of these are combined heat and power (CHP) or cogeneration stations. CHP or cogeneration plays an important role in mitigating the impact of thermal power stations on the environment. The significant reliance on CHP has reduced the use of fuel, and therefore by implication reduced noxious emissions, at 1990 levels, by at least 1.5-1.8 mtoe – a total reduction of about 7-9% of fuel consumption in the sector, and of about 3.5% nationally, compared to meeting the same industrial and heating demand with local boiler plant. Heat produced in cogeneration reduces the amount of water needed by thermal power stations and the losses through evaporation, and therefore reduces the call on water resources. However, Romanian specialists note that conventional cogeneration, associated with gigantic heat distribution systems, also has disadvantages (see Chapter 6). The initial investment in the grid is very costly, as are repairs and maintenance. In the absence of modern insulating technology, heat losses are relatively high. Performance, in terms of the quality of useful energy, is lower than simple quantitative energy efficiency calculations suggest, because these calculations assume that the high-quality, high-value electrical energy is identical to the low-temperature heat extracted from a steam cycle. A more efficient solution would be

**Table 3.1: Trends in electricity use, 1989-1993**

|                                                   | 1989  | 1990  | 1991  | 1992  | 1993  |
|---------------------------------------------------|-------|-------|-------|-------|-------|
| Internal use                                      |       |       |       |       |       |
| TWh                                               | 83.3  | 73.5  | 63.8  | 58.3  | 57.3  |
| MW                                                | 9,516 | 8,396 | 7,289 | 6,655 | 6,537 |
|                                                   |       |       |       |       |       |
| Fall in internal use compared with 1989 (%)       |       | 11.8  | 23.4  | 30.2  | 31.5  |

**Table 3.2: Age structure of RENEL thermal power stations in 1992**

|           | Units |        | Power  |        |
|-----------|-------|--------|--------|--------|
| Age (yrs) | No.   | %      | MW     | %      |
| 0-10      | 37    | 23     | 3,074  | 20.7   |
| 11-20     | 36    | 22.4   | 5,787  | 38.9   |
| 21-25     | 22    | 13.6   | 2,743  | 18.55  |
| 26-30     | 34    | 21.1   | 2,442  | 16.45  |
| >30       | 32    | 19.9   | 782    | 5.4    |
| Total     | 161   | 100.00 | 14,828 | 100.00 |

combined gas and steam cycles with cogeneration, in conditions in which the heat distribution grid is of reasonable dimensions, and therefore has smaller production units. Of course, the insulation technology for steam and hot-water pipework must be cost-effective and energy-efficient. Application of these technologies is now being investigated in Romania.

Several difficult policy issues now confront Romanian electricity specialists. RENEL has many more employees per megawatt installed than electricity suppliers in OECD countries; and much of the installed capacity is under-used or completely idle. The present surplus of nominal capacity means that time is available to refurbish existing stations; but that may not be the most appropriate way to use scarce capital, given that the future performance even of refurbished stations may be limited, as may their operating lifetime. Some Romanian specialists even feel that certain refurbishments already undertaken may have been ill-advised. One alternative might be to 'repower' some thermal stations, stripping out existing boilers and installing modern units, perhaps incorporating so-called 'clean coal technologies' like fluidized-bed combustion. (Both Poland and the Czech Republic have such projects under way.[24]) Another option would be to retire some stations completely, and replace them with new ones – perhaps, for instance, gas-fired combined cycle stations. But the fuel cost of importing natural gas might more than offset the efficiency gains. Yet another option would be to direct most new investment not into supply but into a truly major effort on DSM, while electricity use is still flat (see Chapter 6). That would raise questions about RENEL's statute, which at the moment severely limits its powers to invest in assets other than its own, or to earn revenue from such investments; and it would necessitate a completely different approach to tariff-setting, probably also calling for a regulatory agency outside the present ministry structure. The future of the Cernavoda nuclear station looms as a major uncertainty in its own right, both as to its effect on RENEL's total generating capacity and as to the investments it entails. RENEL's relationships with its suppliers of indigenous coal and lignite must also be clarified, as will be discussed below.

Romania also has significant electricity transmission and distribution capacity. Table 3.3 shows the system in 1991.

The political transformations in eastern Europe in recent years have opened up new possibilities for European electricity business. Until 1989, east-west exchanges were very modest; but in the political and social climate since created, the potential for such exchanges has significantly expanded. Exchanges of electricity can only be increased, however, through adequate development of interconnecting grids. Recent studies have confirmed that eastern and western systems could be interconnected; for the past three years UNIPEDE, the union of European producers and distributors of electricity, and UCPTE, the union for coordination of production and transmission of electricity in western Europe, have had a joint working group on the problem. Romania could have a particular role to play in this interconnection, because of its geographical location and the transverse form of the southern UCPTE

---

[24] Walter C. Patterson, *Coal-use Technology: New Challenges, New Responses*, Financial Times Business Information, 1993.

**Table 3.3: Transmission and distribution of electricity in Romania, 1991**

| Voltage (kV) | Length (km) |
|---|---|
| 750 | 154 |
| 400 | 4,310 |
| 220 | 3,600 |
| 110 | 18,260 |
| 1-60 | 143,620 |
| <1 | 425,550 |
| Total | 595,494 |

– former Yugoslavia, Greece and prospectively Turkey. Romania has enough transmission capacity to handle an eventual exchange between the northern and southern UCPTE systems, or with those of the Commonwealth of Independent States.

Favourable conditions may permit Romania to operate together with the UCPTE system in 1997-8. Romania's electricity system is based on design criteria similar to those accepted by the UCPTE system, and Romania's national energy system has significant exchange and production capacity. Frequency and power regulation meeting UCPTE requirements has been coming into operation. According to Romanian specialists, interconnecting the Romanian national energy system with the UCPTE would enhance the reliability and quality of electricity supply for users, and optimize production potential. In any event, interconnection with the UCPTE system would be a question not just for Romania but for the whole region.

## 3.5 Regia Autonoma a Lignitului (RAL): lignite authority; Regia Autonoma a Huilei (RAH): hard coal authority

As noted in Chapter 1, among the emerging democracies of central and eastern Europe Romania has the distinction that it has long been a major producer of all the fossil fuels – coal, oil and natural gas. However, the depredations of the Ceauşescu era did all these energy industries serious damage. The coal industry suffered particularly badly, as the IEA report has described.

The rate and pattern of development in the coal industry were much influenced by the attempt of the Ceauşescu government in the 1980s to establish an industrial state based largely, if not exclusively, on national resources. Enormous effort was directed towards increasing production of coal, the most abundant domestic energy resource. Ambitious targets were sought, often at the expense of quality and future output; in 1989 the army was deployed to help boost production. After the revolution, it became clear that this frantic pace was unsustainable, and the legacy of poor maintenance, exhausted machinery, substandard materials and inadequate investment became apparent.[25]

Bringing Romania's coal industry up to modern standards for safety, efficiency, productivity, competitiveness and environmental acceptability presents a severe challenge. Work has begun, but it has a long way to go.

After December 1989, the Romanian coal industry was reorganized into two RAs, one for lignite, the Regia Autonoma a Lignitului (RAL), and one for Romania's type of hard coal, called *huila*, the Regia Autonoma a Huilei (RAH). Both were founded in 1990 by government decree. Although each is a legal entity and operates with its own economic administration and financial autonomy, the MoI, which represents government interests on the administrative council of each RA, appoints its director general, who is also president of the council.

RAL administers the industrial reserves of lignite, brown coal and peat within the boundaries accredited for exploitation. It extracts lignite, brown coal and peat from underground and opencast mines in the deposits and mining areas supplying the RA. It opens and prepares underground mines, and removes overburden from opencast mines. It does geological and technological research, draws up studies, designs and documentation, and develops both existing and new deposits. RAH has the same aims as RAL, but for hard coal, shale coal and refractory clay within other perimeters accredited by the government.

RAL's subordinates include mines, opencast mines, sections, workshops and territorial sub-units, as well as its own research and design units. The components of RAH include operations, mines, opencast mines, preparation

---

[25] *Energy Policies of Romania.*

plants, repair plants, sections, workshops and territorial sub-units, and its own research and design units.

In 1992 coal, of the specifications shown in Table 3.4, accounted for 22.9% of total primary energy consumption. According to Romanian specialists, the Romanian coal industry has both positive and negative features. On the positive side, at the level of output officially estimated for the year 2000 (87 million tonnes/year (t/y) of lignite and 12 million t/y of hard coal), industrial coal reserves in the areas now being exploited or opened represent 38 years' supply of lignite and 125 years' supply of hard coal. Data about the coalfields are good enough to base development of both deep mines and opencast mines on them, and investment programmes in earlier years have created a significant potential in the form of facilities and corresponding infrastructure. Through activities over many years, Romanian mining engineers have developed, tested and demonstrated methods and technologies to exploit all the varieties of coalfields and geological and mining conditions existing in Romania on an industrial scale. Romanian miners are well qualified, and have experience adapted to existing mining conditions. On the negative side, however, technical equipment is obsolescent and deteriorating, and short of spare parts, so that coalfaces advance only slowly and capacity is under-utilized. Moreover, output from the deepest mines is falling, as lignite workings penetrate below the water table and geostatic pressures affect hard coal seams. As Table 3.4 indicates, the quality of the lignite is low. One Romanian specialist has noted wryly a comment from a foreign mining engineer; asked how Romanian lignite might be improved, the foreign engineer responded 'Leave it in the ground a few more centuries'.

The majority of coal output is used to produce electricity and heat. According to Romanian specialists, in the final years of the Ceauşescu era, coal mines trying to meet the production quotas set for them increased the tonnage of raw output simply by mining rock as well as coal; so statistical comparisons before and after December 1989 are even more misleading than usual. With that proviso, however, indigenous coal output has declined continuously since 1989, from 53.1 million tonnes of lignite in 1989 to 34.3 million tonnes in 1992, and from 11.6 million tonnes of hard coal to 4.1 million tonnes in 1992, making imports necessary; see Table 3.5.

**Table 3.4: Coal and lignite specifications**

| Mine and product | Calorific value (kJ/kg) | Ash content (% db) | Moisture (% as mined) | Sulphur (% daf) |
|---|---|---|---|---|
| Lignite, unwashed | | | | |
| Rosia Jilt | 6,780 | 40 | 43 | 1.2 |
| Rovinari | 6,800 | 43 | 43 | 0.9 |
| Motru | 6,700 | 49 | 40 | 1.1 |
| Voievozi | 7,285 | 32 | 36 | 2.3 |
| | | | | |
| Hard coal, washed | | | | |
| Jiu Valley | 25,120 | 48* | 11 | 2.5 |

db = dry basis
daf = dry ash-free basis
* suggests coal washeries not working to design standards

*Source*: Ministry of Industries, cited in *Energy Policies of Romania* (IEA, 1993).

**Table 3.5: Coal and lignite production and use, 1990-1992 (mt)**

| | 1990 | 1991 | 1992 |
|---|---|---|---|
| Production | | | |
| Lignite | 32.4 | 28.6 | 34.3 |
| Hard coal | 3.2 | 3.8 | 4.1 |
| Destined for production | | | |
| of electricity and heat | | | |
| Lignite | 29.9 | 26.5 | 32.0 |
| Hard coal | 2.4 | 2.2 | 2.7 |
| Import | 4.1 | 2.6 | 2.2 |

*Source*: Ministry of Industries, cited in *Energy Policies of Romania* (IEA, 1993).

According to Romanian specialists, the strategy of the coal industry until the year 2000 is to maintain existing production capacity; to increase the quality of the coal mined and prepared; to modernize facilities to increase coal output; to reduce production costs; and to lower subsidies gradually until they are eliminated. The estimated demand for electricity and heat in the year 2000 will require more than 50 million tonnes of coal, compared with the 40 million tonnes burned in 1990. According to some government estimates, the investment needed to attain this objective will be US$900-1,000 million, one-half of this in Romanian currency.

Analysis of the efficiency and competitiveness of underground mines has led to the conclusion that, in spite of the technical and managerial measures foreseen, twenty-nine mines and sectors – eighteen lignite and eleven hard coal – still remain so inefficient that they will have to close. Of these twenty-nine mines, nineteen – thirteen lignite and six hard coal – will be closed by 1995, and the others will be closed between 1996 and 2000. In the following decade, extraction of lignite is forecast to increase to about 50 million tonnes in the year 2005 and about 55 million tonnes in the year 2010. For net hard coal, in the period 2005-2010 annual output is forecast to be 6.5-7 million tonnes. How production can be increased while closing mines has not, thus far, been clarified.[26]

Neither RAL nor RAH covers its expenses with the income from its own activities; both receive subsidies from the government budget. Romanian specialists consider that their activities are on the whole economically useful and productive although unprofitable. The IEA report takes a more sombre view.[27] It draws a sharp distinction between lignite and *huila*. According to the IEA report, 'The prospects for lignite mining are inextricably linked with those for rehabilitation of power plants,' since most lignite is burned in power stations close to the mines. The report warns that even if the mines themselves were upgraded with proper management and equipment, to bring the cost of lignite down to a competitive level, 'the future of the mines would still depend upon having rehabilitated or new power stations capable of burning the product'. It endorses an 'integrated approach' to developing the lignite and power sectors. The IEA report reserves its most severe strictures for *huila*. 'The management of RAH appears to be little aware of the demands of a market

---

[26] Romania is by no means the only country facing difficult policy issues relating to its coal industry; others include the UK, Germany and Spain. See for example Mike Parker, *The UK 'Coal Crisis': Origins and Resolution*, Royal Institute of International Affairs, 1993, and *The Prospects for Hard Coal in Europe*, Royal Institute of International Affairs, 1994, forthcoming.

[27] *Energy Policies of Romania*.

economy. The resource appears to have few economic prospects and the gross value of the product is only $18 per person per day. Subsidies approximately equal the value of the output. It is hard to believe that any increase in productivity could essentially change the economic characteristics of the industry'. If this judgement is accepted, resolving the dilemma, especially as it affects the miners themselves, and their communities, will not be easy. The IEA report calls for 'bold, determined intervention by government, accepting the inevitable costs and devising a programme that balances as well as possible within a restricted budget three essential elements: urgent concentration on the most effective mines, guarantee while necessary of subsidies and markets, and compensation and retraining of personnel'. It acknowledges that the Romanian government 'faces very difficult decisions over the future of the industry'. The decisions taken will affect profoundly and directly the lives of tens of thousands of people and the communities in which they live. The plight of Romania's hard coal industry throws into sharp relief the human dimension of rebuilding Romania.

### 3.6 Regia Autonoma a Gazelor Naturale (ROMGAZ RA): natural gas authority

As noted in Chapter 1, Romania was for many years the largest producer of natural gas in Europe. However, the recent upsurge of enthusiasm for natural gas may be late in the day for Romania, whose domestic gas reserves were severely depleted under Ceauşescu. Romania's natural gas authority, ROMGAZ, was founded in 1991 by government decree. Although it is a legal entity and operates with its own economic administration and financial autonomy, the Ministry of Industries, which represents government interests on its administrative council, appoints the whole council, including its president, who is the director general of ROMGAZ.

ROMGAZ administers Romania's deposits of natural gas, except for deposits of associated gas exploited by petroleum extraction on land and in the sea. It does geological research to discover reserves, develops new deposits, and drills wells. It extracts and stores natural gas, and operates main pipelines, grids, and distribution and commercial installations for natural gas. It maintains installations, manufactures spare parts, and does industrial and civil building and erection work. Service functions, such as production of gas meters and construction of pipelines, have, however, already been separated from ROMGAZ's main business centres and established as commercial companies. ROMGAZ likewise intends to split off drilling and distribution units as soon as possible.

ROMGAZ imports and exports products, plant, equipment and specialized technology. It collaborates economically, scientifically and technically with other organizations, and also works abroad. ROMGAZ dispatches gas and oversees its use by all categories of users. It carries out research and design, does work and provides services for natural gas activities both within and outside Romania. ROMGAZ includes subsidiaries, plants, factories, sub-units for research and design and computation, building sites, workshops and other sub-units. Unlike the coal and lignite authorities RAH and RAL, ROMGAZ covers all its expenses with income from its own activities.

In addition to ROMGAZ, PETROM (see below), ROMPETROL (see below) and WIEH (a joint venture between the German firm of Wintershall and the Russian agency Gazprom) are now involved in producing, transporting, distributing and doing business with natural gas. Some international companies, including Shell, are engaged in exploration activities. The Romanian gas industry is vertically integrated. ROMGAZ is responsible for producing some 60% of Romania's natural gas, and for transporting and distributing it. PETROM is responsible for producing some 40%, in the form of associated gas from petroleum production, which is largely transmitted and distributed by ROMGAZ. ROMPETROL has been responsible for gas imports, by negotiating contracts with the former Soviet Union, and is also responsible for barter exchange. Since March 1993, however, ROMGAZ has had exclusive authorization to negotiate pricing for imports for general gas supply.[28]

Natural gas is transported through a network of 12,000 km of transmission pipelines with diameters from 250 mm to 1000 mm, extending radially from the main gasfields in the centre of the country. The maximum pipeline capac-

---

[28] For the background to the burgeoning international market in natural gas, see Jonathan Stern, *European Gas Markets: Challenge and Opportunity in the 1990s*, Royal Institute of International Affairs, 1990; and for a key policy issue see Jonathan Stern, *Third Party Access in European Gas Industries*, Royal Institute of International Affairs, 1992.

ity is 135 million cu m/day or 40 billion cu m/year at a maximum pressure of 50 bar. The distribution system totals 11,150 km. The pressure of distributed gas is nominally 6 bar; during the old regime it sometimes fell as low as 0.5 bar, but now does so only locally, for a few days in the winter. Natural gas storage capacity is 670 million cu m/cycle, concentrated in three deposits with a maximum exit capacity of 4.65 million cu m/day, working at a pressure varying from 60 bar to 80 bar.

At present, gas from the former Soviet Union is routed through Romania to Bulgaria and Turkey. To Bulgaria the transit began in 1972, utilizing a 200 km pipeline of 1,000 mm diameter, and to Turkey it began in 1988 through a 200 km pipeline of 1,200 mm diameter. The volume transported varies according to the contracts signed, between 10 and 12 billion cu m/year.

As the IEA report notes,[29] gas is imported in five different ways:

- From Gazprom through government contracts, as payment for the Romanian contribution to the development of gasfields in Russia. The volume of this import is 1.8 billion cu m/ year.
- Barter exchanges through government contracts. The limit of these exchanges is 38% of the volume of imports and is 0.7-0.8 billion cu m/year.
- Barter exchanges between WIEH and the Romanian fertilizer industry. The volume of these exchanges is rising to 2 billion cu m/year.
- Tax for transit to Bulgaria and Turkey (0.35 billion cu m/year).
- To cover the balance temporarily, hard currency purchases from Gazprom.

With regard to contracts with Russia based on the existing infrastructure, Romania intends to diversify import possibilities. On the basis of estimates of the possible evolution of natural gas demand in Romania, ROMGAZ projects, as a minimum scenario, the values shown in Table 3.6. The doubling (by 1995) or indeed tripling (by 2000) of gas consumption by the public and the service sector will necessitate major investments to create the corresponding infrastructure. Demand in these sectors will have to be reassessed periodically, especially in the light of increasing gas prices.

---

[29] *Energy Policies of Romania.*

**Table 3.6: Natural Gas Balance (Minimum Scenario) (billion cu m at 15° Celsius)**

|                                | 1986 | 1990 | 1991 | 1992 | 1995 | 2000 |
|--------------------------------|------|------|------|------|------|------|
| Internal production            |      |      |      |      |      |      |
| Free gas                       | 26.8 | 19.2 | 17.2 | 15.1 | 12.6 | 9.0  |
| Associated gases               | 12.5 | 8.9  | 7.5  | 6.9  | 5.7  | 4.0  |
| Total internal production      | 39.3 | 28.1 | 24.7 | 22.0 | 18.3 | 13.0 |
| Imports                        | 2.5  | 7.2  | 5.3  | 4.5  | 9.0  | 15.0 |
| Total resources                | 41.8 | 35.3 | 30.0 | 26.5 | 27.3 | 28.0 |
| Structure of use (%)           |      |      |      |      |      |      |
| Industry                       | 58   | 57   | 49   | 48   | 44   | 38   |
| General public and services    | 7    | 8    | 11   | 12   | 23   | 34   |

## 3.7 Regia Autonoma a Petrolului (PETROM RA): petroleum authority

As noted in Chapter 1, Romania was historically the first country in the world to produce petroleum commercially. Petroleum production, refining and petrochemicals have long been a major Romanian industry; but under Ceauşescu the industry suffered serious degradation, and will need major investment to modernize its facilities, as the IEA report has described.[30] The Romanian petroleum authority, PETROM, was founded in 1991 by government decree. Although it is a legal entity and operates with its own administration and financial autonomy, the MoI, the Ministry of Finances and the Ministry of Commerce and Tourism together represent government interests on its administrative council, which is appointed by the Minister of Industries. The director general of PETROM is also president of the administrative council.

PETROM discovers, exploits and administers deposits of petroleum and gas on Romanian territory, on land and on the Black Sea continental shelf, except for the gas deposits of ROMGAZ (see above). It recovers gasoline and ethane fractions from gases, and extracts carbon dioxide from wells. It

---

[30] Ibid.

does research and design, drills wells, and maintains and repairs wells, production equipment and installations. It imports and exports products, plant, equipment and technology. It collaborates economically, scientifically and technically with other organizations, and does petroleum business abroad, on its own account and at its own risk. The structure of PETROM includes production derricks, drilling derricks, the PETROMAR enterprise in Constanţa for offshore production, plants, factories, sections, building sites, workshops, centres and offices, as well as research, design and training units. PETROM covers all its expenses with income from its own activities.

ROMPETROL, formerly part of the same communist-era ministry as PETROM, is now a separate organization, involved particularly in international oil activities. RAFIROM, a state-owned holding company constituted as an SA, is responsible for refining.

Among primary resources in Romania, petroleum is the second largest energy resource. Romania's deposits of petroleum and gas are at an advanced stage of exploitation; the deposits discovered more recently have relatively small reserves compared to older deposits. At the moment about 460 deposits of petroleum and about 120 gas-bearing structures are being exploited. They are located in the sub-carpatic regions of the Southern and Arc Carpathians, in Moldova, and – recent discoveries – in the Western Plain, in the Dobrogea region and on the continental shelf of the Black Sea. The last, discovered in 1980, entered into production in 1987, producing about 1,800 tonnes of petroleum and 55,000 cu m of gas a day.

In Romania petroleum is extracted both by derricks and by enhanced (secondary and tertiary) recovery. Production with derricks is expected to fall, as a consequence of the natural decline of deposits and of production from old derricks, and of the fall in the contribution from new derricks. Production by secondary recovery uses water injection, gas injection, or steam injection, and by tertiary recovery uses subterranean combustion (wet and dry), polymer injection, and even mining – recalling the very first petroleum production in Romania, and very rare elsewhere in the world. The efficiency depends both on natural factors, such as the geological and physical characteristics of the deposit, the depth to which the derricks can reach and the existing reserves, and also on technical and economic factors.

According to Romanian specialists, studies indicate that the volume of newly discovered recoverable reserves of petroleum will continue to fall in the period 1991-95, from approximately 4.6 million tonnes of petroleum reserve in 1991 to 3.5 million tonnes in 1995. In consequence the annual production of petroleum will fall from 7.6 million tonnes in 1992 to approximately 6.5 million tonnes in 1995. International oil companies have returned to Romania, and are already involved in exploration activities; one foreign specialist commented wryly that Romanians were initially wary, expecting oil industry people to be like 'J.R.' in the television series *Dallas*. For both petroleum and natural gas, foreign specialists suggest that modern exploratory techniques such as three-dimensional seismic studies might reveal additional Romanian reserves; they comment that old provinces invariably benefit from re-examination with modern techniques. They add that modern drilling technology, including directional and horizontal drilling, might improve production from both oil- and gasfields.

Romania has significant petroleum refining capacity – 34 million tonnes of petroleum a year, as shown in Table 3.7. Romanian specialists note that the IEA report found that Romania's petroleum refining industry compares favourably with those of other east European countries on various criteria:[31]

* Complexity: it is the most sophisticated of those in the countries of eastern Europe, and comparable with the average of those in the countries of western Europe.
* Access to resources: it has access to its own resources and does not depend on petroleum from the former Soviet Union.
* Integration of refining and petrochemistry: four of the five large refineries – Arpechim, Petromidia, Petroţel and Petrobrazi – have integrated capacity to process olefines and aromatics, based on a combination of stocks of naphtha and also light fuel oil from the adjacent refineries.
* Infrastructure: it has access to the most complex network of interconnecting pipelines, in three refineries and harbour terminals, in Europe.

On the other hand, the IEA report also comments that 'While the nominal capacity of the Romanian refining industry is impressive, its economic and

[31] Ibid.

**Table 3.7: Romanian refining capacity, end 1992 (m t/y)**

| Refinery | Location | Atmospheric Distillation | Vacuum Distillation | Catalytic cracking | Vis-breaking | Thermal cracking | Coking | Catalytic reforming | HDS | BTX | Others |
|---|---|---|---|---|---|---|---|---|---|---|---|
| Arpechim | Pitești | 6.5 | 3.0 | 1.86 | 1.0 | - | - | 1.0 | 3.16 | 0.44 | Bitumen, lubes |
| Petrobrazi | Ploiești | 7.5 | | 1.1 | - | - | 1.92 | 1.85 | 3.67 | 0.84 | Bitumen, |
| Petrotel | Ploiești | 4.7 | | 1.0 | 0.36 | - | 0.7 | 0.5 | 1.9 | - | alkylation, lubes |
| Petromidia | Navodari | 4.8 | | 1.0 | - | - | 0.8 | 0.5 | 2.7 | 0.42 | |
| RAFO | Onești | 5.25 | | 1.78 | - | 0.36 | 0.3 | 1.0 | 3.77 | 0.64 | |
| Astra | Ploiești | 2.0 | 0.35 | - | - | - | 0.45 | - | - | - | Bitumen, white oils |
| Darmanești | Darmanești | 1.5 | - | - | - | 0.41 | 0.46 | - | - | - | |
| Steaua Romana | Cimpina | 0.4 | 0.29 | - | - | - | - | - | - | - | Lubes, bitumen |
| Vega | Ploiești | 0.8 | 0.17 | - | - | - | - | - | - | - | Lubes, bitumen |
| Crișana | Suplacu de Barcau | 0.4 | 0.25 | - | - | - | - | - | - | - | Bitumen |
| Total | | 33.85 | 4.06 | 6.74 | 1.36 | 0.77 | 4.63 | 4.85 | 15.2 | 2.34 | |

technical performance has been less so. The sector has been beset by poor operational performance, extended downtime, extensive losses and disregard for energy conservation and the local environment'.

After 1989, production of petroleum products fell from 26.55 million tonnes to 12.29 million tonnes in 1992, as a consequence on the one hand of the decline of indigenous production of petroleum, and on the other hand of difficulties with hard currency to pay for imports. In 1992 approximately 50% of the petroleum processed was imported, compared to a maximum of 70% in 1989. Table 3.8 shows the evolution of indigenous production and of imports of petroleum, as well as the structure of petroleum products from refining and processing.

Crude oil from different oilfields reaches the refineries through pipelines. Imported crude is brought to the petroleum terminal at Constanţa, where it is unloaded, mixed and pumped to the Piteşti, Ploieşti and Oneşti refineries through 10- 20- and 24-inch pipelines. The pipelines are interconnected through a collector at Baraganu, thus depriving the refineries of the facility to choose among sources of import supplies, and therefore among qualities and quantities imported. The investment needed to rectify this is not available. Table 3.7 (see above) shows the capacities of Romanian refineries by process. Petroleum products are exported through Constanţa, which has specialized zones and terminals, and through the Giurgiu barge-loading terminal, which has a capacity of 1 million t/y of white and black products for export along the Danube.

As the IEA report observes, the future of the Romanian refining and petrochemical industry will depend not only on appropriate upgrading and improvement of existing facilities, but also on the international markets for refining services, petroleum products and petrochemicals.[32] Unfortunately for Romania, the whole of Europe at the moment has surplus refining capacity. Forward planning for the Romanian industry will have to take this international dimension into account.[33]

---

[32] Ibid.

[33] One proposal perhaps worth noting is that of increasing the use of fuel oil for power generation, as a way to ease the problems both of refinery mix and of environmental pollution; see John Mitchell, *An Oil Agenda for Europe*, Royal Institute of International Affairs, 1994, forthcoming.

**Table 3.8: Refinery throughput and production, 1980-92**

|  | 1980 | 1985 | 1988 | 1989 | 1990 | 1991 | 1992 |
|---|---|---|---|---|---|---|---|
| *Crude input* |  |  |  |  |  |  |  |
| Domestic | 11.51 | 10.72 | 9.39 | 9.05 | 7.77 | 6.64 | 6.54 |
| Imported | 15.96 | 14.63 | 20.96 | 21.56 | 15.89 | 8.55 | 6.76 |
| Total | 27.47 | 25.34 | 30.35 | 30.61 | 23.66 | 15.19 | 13.30 |
| *Product output* |  |  |  |  |  |  |  |
| LPG | 0.22 | 0.19 | 0.21 | 0.19 | 0.22 | 0.22 | 0.23 |
| Naphtha | 0.94 | 1.34 | 1.80 | 1.61 | 1.28 | 0.34 | 0.25+ |
| Gasoline | 2.68 | 3.79 | 4.64 | 4.35 | 3.38 | 2.78 | 2.67+ |
| Kerosene | 0.87 | 0.49 | 0.63 | 0.51 | 0.45 | 0.41 | 0.39 |
| Gasoil | 7.48 | 6.84 | 8.35 | 8.31 | 6.23 | 3.90 | 3.99 |
| Fuel Oil | 10.23 | 8.43 | 9.95 | 10.11 | 8.12 | 4.96 | 3.88 |
| Coke | 0.61 | 0.43 | 0.54 | 0.54 | 0.37 | 0.29 | 0.27 |
| Lubes | 0.29 | 0.49 | 0.47 | 0.48 | 0.37 | 0.27 | 0.25 |
| Bitumen | 0.67 | 0.46 | 0.47 | 0.45 | 0.41 | 0.37 | 0.36 |
| Total* | 23.99 | 22.46 | 27.06 | 26.55 | 20.83 | 13.54 | 12.29 |

+ Estimated
* Excluding refinery gas, speciality products, refinery fuel and losses.

*Source: Romanian Statistical Yearbook 1991*, National Statistics Commission, RAFIROM.

## 3.8 Renewable energy

As well as coal, oil and natural gas, Romania also has significant opportunities for developing renewable energy. The Directorate General for Energy of the MoI has launched a programme to promote new and renewable sources of energy nationally. The programme includes five subprogrammes, each for a particular renewable source. RENEL is coordinating subprogramme A for microhydro stations and subprogramme B for wind energy. The firm of FORADEX SA is coordinating subprogramme C for geothermal energy. The Building Research Institute IMCREST, in collaboration with the firm of ICPAIUC SA, is coordinating subprogramme D for solar energy. AGROPROIECT SA, in collaboration with the Design Institute for the Food Industry (IPIA), is coordinating subprogramme E for biomass. The MoI is coordinating the whole programme with the direct collaboration of ARCE. Each of the five subprogrammes includes consideration of a legislative framework and a fiscal and customs policy, to encourage both investment and the development of industry to manufacture the energy equipment for such investment.

Foreign specialists comment that the data on Romania's renewable resources warrant upgrading and expanding, perhaps including preparation of a detailed atlas of renewable resources in Romania. The present study, which focuses more on end-use than on supply, can offer only a brief summary of the potential for renewable energy in Romania. Nevertheless, even this cursory overview suggests that Romania's sunlight, waterways, forests and arable land may represent a future energy resource of some importance, which would benefit from closer assessment. The Annex (see end of chapter) summarizes the currently available information about the potential and the activities for hydroelectricity, geothermal energy, solar energy, wind energy and biomass energy in Romania. In the context of the present study, foreign specialists also emphasize that renewable energy supplies and energy efficiency are frequently 'synergistic', complementing each other effectively, because renewable resources tend to be diffuse and dispersed. Passive solar techniques, for instance, can be combined with building refurbishment to improve thermal performance. Active solar heating can meet requirements more effectively if the heat load for a building is reduced by improving its efficiency. Active water heating can be used to top up district heating, or be combined with long-term heat storage; and so on.

### 3.9 Energy research institutes

In the old centrally planned economy, the government controlled all research and development. All industrial sectors had their own research and design institutes, funded by the government and responsible to the appropriate ministry. Since December 1989 this arrangement has undergone a gradual metamorphosis, but still broadly resembles the previous system. For the energy research institutes, as for many other research institutes in Romania, finances from the so-called 'special fund' remain essential. The fund was set up for the first time in December 1990, following vigorous demonstrations by research and design staff in Bucureşti on 22 November 1990. The Romanian parliament has since reconfirmed the fund annually, as a special budgetary source, made up from legally obligatory monthly payments of 1% of the income of all enterprises, whether state-owned, private or mixed. The Ministry of Research and Technology administers the fund, through a consultative committee made up of representatives of research and design institutes from all industrial sectors. The consultative committee considers only applied research and development of an interdepartmental and multidisciplinary character, of broad interest for the economy. In the energy field the research institutes, each with its own specialization, operate with finances from the 'special fund' and from contracts with clients, either within the relevant industrial branches or outside these branches.

Scientific research in Romania is departmental, and frequently combined with design. This is the result of the social and political regime before 1989, which emphasized industrialization and investment. Romanian applied scientific research was nevertheless able to develop without being suffocated by the political limits of the communist regime, training competent specialists and obtaining notable results. Some Romanian specialists consider that both applied and fundamental research faced the same problems and the same disadvantages; others, however, consider that fundamental research with technical and technological implications was not sustained consistently and continually, and fell behind both applied research and behind research outside Romania. After 1989, the authorities radically altered the content of the research programmes, because funds for investment, for research design, were so scarce. Design was almost abandoned, even though, generation after generation, Romania had produced many able design engineers and scientists, whose designs had been applied both within Romania and abroad.

As Romania moves through a transition period in which the economy is struggling, the prevailing view is that support should be focused on applied research, to find technological solutions to relaunch industry, agriculture, transport and services in the near future. Relaunching the economy will require not only financial resources but also effective solutions, able not only to create new industrial potential on the bases of modern and economically efficient technologies, but also to restore existing industrial potential, by improving, retooling and modernizing. The situation for energy research is analogous to that for the entire economy. The energy research institutes are therefore concentrating on applied research. They draw up studies of requirements, opportunities and feasibility; they pursue technological development and disseminate new and prototype solutions; and they obtain material resources and train personnel.

Appendix 2 lists and describes many of the main energy research institutes, including the Energy Research and Modernizing Institute (ICEMENERG), some of whose senior staff have prepared most of the material presented in this study. Many other organizations play a part in energy activities in Romania, in particular the enterprises that manufacture energy technology. Appendix 2 also describes some prominent non-governmental groups with energy interests, and Appendix 3 is a contact list for Romanian governmental, non-governmental and industrial organizations involved in energy.


### 3.10 Changing the groundrules

In the aftermath of December 1989, the provisional government that took over in Romania at once abolished the old quotas on energy supplies to the public, and removed the upper limits on the amount of energy that individual households could use. It lifted the ban on connecting new consumers to the natural gas distribution networks, and drew up a programme to extend these networks. It eliminated official restrictions on personal car travel; and it banned the disconnection of household electricity, even in difficult situations. These measures were very popular; to reverse most of them is now inconceivable. As a result of these measures, the use of energy in the household sector quickly increased significantly, both in absolute terms and in the percentage of final consumption – between 1989 and 1991 from 4.3 TWh to 6.7 TWh, and from 6.1% to 13.0% of final use of electricity. Consumption of heat produced centrally increased from 2.0 mtoe to 2.7 mtoe over the same period. For other forms of energy the picture was similar, at least qualitatively. For everyday Romanians, fuels and electricity are still sometimes difficult to obtain; but the obstacles are now exclusively technical or commercial, and not generated by laws or regulations. Similar difficulties still exist for supplies of bottled liquid gas, petrol and heat produced centrally, and are all related. On the other hand, the government subsidized energy supplies to the public until 1 May 1993, when most direct subsidies were withdrawn; the subsidy on heat was phased out more gradually through 1993. Foreign specialists note, however, that extensive cross-subsidies still exist between industry and households; Romanian households pay at rates much lower than Romanian industry – an average of some US$25/MWh for households, as against US$45/MWh for industry – whereas in OECD countries household rates are usually much higher than industrial rates, reflecting the difference in cost of supply. Cross-subsidies also exist between electricity and heat, such that heat is sold at a price only half of what would be appropriate.

The provisional government also abolished norms and reports about specific energy use for products and services in activities considered 'productive' – industries, transport, agriculture and construction. This was a logical step, for the norms and limits laid down had by that time become arbitrary and without any technical basis, and the funds that would have been needed to implement economy measures had not been allocated. On the other hand, some Romanian specialists stress the need for some kind of central agency to gather genuine data on energy use, so that the government can compile and analyze data on energy efficiency to define and justify national energy policy. Obtaining data from enterprises about energy use and energy efficiency still depends essentially on their goodwill. A law about the statistical reports that enterprises are required to prepare for the National Statistics Commission has been drafted for the government and laid before the Romanian parliament. The draft also envisages an obligation to communicate data on total and specific energy use. The hope is that parliament will soon discuss and vote on this draft law.

As yet, Romania does not have a coherent and comprehensive set of laws on energy and energy efficiency – using the word 'law' in the sense of legislation voted by parliament. Old laws have mostly been abrogated; but those that are still formally in effect contain many articles that refer to the old mode of economic organization. These articles compromise the ones that could, in principle, be applied, and make the law as a whole inapplicable. Efforts to put a coherent set of energy laws in place are under way. Parliament has already received some drafts that await discussion; others are being drawn up. One of these draft laws – usually referred to as the 'energy law' – concerns electricity and heat supply; another covers energy conservation; and a third, drawn up by the government and sent to parliament for analysis, is on protecting the environment (see Chapter 8). The law on environmental protection is part of the effort to bring Romanian legislation into line with that of western Europe, an obligation the Romanian government accepted by acceding to international conventions on environmental protection. Implementing such a law on environmental protection will pose problems for RENEL and for energy users. Some Romanian specialists consider that it would lead to an increase in the proportion of electricity in final energy use, and in the efficiency of end-use of energy. Whether this will happen and to what extent, however, remains to be seen.

The Directorate General for Energy of the MoI has been working for more than a year to prepare the draft 'energy law'. Interested bodies, including RENEL and ARCE, have also submitted comments and alternative drafts; and the process of reconciling the different views and producing a draft acceptable to all has proved to be demanding. The Synergy Programme of the European Commission has seconded an advisor to the Directorate General in Bucureşti, one of whose tasks is to assist in furthering the drafting. At one stage the 'energy law' itself contained a chapter on efficient use of energy. This was subsequently split off into an entirely separate law, whose draft provisions envisage, for instance, placing efficiency obligations on Romanian manufacturers and importers of appliances and equipment, as well as on energy users. The draft laws must be approved by the government and placed before parliament for debate. Until parliament passes the legislation, in the absence of a specific law – often the case these days, as Romania's transition evolves – many problems are dealt with in legal terms by government or ministerial decree, and in particular by the MoI.

Because indigenous resources and production of energy are limited, and procuring hard currency to pay for imports is difficult, the government has taken some time to phase out the quota system for distributing energy produced indigenously – that is, Romanian crude oil and all electricity, heat and gas – that can be paid for in Romanian currency. For electricity, for instance, the quota system was terminated only on 1 July 1994. The government did, however, abolish planning control of industrial production and specific energy use. Where the quota system remained in effect, each industrial user was assured of a certain amount of energy that could be paid for in Romanian currency, to use as desired. As noted above, the household sector has not been subject to these limits. The government has also decreed that commercial enterprises with access to hard currency may import energy on their own account; but transport and distribution services by specialized suppliers on Romanian territory must be paid for in Romanian currency. According to Romanian specialists, the government expects this approach to increase both the efficiency of energy use and productive output for export. No longer constrained by rigid planning and targets for specific energy use, industrial users themselves should then redirect their activities, to make the economic and efficient products that Romanian and international markets demand. IEA specialists, however, remain sceptical that any measures short of full privatization will adequately improve product output and quality, or energy efficiency. They have noted that from 1989 to 1992, although total energy use in industry fell, the proportional decrease in each industry was about the same – suggesting that the quota system merely allocated a smaller quantity of energy according to the former criteria, with no regard to the comparative commercial status of the various outputs. IEA specialists have questioned the official rationale for maintaining any remnant of the quota system, insisting that market forces will allocate resources more effectively than any bureaucracy.

In any event, because the Romanian economy has been suffering economic upheaval and high inflation, the effects of these measures on efficiency of energy use have thus far been debatable. In the early months of 1994, however, the monthly rate of inflation fell to about 5%, and measures taken by the Romanian National Bank, notably high real interest rates, helped to bring official and unofficial exchange rates much more close together, although the exchange rate has not yet been completely liberalized (see Chapter 4). Whether or not the official rationale for maintaining energy quotas has been plausible, Romanian specialists say that the pronounced drop in energy use, easing pressures on indigenous supplies, means that the quota system will be replaced by freely negotiated contracts between suppliers and users for the amount of energy desired. The role of the bureaucracy in steering the economy will therefore continue to decline, and the role of economic players will increase, according to the laws of the market.

# Annex to Chapter 3

Romania is located in a geographical zone with moderate resources of renewable energy, including hydro, geothermal, solar, wind and biomass. According to Romanian specialists, some estimates of the potential of these renewable energies suggest that in the longer term – by 2020 – they will cater for 5-10% of the primary energy needs of the country, with corresponding savings of fossil fuel and related reduction of polluting emissions to the surrounding environment. Appendix 2 describes specialist organizations involved in these fields, and Appendix 3 gives contact information.

## Hydroelectricity
Romania has long had significant hydroelectric capacity; indeed it is ranked twenty-seventh in the world for power and installed capacity. The theoretical gross potential for hydro power is approximately 70 TWh, of which in practice some 38 TWh could be utilized in stations of more than 2 MW, and a further 2 TWh in stations of less than 2 MW. At the end of 1992, hydroelectric stations with a total capacity of 5,700 MW were in place, and generated 16.6 TWh – that is, 41.5% of the 40 TWh of available potential. Of this installed capacity, the installations on the Danube, Porţile de Fier (Iron Gates) 1 and 2, represent about 40%; the rest are on rivers in the interior of Romania, 1.5% in the form of microhydro stations of less than 1 MW. At present sixty-seven hydro stations are under construction, with a total production capacity of about 3,645 GWh/y. Among these, twelve are in partial operation and three are in the final phase of construction. Completing these would increase electricity production by about 1,390 GWh/y. The total production capacity of other work under way is about 2,225 GWh/y. Completing all these installations would utilize 47.8% of Romania's hydroelectric potential. Many existing installations, especially the smaller ones, would benefit from automation of control systems.

## Geothermal energy

Romania has an estimated long-term (by 2020) potential of about 0.21 mtoe/year for geothermal energy, with supply assured for twenty-seven years, consisting of hot and boiling water at temperatures from 40 to 120° Celsius. In the medium term (2010), the Romanian potential for geothermal energy is estimated at about 70,000 toe/year. Some 90% of the zones of interest, considered natural reserves of geothermal energy, are located in the Western Plain. At present, geothermal sources achieve fuel savings of 37,100 toe/year, with plants in operation mainly for district heating, domestic hot water and greenhouse heating.

## Solar energy

For Romania, in which only very few localities are not connected to the electricity grid, self-contained solar photovoltaic systems are of little relevance. However, solar-electric technologies with installations of high output, based on photovoltaic systems, are of interest. These technologies may become available after the turn of the century; if the prices of fuels increase, importing photovoltaic modules may become suitably economic.

Although active solar-thermal technologies with flat-plate collectors to supply hot water – 45-75° Celsius – for household and technical use were developed some years ago, they are now in a period of stagnation, even in favourable locations in the southeast of the country. In the medium term (by 2010) these technologies could save an estimated 21,000-35,000 toe/year, and in the long term (by 2020) about 1m toe/year. At favourable locations in the southeast of the country, adjacent to the Black Sea littoral, energy capacity totalling about 1,200-1,500 MW could be installed; but the cost would have to be assessed.

## Wind energy

For wind energy, the principal favourable zones have been evaluated. They include the northern part of the Black Sea littoral, including the continental shelf, which benefits from multi-year average wind speeds of 5-7 metres/second; the high mountain zone – the plateau of the Semenic Mountains, the Carpathian Mountains, the curvature of the sub-Carpathian hills and others – with multi-year average wind speeds of 6-10 metres/second; and the zone of hills and plateaux in Dobrogea and south Moldova, with speeds of about

5.5 metres/second. Favourable locations have also been identified in these zones for installation of wind-energy stations totalling about 550 MW, with an average utilization of 2500 hours per year. This is the economic potential that could be installed in the medium term (by 2010); experts have estimated that the long-term potential will be around 3,000 MW. For these wind-energy stations, experimental work is being done on industrial assimilation of 100 kW vertical axis wind turbines at Tulcea, and 300 kW horizontal axis wind turbines at Semenic; 1,000 kW horizontal axis turbines for the mountain zone are at the design stage at Sulina. Wind turbines might also be imported.

**Biomass energy**

For biomass, on the basis of a recent evaluation by specialist institutes and the Romanian National Commission for Waste Recycling, the annual potential could rise to an estimated 6m toe/year, including biogas and byproduct wastes from agriculture and forestry, but not including firewood. Technologies to take advantage of this significant energy potential are in various stages of development, for energy use especially in the rural environment. For example, to make practical use of agricultural, forestry and vineyard wastes for energy purposes, specialists at the FRUVIMED SA winery in Medgidia have developed a Romanian technology, now in the experimental pilot phase and also patented in France and Germany, with which they can supply all their own site energy requirements by burning vine trimmings baled from their own 2,000 ha of land. In 1993 this large wine producer began to sell its surplus biomass fuel to ceramics factories nearby.

Projects are likewise under way to fabricate construction materials such as composites incorporating agricultural wastes – straw, branches, stalks and so on. Thus far the majority of fermentation units, with medium (50-500 m³) and large (1,000-1,200 m³) capacity, have been installed at former collective farms and animal-husbandry complexes. As these applications are extended, the accent will be on fermentation units of small capacity, accessible to private users.

These activities are supported nationally by arguments connected with the much lower prices of these resources, and their relatively clean energy, since they absorb $CO_2$ that they themselves inject into the atmosphere, and contribute only a small amount to emissions of sulphur and nitrogen, the precursors of acid rain that come mainly from burning fossil fuels. The European Parliament considers biomass as the only low-cost reserve of solar energy; it has asked the European Union to intensify efforts to use agriculture and forestry byproducts and to produce biomass, and proposes that the EU increase production of biomass for energy and industrial use. In light of this, Romanian specialists agree on the need to encourage direct users, local authority users and government users to take an interest in biomass, by drawing up programmes and integrated activities of appropriate kinds and on an appropriate scale, to accelerate technical development and extend economic applications.

For firewood, according to the latest data from the National Statistics Commission, a total forest area of 6,369,000 ha in 1991, of which approximately 5,200,000 ha are productive, produced 750,000 toe of energy in 1991. Firewood represents less than 2% of the primary energy resources of the country.

Foreign specialists suggest that data on Romania's renewable energy resources should be refined and updated, to reduce uncertainties and incorporate the latest technical developments. Romanian specialists believe that research and development efforts should be sustained, to make renewable energy technologies competitive as quickly as possible, and thus to lighten the pressure on exhaustible fossil resources, reduce the need to import fuel and reduce environmental impacts of energy use and supply.[34]

---

[34] For a detailed analysis and commentary on policies for renewable energy in Europe see Michael Grubb, *Renewable Energy Strategies for Europe*, Summary and Reports I-IV, Royal Institute of International Affairs, forthcoming (Summary and Reports I and II, *Renewing Europe's Energy* and *Renewable Electricity for Europe*, forthcoming early 1995).

# Chapter 4

## Financing Transition

### 4.1 Leu trouble

In Romania in December 1989 the financial situation was far removed from that usually taken for granted in OECD countries. Romania was almost isolated, a closed society and a closed economy. Very few people crossed its borders, and very little money. In principle, to be sure, an 'island economy' could function perfectly well, given adequate internal resources and an effective market economy to establish their value. In Romania, however, the value of resources was decreed by edict from the centre. 'Prices' were arbitrary. Resources were allocated centrally; most financial transactions involved the government in one of its multifarious guises, moving money from one pocket to another. The money in the pockets of ordinary Romanians was limited both in quantity and in what could be done with it. Again, in principle, prices for 'essentials' were low; set centrally, they bore little relation to the cost of producing bread or milk or electricity. Essential though they might be, however, these goods and services were often in short supply. Bread or milk, of whatever quality, might be available only fleetingly at selected outlets; electricity supply might be cut off instantaneously, and was, routinely – for five hours a day in urban households and for sixteen to eighteen hours a day in rural households. Few of the consumer goods clamouring for purchasers in most OECD countries could be found in Romania's state-run shops; even those that sometimes appeared in the windows or on the shelves tended to be of mediocre quality. What Romanians lacked was not money, but the goods and services that money can buy. The Romanian currency, the 'leu' or lion (plural 'lei') had been for decades a recognized international currency, in the years when Romania had been a substantial exporter, particularly of agricultural products. But the final years of the Ceauşescu era disconnected the leu almost completely from the global financial system; and its eventual re-entry proved painful and debilitating. Even within Romania the leu was of questionable value, simply because so little was available to purchase.

Financial transactions between Romanian industries were denominated in lei; but the role of the currency was peripheral and of little practical meaning, since the transactions were effectively transfers within a single government budget, on the basis of allocated resources, goods and services. As a result the Romanian economy was itself almost as disconnected from Romania's national currency as it was from the rest of the world. Needless to say, the structure of the economy, as directed by the central planners and ultimately by Ceauşescu himself, grew more and more distorted. From year to year the difficulties increased. Ceauşescu's preoccupation with repaying Romania's foreign debt drastically reduced imports, and promoted selective exports, arbitrary and inappropriate, of goods and commodities often already in short supply within Romania. The restrictions on imports led to a shortage of imported primary materials and equipment, spare parts and other essentials. This progressively crippled many economic activities. Many industries were unable to work at full output capacity because they could not obtain enough indigenous fuel and electricity, raw materials or components. Even so, they often began to accumulate unsold stocks, because of lack of orders for their products. The problems were aggravated by the decline in the total output and in the quality of domestic fuel resources. Relations between the various state-owned industries, their suppliers and their customers were frayed and tense, as competent, frustrated managers watched the system crumbling. Indeed, even the banknotes themselves, dingy 100-lei notes that had passed through countless hands, were amorphous and tattered, utterly unpersuasive as repositories of national value. Rebuilding Romania's national currency was to pose a daunting challenge.

After December 1989, when Romania began to re-establish links between its economy and that of the rest of the world, the parlous state of the leu became all too evident. The lack of connection between the leu and the goods and services people needed and wanted drastically complicated efforts to restructure Romania's economy. Wages and salaries were increased, but not on the basis of any rational assessment of the cost or revenues associated with running state-owned enterprises. The rapid upsurge of private enterprises gradually filled shops and markets with goods. Some – for instance housewares, cosmetics, consumer electronics and appliances – were imported; some – fresh fruit and vegetables – were produced on private farms. But the prices the new private suppliers were charging, more realistically related to the cost of acquiring the goods for sale, were far higher than those that people were used to paying, and far higher than many could afford on the incomes they were being paid. The purchasing power of the leu plummeted, and inflation took off. Romanians with savings in lei saw the value of their deposits evaporate.

The government itself had long been the locus of almost all significant financial activity in Romania; but both its revenue-raising and its expenditure had borne little relationship to the budgetary procedures common, for instance, in OECD countries. After December 1989 these procedures had to be fundamentally rethought; but popular and managerial expectations were more difficult to change. Taxation to raise government revenue had been inextricably interwoven with the operations of state-owned enterprises; and Romanians had come to assume that 'the budget' – the government budget – was, directly or indirectly, the appropriate source of all substantial outlay. Reorganizing the basis of government finances, both income and expenditure, affected the entire power structure of the system, and met with stumbling-blocks at almost every turn.

Two financial conflicts emerged almost immediately. They can be characterized as 'consumption versus investment' and 'the leu versus the dollar'. As soon as Ceauşescu's grip was broken, the long-suppressed desire of ordinary Romanians to emulate the consumer societies of OECD countries burst out across the country. Romanians knew what could be purchased in western Europe; they had seen the cars, the TV sets, the washing machines, the stereos and so on in films and on television, and they were desperately eager to acquire them. Some of these items, to be sure – for instance cars – had long been manufactured in Romania; but Romanians wanted the higher quality available only from beyond the country's borders. Small quantities of high-quality foreign products like cars and electronics had been smuggled into Romania for years; but the new freedom opened the floodgates. As soon as the barriers went down, Romanians with access to hard currency thronged through the border posts into western Europe, and returned home laden with new goods, either for themselves or to sell. By 1992 the streets of Romanian cities were filling with BMWs and Audis, and the windows of private-enterprise shops were crammed with Japanese electronics. This urge for imported consumer goods put yet further pressure on the national currency; it also aggravated the problem of finding the investment desperately needed to restore the country's run-down infrastructure. A major conflict arose between the craving for gratification, even at a basic level, of desires long denied, and the need to forgo such immediate satisfaction and plough the available funds into longer-term benefits. The problem was compounded by low wages and salaries, and by the falling value of the leu – both its domestic purchasing power and its value in foreign exchange. Rather than holding lei and watching their worth diminish, people tended to spend them as fast as they could; and for a time the dollar threatened to supplant the leu as the de facto national reserve of value, at least in the minds of most Romanians. The pavements around the Hotel Intercontinental in Bucureşti swarmed with freelance money-changers, accosting likely-looking passersby with offers to buy dollars at rates far above those officially on offer. This thriving currency black market continued even after such transactions were made illegal, although it became more discreet.

In early 1993 the OECD published *Romania: An Economic Assessment*, the opening of the preface to which acknowledged Romania's achievements since December 1989.

Although frequently underestimated abroad, Romania has undertaken major structural reforms over the past three years. Romania started from extremely difficult initial conditions – extreme centralization, a high degree of autarchy, and no experience of partial reforms such as those undertaken in other central and eastern European economies during the 1980s. Today the legal infrastructure for a market economy has now been largely established, agriculture has been privatized, a private sector is emerging in other sectors, trade has been liberalized and the framework of an ambitious mass privatization programme is nearly complete.[35]

---

[35] *Romania: An Economic Assessment*, OECD 1993.

But it continued: 'The macroeconomic performance has, however, been disappointing, offsetting these impressive achievements: the collapse in output is now longer and deeper than in most other countries in transition, inflation remains very high and there is a chronic shortage of foreign currency'. The OECD report then analyzed the problems of establishing the necessary macroeconomic stability in the circumstances and context of Romania, including the energy sector, underlining the need to reform prices and to impose financial discipline on industrial enterprises.

## 4.2 Industrial problems

After 1989 the Romanian economy in general and Romanian industry in particular faced a new crisis. The structural distortions that had accumulated in the 1980s left Romania ill-prepared for a transition to a market economy. Whereas other countries of central Europe – Poland, the then Czechoslovakia and Hungary – had begun to relax constraints and introduce market mechanisms even before the overthrow of communism, in Romania the institutional and organizational framework changed abruptly, almost overnight. Market mechanisms were injected rapidly into some – but not all – parts of a system that had no easy way to accommodate them. Other parts of the system remained effectively part of a command economy still reminiscent of the old regime.[36] In the transition that Romania is still undergoing, the new economic system has been effectively ad hoc, with ample opportunity for obstruction, especially by bureaucracy. The brusque switch to the new system did not allow time to create the necessary conditions for, or to evaluate the socioeconomic effects of, the new situation. Many measures directed at economic normalization under-estimated the existing productive potential; this generated, especially in industry, a series of radical and rapid restructuring moves, including refitting without an economic basis or preparatory stages. Techni-

---

[36] Although Romania was less prepared than Poland or Hungary to inject market mechanisms into its domestic economy, Romania in fact had much more extensive recent experience of international markets than other former Comecon countries. In the 1960s and 1970s Romania was a major exporter at the standards of the international marketplace – more so than either Poland or Hungary, which exported almost exclusively to other Comecon countries. Romania redirected its exports to Comecon countries only in the 1980s.

cal, economic and administrative leaders acted under the influence of strikes and other opposing pressures, making the economy more unstable. The evolution of productive branches of industry was permanently marked by shortages of material, finances and hard currency. In agriculture, the progress of privatization based on the law of the Land Fund, passed in 1990, led to significant structural changes in the form of property, and greatly increased production from the private sector. However, even agriculture, the one-time mainstay of Romania's economy, had its problems. On an arable land area of about 9.4 million ha and with an irrigation system that covers 3.1 million ha, the efficiency of vegetable production fell below that of other countries – for example, to one-half of that of Germany, France, the Netherlands or the former Czechoslovakia – because high prices forced cutbacks in the use of fertilizers and irrigation, because integrated irrigation systems for large-scale collective farms along the Danube were too inflexible to use for smaller farms, and because agricultural work was delayed.

## 4.3 Finances in transition

### 4.3.1 Emerging from turmoil

Between 1990 and 1993 inflation in Romania was very high. The average monthly rate of inflation was 10.3% in 1991, 9.6% in 1992 and 12.6% in the first eleven months of 1993. Such high inflation inflicts damage on organizations like RENEL that must wait some time after supplying goods or services before customers pay their bills. High inflation creates conditions for commercial speculation, and reduces interest in real efficiency. At a press conference on 22 November 1993, prime minister Nicolae Vacaroiu declared that in 1993 the economic decline had stopped, that 1994 would record a growth in gross domestic product of some 0.5% and in industrial production of some 1% compared to the previous year, and that in the following period the government would limit inflation to about 70% per year. In fact, by mid-1994 government figures recorded GDP growth of 1% in 1993 and were estimating growth of 1.5% in 1994. As economic growth returns, an important indicator of performance will be the relationship between GDP and energy use. Will the energy intensity of the Romanian economy fall, as Romania energy specialists hope? If so, how rapidly? Romanian energy policy will depend critically on the behaviour of the whole economy; and its evolution is still both rapid and unpredictable. If energy efficiency improves, how will economic growth respond? Will Romanian statistics allow appropriate analysis to be carried out?

Bank interest charges have been relatively high, from 80% to 120%, differing from one bank to another, from one month to another, and from one debtor to another. Even so, until 1994 bank interest has been less than the rate of inflation. This has provoked deep differences of opinion. Actual or potential debtors insist that interest charges are too high, and thus impede productive activity and investment. Each in part wants to demonstrate that his or her activity is particularly important, and should benefit from reduced interest charges – which would be equivalent to receiving a subsidy. In practice this sort of credit, with interest charges of 15%, is granted to agriculture, the difference being supported by the government budget. Opposition parties, on the other hand, say that interest charges are too low, and that the government wants to rescue unprofitable industrial units through the intermediary of the banking sector. The opposition agrees that small and medium-sized enterprises in the private sector should receive preferential credit. The government says that this is a problem for the banks, and declares that neither the National Bank nor commercial banks are subordinate to the government. The banks believe in the principal of banking secrecy.

At the beginning of 1994, to reduce inflation, the banks increased the interest rates on loans to between 100 and 135%, while also raising interest on deposits to 100-110% yearly. The objective was to have both loan and deposit interest rates higher than inflation, which is estimated to be 70-75% in 1994. Both companies and private individuals can have separate bank accounts in lei and in hard currency. Thus far, account-holders have avoided holding deposits in lei, because of their loss of value; customers have preferred to buy hard currency, even at higher prices, and deposit this instead. Interest on hard currency accounts is some 4-8% yearly, depending on the particular hard currency and the particular bank. However, the new interest rates on lei deposits have decreased the demand for hard currency, and trust in the national currency appears to be growing.

One of the most stubborn and intractable problems of Romania's transition has come to be called *blocajul financiar*, 'the financial blockage'; foreign specialists call it the 'financial gridlock'. It manifests itself like this. An industrial enterprise makes products but does not sell them, either because no one will buy them or because it wants to sell them later when prices will be higher. It does not get a loan from the bank, because interest charges are high or because it cannot get credit. The enterprise cannot therefore pay its suppliers of raw materials, other materials or energy. In their turn the suppliers, too, cannot pay their debts. The phenomenon propagates itself throughout the national economy; more and more enterprises find themselves short of money to pay bills, to purchase or to invest, even though all believe that they should be receiving substantial sums.

The government, in collaboration with the banks, has been making periodic efforts to remove the blockage, by reciprocal compensation of debts and by granting subsidies or credits to some enterprises with debts; but some concerns have simply fallen back into arrears. In the autumn of 1993, thirty enterprises were singled out as 'bad payers'. They will be supported in efforts to become efficient; if they cannot, they will be declared bankrupt.

The opposition declares that the phenomenon has arisen because the government continues to support unprofitable enterprises, and delays privatizations that would distinguish efficient from inefficient enterprises. In their turn, the parties that support the government declare that hasty privatization of enterprises going through a bad patch would lead to large losses for the state. The debate continues. Beyond this political dispute, Romanian specialists argue that laws addressing the point – including a bankruptcy law – are certainly necessary. The IEA report argues that measures could be taken against non-payment of bills, without waiting for a bankruptcy law.[37] Bankruptcy is almost certainly an essential sanction, but the social implications cannot be underestimated – and in a democracy social implications are also political implications. If a state-owned enterprise is to be declared bankrupt, some safety net will have to be provided for its employees – involving perhaps compensation and retraining in more appropriate skills.

The difficulty of obtaining hard currency has created major problems for enterprises, especially those that do not export but do import – as is the case, for example, with RENEL. The present law permits those who export

---

[37] *Energy Policies of Romania*, International Energy Agency, 1993.

to keep hard currency in special accounts. Until mid-1994, hard currency auctions took place every day at the National Bank, at which both those holding hard currency and those seeking it were represented by commercial banks at which they had opened accounts. Until 1994 the demand for hard currency always exceeded the supply. Firms with state capital were likewise obliged to sell or procure hard currency at such auctions. At the same time, a parallel market, also official, developed, open exclusively to private firms and individuals, but with a more reduced scope. For many months the exchange rate in this market was 60-70% higher than that in the auctions at the National Bank; on 21 November 1993, for instance, the rate was 1,074 lei to the dollar at the National Bank and 1,700-1,900 lei to the dollar in the private market. The IMF, in its negotiations with the Romanian government, made the offer of a major loan conditional on liberalization of the exchange rate to a market value, and withheld financial commitment until the condition was met.

In 1994, however, the position has markedly improved. As noted earlier, demand for hard currency has recently fallen. On 6 April 1994 the exchange rate of the National Bank was 1,670 lei to the dollar, and that of the private market was 1,700-1,780 lei to the dollar; the difference is now very small. Romanian specialists conclude that the Romanian government has fulfilled its commitment to the IMF; but they add that preventing future divergence between the rates will be very important. When the government achieves its stated aim of 'internal convertibility' of the leu, any Romanian company will be able to buy and sell hard currency both inside and outside Romania. By mid-1994 the exchange rate was stabilizing on the interbank hard currency market; and as a rule hard-currency exchange houses were offering fewer lei per dollar than the interbank rate. The last components of the interbank market were to be put into practice in July 1994, thus replacing completely the mechanism of hard-currency auctions. A communiqué from the National Bank declared that banks and exchange houses would be able to carry out direct operations of buying and selling hard currency, for unlimited sums, at freely negotiated rates. Economic agents would still, as before, be able to keep hard currency deposited as the proceeds from exports.

## 4.3.2 Financing investments

The problem of financing investments in Romania is delicate enough at the moment even apart from specifically financial reasons. The very concept of 'investment' has to be rescued from the habits of mind instilled during four decades of rigid central planning, brutally enforced. Only five years ago all investment decisions except the purely personal were dictated from the centre, in a context in which financial analysis was functionally meaningless. Romanian specialists concede the urgent necessity to learn the disciplines of financial analysis in a market context – establishing real rates of return on investments, assessing marginal costs and payback times, comparing alternative investments, evaluating price signals and so on.[38] In the mid-1990s the tendency is still to assume that major investments are the province of government. Until the managers of enterprises have the freedom to reach their own decisions, on the basis of appropriate financial analysis of proposed investments – including, for example, the purpose of the investment and the real rate of return anticipated – the whole process of investment will fall short of market requirements. As matters stand, enterprises with state capital – old socialist enterprises – are themselves in transition, from the legal point of view, on the way to privatization. In this situation, and because of the continuing economic turbulence in Romania, managers in charge of such enterprises have held back from any major measures, including investment, and prefer to keep a unit operating until the picture clarifies. The existence of significant unused production capacity, and the drastic fall in internal de-

---

[38] The novelty of financial operations in a market context has left loopholes allowing confidence tricksters to fleece unwary Romanians of enormous sums of money. The best-known but no means the only example of such shady dealing was the so-called 'Caritas' scheme of 'mutual assistance', promoted in Cluj and elsewhere. It was a classical 'pyramid' swindle; an investor was persuaded to contribute a certain sum with the guarantee that the scheme would repay a multiple of this sum a few weeks later. As long as more and more 'investors' contributed, their money could be passed back to earlier 'investors' as promised, while the promoters creamed off substantial proceeds for themselves. Eventually and inevitably, however, new contributions began to tail off. The scheme began defaulting on promised payouts, making prospective contributors more and more uneasy, until the whole fabrication collapsed. By the time the 'Caritas' swindle came down in a heap in the spring of 1994 many thousands of Romanians had seen their savings disappear. Newspaper estimates of the losses inflicted by 'Caritas' and similar scams ranged into hundreds of billions of lei.

mand for industrial output, make new investments risky. A related and important question also arises: should an enterprise be privatized before improvement or after? If it is privatized before improvement, the capital injected may hasten the improvement; but the government will get low proceeds from privatization. On the other hand, if the government attempts to gain higher proceeds by delaying privatization until after an enterprise has been improved, the improvements may be hampered by the shortage of available funds. Units with private capital show much more initiative, but their possibilities are as yet relatively limited.

Romanians still tend to make a revealing distinction between 'commercial' activity, by which they mean buying and selling, and 'productive' activity, by which they mean extraction and processing of raw materials, energy supply, manufacturing and so on. In many cases, private enterprises have begun with 'commercial' activities, to enable them to accumulate a minimum of capital, after which they have moved to 'productive' activities, in which the rate of profit is less but which are considered more secure in the medium and long term. In due course, as habits of mind imprinted during the communist decades fade out, the essential link between production and commerce must be re-established, so that a product that cannot be sold at an acceptable price is regarded not as an asset but as a liability.

Loans from Romanian banks are a source on which all investors can call, despite the problem of interest rates described earlier. A Romanian bank, like any other bank anywhere in the world, demands material guarantees that loans will be repaid, in the form of mortgages on houses, cars, furniture and so on. For example, one Romanian entrepreneur mortgaged himself right down to the kitchen utensils – plates, pots, even cutlery – that had been his wife's dowry, to get credit to buy agricultural machinery for a private farm. Many Romanian firms have agreed to associate with foreign investors and establish joint ventures, both for products that can be brought from abroad and for the fiscal advantages that Romanian legislation offers to joint ventures. As noted earlier, many important international companies, including Shell, Amoco, ABB and Coca-Cola, have already begun to invest in Romania. Some Romanians believe that too many small foreign investors want to enrich themselves overnight in Romania, without contributing to increasing the technical level of indigenous industry; but large firms are eagerly awaited.

Romanians hope that large western firms will recognize the signs of political stability and of the beginning of economic reform. Romania has received funds from groups of western countries or from individual governments – the PHARE programme of the European Union, the US Agency for International Development, the Know-How Fund of the UK government, and so on – for feasibility studies, training and seminars, creating a favourable climate for investment, although the investment funds themselves have usually come from multilateral development banks and private finance.[39]

For this study, the investments of particular interest are those made in pursuit of enhanced energy efficiency – although, as discussed in Chapter 5, investment should not be the top priority for energy efficiency. As described earlier, the Romanian Energy Conservation Agency, ARCE, offers grant support, with funds from the government budget, to encourage enterprises to invest in improved efficiency; and other related activities are rapidly expanding, as later sections will describe. As yet, however, no international investments to support energy efficiency improvement have been forthcoming. In part this may be a reflection of a general problem by no means peculiar to Romania: international funding agencies like the World Bank still almost invariably support investments in supply, not in end-use efficiency, even though analyses often indicate that efficiency investments would offer more rapid and certain paybacks. In Romania in particular this overall predilection may be reinforced by uncertainties about Romanian economic priorities and future development of the nation's economy; but the efficiency options nevertheless deserve closer study, in Romania as elsewhere. The distinctive problems of domestic and international financing of energy efficiency in Romania will be discussed in more detail in Chapters 5 and 6.

### 4.3.3 Financing foreign trade

At the current stage of reconstruction in Romania, importing machines and plant of a superior technical level is sometimes necessary, although by no means always. Sometimes existing equipment can be used, importing only

---

[39] In the case of the PHARE programme, although it has hitherto been confined to technical assistance, from 1995 onwards it is to be oriented much more towards investment; in Hungary, for instance, 80% of PHARE funding in 1995 is to be for investment, according to Ian Brown, director of the Hungary-EC Energy Centre in Budapest (private communication).

certain components, in particular control devices, and introducing modern managerial systems. Access to hard currency is however, difficult enough, as explained earlier. The problems are simpler for firms that export and have access to hard currency. For other enterprises, including import-export firms, the solution is to obtain hard currency at the National Bank auctions or on the private market. A few banks offer credit directly in hard currency – for example, the Romanian Bank of External Commerce and the Ion Tiriac Bank. Very substantial guarantees, however, have to be offered. The loan must also be repaid in hard currency, including interest. This in turn requires hard currency revenues, or buying hard currency at auctions.

The danger is that old plant – cheaper, but with low energy performance – will be imported; the phenomenon is already occurring elsewhere in eastern Europe, and may become more prevalent in Romania. To avoid this, the MoI has drawn up a programme of performance standards for different types of appliance. A law that could ban the import of appliances not complying with Romanian standards is in the course of preparation.

## 4.3.4 Financing research and development

After 1990, because of the reorganization of the economy and the accompanying upheaval, financing research became a major problem. The state budget was already in deficit, and large enterprises were already confronted with their own economic and organizational problems. The danger appeared to be that the best specialists would emigrate. In these conditions, as noted earlier, the government decided to set up a 'special fund' for research and development activities. The fund, made up of contributions from all enterprises in industry, construction, agriculture, commerce, tourism and so on, is administered by the Ministry for Research and Technology. The ministry is supported by a consultative council drawn from the various specialized fields – including energy – made up of nationally recognized specialists in research, education, industry and administration.

When an institute desires finances from the 'special fund', it has to present documentation about the work in question, accompanied by recommendations from outside the institute about the opportunity and the need for the work. The consultative commission from the relevant field analyzes all the requests, and expresses its view to the ministry on which proposals should be given contracts. A certain sum from the government budget is also allocated to research, but this is intended especially for research in the humanities – history, philology and so on. The government budget also finances some research on new sources of energy, for instance solar and wind energy.

Many large firms in Romania have their own research groups, and continue to finance them. Many small and medium-sized firms need the results of research, or at least advice, but as a rule they do not have sufficient funds to finance research activities by themselves. They do, however, contribute to the special fund, and can benefit from the results of work done.

Financing research and development for energy efficiency will be discussed in Chapter 5.

## 4.4 Energy prices

Previous studies of Romania in the 1990s, notably the OECD and IEA reports already cited,[40] have emphasized, with ample justification, the essential role that sensible pricing must play in rebuilding Romania – including cost-based pricing for fuels, electricity and heat. The general observation is also valid for energy efficiency. If measures to improve energy efficiency are to succeed, they must do so on a valid economic basis – that is, because they genuinely constitute a cheaper way to deliver the desired energy services than augmenting supply. During the old regime, the government set energy prices at arbitrary low levels, subsidizing them from elsewhere in the government budget. Some energy-intensive industries were therefore assured of relatively cheap energy, albeit in limited quantities, through the mechanisms of central planning. This artificially and unrealistically cheap energy in turn engendered indifference to waste and inefficiency. If fuel, electricity and heat are priced unrealistically cheaply, these low prices distort the relevant comparisons with the costs of efficiency measures, to the disadvantage of efficiency. Moreover, users themselves must at the outset be interested and motivated. Cost-based prices for fuel, electricity and heat – which will be higher than the subsidized prices of previous years – will therefore help to convince users to take a positive attitude towards efficiency, as a way to cut their costs.

---

[40] *Romania: An Economic Assessment; Energy Policies of Romania.*

Efforts are now in progress to set fuel and electricity prices at the 'right' levels, partly to stimulate efficient energy use. But a stubborn problem persists: who is to decide the 'right' level, and on what basis? The grid-based energy carriers – electricity, natural gas and delivered heat – have an element of natural monopoly associated with their fixed infrastructure, and even in market economies their prices are set by reference to some regulatory mechanism. But the fuels themselves – oil, coal and natural gas – are commodities. The OECD view, and that of the IEA report, is that the prices of these fuels should be determined not by government but by the market, although some others might insist on reservations about the meaning of the word 'market' as it applies to these fuels internationally. At present, however, in Romania all energy prices, including tariffs for electricity, gas and heat supply, are set by the government, on the basis of discussions and negotiations between the Ministry of Finance, the MoI and the energy RAs. These prices apply to the whole of the country. The World Bank and the IMF have insisted that the Romanian government periodically align these prices with actual costs and world market levels. The evolution of energy prices has to be considered in the general context of the evolution of prices for all products, and of the pronounced inflation recorded in Romania in recent years, and the falling value of the leu on foreign exchange markets. For products whose prices are established by a free market, the market takes inflation and exchange rates into account more or less continuously. For energy, however – and in particular for electricity, gas and delivered heat – when the price is fixed by governmental decision, it changes in periodic jumps. This means that for much of the time real energy prices are steadily falling, in inverse proportion to the rate of inflation. International agencies like the IEA and the OECD stress that the reform of energy pricing is one of the key measures in rebuilding Romania's economy. In addition to its importance as a manifestation of market economics, energy price reform will be essential as a stimulus to improve energy efficiency.

# Chapter 5

## Promoting Efficiency

### 5.1 'Freezing in the dark'

The effects of energy prices can be dramatic. In late 1973 the Organization of Petroleum Exporting Countries (OPEC) quadrupled the world price of petrol. Amid the global confusion that ensued, many countries launched programmes to promote so-called 'energy conservation'. In OECD countries the programmes generally took the form of urgent official exhortations to turn off lights, turn down thermostats, walk instead of driving, and otherwise reduce the use of fuels and electricity simply by reducing the level of services that people had previously enjoyed. This approach had limited public appeal, to put it mildly. The call for such personal sacrifices had some brief and modest success, but rapidly lost what effectiveness it had. In the process it tainted the concept of 'energy conservation'. In people's minds, energy conservation came to mean 'doing without', cutting back on comfort and convenience, undermining lifestyles: 'freezing in the dark'. In a modern democratic society such an approach to energy policy was doomed to fail; voters would not put up with it. A democratically elected government that moved beyond exhortation and inflicted prolonged cutbacks of fuel and electricity use by depriving its electorate of services would be voted out of office.

In a country like Romania under Ceauşescu, however, with the mechanisms of central planning backed by authoritarian repression, and with no fear of repercussions from a democratic electorate, this latter consideration did not apply. As it happens, the OPEC 'oil shock' of 1973 had less effect in Romania than it did in OECD countries, because of Romania's own oil production. However, by the mid-1980s, as Romania's indigenous resources were overstretched, Ceauşescu's government could and did enforce 'energy saving' and 'energy conservation' by direct intervention, simply by denying Romanians access to supplies of fuel and electricity. In the minds of Romanians, the concept of 'energy conservation', as practised under Ceauşescu, eventually became anathema.

In OECD countries, by the late 1970s, a more profound transformation of thinking about energy was beginning to emerge. In Sweden, the US, the UK and elsewhere, innovative analysts were starting to develop an alternative approach to energy policy, focusing not on how fuels and electricity were supplied but on how they were used, and for what purpose. The analysts pointed out that people do not, in fact, want fuels and electricity – not as such. People want comfort, whatever the season or the weather. They want illumination when the sun is not shining. They want to store and cook food. They want to move quickly and conveniently from place to place. They want to exert forces and lift weights – and so on. People want the benefits that fuels and electricity can provide; they want 'energy services'. But these services are not provided by fuels and electricity alone. The fuels and electricity are used in many types of equipment: buildings, lights, appliances, boilers, motors, computers, vehicles: a vast and continually expanding range of 'end-use' energy technologies. Studies rapidly demonstrated that these end-use technologies could be improved, often substantially, to deliver better services while using less fuel or electricity; that is, they could be made more 'efficient'. Moreover, analysis revealed that improving the efficiency of energy use would often cost less than augmenting fuel or electricity supplies.

One of the first influential studies taking this new approach, *A Low Energy Strategy for the United Kingdom*, was published by the International Institute for Environment and Development (IIED) in London in January 1979.[41] Traditional energy policy had tended to assume that growth in GDP was invariably accompanied by equivalent growth in the use of fuels and electricity. The IIED study showed that this assumption was incorrect. The OPEC oil price rise, while triggering a global recession, had also spurred efforts to improve the efficiency of energy use; in a number of OECD countries GDP had continued to grow while fuel and electricity use remained stable or even

---

[41] Gerald Leach *et al.*, *A Low Energy Strategy for the United Kingdom*, Science Reviews, 1979.

declined. The study, by examining the structure of GDP and end-uses of fuels and electricity, also showed why this was so. Breaking down energy end-use into nearly 400 separate categories, it demonstrated that GDP could continue to grow for the following twenty-five years as official projections indicated, while fuel and electricity use declined sharply – provided the necessary effort and investment were redirected away from fuel and electricity supply and into improving the efficiency of buildings, lighting, appliances, industrial plant and other end-use technologies. At the time the study was hotly controversial, and official critiques fiercely challenged its findings. It is now remembered as a landmark pointing to a new direction for energy policy.[42]

One key difference in this new approach to 'energy saving' or 'energy conservation' was that it did not imply reducing the energy service delivered. On the contrary, it frequently enhanced the service delivered. As noted above, the concept of 'energy saving' or 'energy conservation' by this time carried with it an implicitly negative psychological message of 'doing without'. The new concept of improving the equipment to deliver better services at lower cost with less fuel and electricity – that is, making energy use more effective – soon acquired an appropriately positive new label: 'energy efficiency'.

In modern democratic societies, in which governments have to rely on persuasion rather than coercion, the positive message of 'energy efficiency' was much more appealing to voters than the negative self-denial by this time associated with 'energy saving' or 'energy conservation'. By the early 1980s 'energy efficiency' was featuring in official programmes throughout the OECD. In Romania in the 1980s, on the other hand, as Ceauşescu determined to make Romania entirely self-sufficient, in energy as in everything else, persuasion had a darker subtext, and coercion was the essential instrument of policy. Radio and television bombarded Romanians with slogans exhorting self-denial, but the slogans did not have to persuade Romanians to comply

---

[42] Other formative studies pointing in a broadly similar direction included Amory Lovins, *World Energy Strategies*, Ballinger 1975, and *Soft Energy Paths*, Penguin 1977; Mans Lonnroth *et al.*, *Energy in Transition*, University of California 1980; Mans Lonnroth *et al.*, *Solar versus Nuclear*, Pergamon, 1980; and Robert Stobaugh and Daniel Yergin for the Harvard Business School, *Energy Future*, Random House, 1979. A concise history of this transformation in energy thinking and policy can be found in Walter C. Patterson, *The Energy Alternative*, Optima 1991.

with the exhortations; the authorities routinely shut off electricity supplies to households anyway. In Romania, energy conservation came to mean all too literally 'freezing in the dark'.

Industrial energy use, too, came under similar coercive pressure, distorting what had been a useful and respected programme. Until the end of the 1960s, a so-called Energy Inspectorate functioned within the framework of the old Ministry of Electrical Energy. This inspectorate had a central directorate in Bucureşti and sixteen territorial branches in large cities, each responsible for a certain zone of the country. Their role was to advise industrial consumers about more efficient use of energy. The inspectorate laid down various technical prescriptions or instructions about using installations efficiently; specialists in energy-using industries appreciated this guidance. For example, the inspectorate promulgated 'instructions to carry out and analyze energy diagnoses for industrial consumers' – in effect, energy audits – as early as 1967. In 1969, however, the inspectorate came under the control of the former Ministry for Technico-Material Supplies, one of the most important centralized planning bodies in the old regime. As economic centralism grew tighter, the technical role of the inspectorate also diminished. It policed energy use in compliance with central planning, ensuring that as much energy was used as the plan stipulated – not more, but also not less. In time the inspectorate became less and less an advisory body and more and more an agency for repression in line with Ceauşescu's policy.

The nature of the collaboration between specialists from the inspectorate and specialists at energy-using enterprises changed. In 1984, as Ceauşescu's self-sufficiency drive intensified, the former Ministry of Electrical Energy was invested with the title of sole national administrator of energy resources. In this capacity its role was also to advise about efficient use of electrical and thermal energy. New collectives were organized to advise users, within their branches of the electricity network. The 'advice', however, was by this time ominously different in tone. Through the mechanisms of centralized planning and control, any information obtained about energy use could ultimately be turned against the users. As one Romanian specialist put it, 'As in American justice – "Anything you say may be used against you"'. The role of the Energy Inspectorate in the 1980s was later to create difficulties when it was transformed into the Romanian Energy Conservation Agency, ARCE, as will be discussed below.

The research institute of the Ministry of Electrical Energy likewise became increasingly concerned not only with supply but also with the use of energy; but Ceauşescu's coercive approach to energy conservation hampered these activities. After December 1989 the institute became ICEMENERG; and ICEMENERG specialists are now acutely conscious that the old concept of 'energy conservation', as practised under Ceauşescu, is unacceptable in the emerging Romanian democracy. Promoting energy efficiency in Romania in the 1990s will require a very different approach if the effort is to succeed.

### 5.2 Impetus and impediments

Even in OECD countries, promoting energy efficiency has proved to be more difficult than anticipated. At the end of the 1970s, the Iranian revolution and the Iran-Iraq war sent world oil prices soaring, with other fuel prices following suit. As before, prices proved to be a key stimulus to improving energy efficiency; throughout the OECD, governments and companies sought to reduce their costs by boosting efficiency. They provided information, advice and training for energy users. They encouraged 'good housekeeping', to avoid unnecessary energy losses. They appointed specialist 'energy managers' specifically responsible for overseeing fuel and electricity use and end-use equipment in buildings and industrial facilities. They set up practical demonstrations of ways to improve efficiency, for instance by installing insulation, upgrading lights and fittings, upgrading heating and ventilating plant and so on. Some governments offered grants, low-interest loans and tax incentives to help fund efficiency improvements. Utility regulators for electricity and gas supply systems fostered concepts called 'least-cost planning', 'demand-side management' (DSM) and 'integrated resource planning' (IRP), through which electricity and gas suppliers could finance investments to improve the efficiency of their customers' end-use equipment (see Chapter 6).

From 1986 onwards, however, oil prices collapsed, taking other fuel prices down with them. Efficiency measures that looked attractive with an oil price above $25 a barrel looked much less so when the price fell below $15 a barrel. Throughout the 1980s, nevertheless, another factor was coming into prominence. Abundant evidence was accumulating to show that energy use was inflicting damage on the environment. Some damage was local, for instance, smoke from power stations, industries and car exhausts; some was regional, for instance, so-called 'acid rain', again from power stations, industries and car exhausts; and some was global, in particular the increasing concentration of $CO_2$ in the atmosphere from burning fossil fuels, causing scientists to warn that the so-called 'greenhouse effect' might be upsetting the world's climate. In OECD countries during the 1980s, while the fear of high energy prices and shortages faded, reducing the impetus towards improving energy efficiency for financial reasons, the fear of environmental side-effects of energy use mounted; improving efficiency came to be seen as an important way to mitigate the environmental damage from energy use, while retaining the benefits.

In OECD countries, nevertheless, efforts to improve energy efficiency still encounter obstacles. Analysts have identified many economically attractive opportunities that have not been realized, because of so-called 'market imperfections' and other barriers.[43] People often lack the knowledge, know-how and technical skills to identify and take advantage of potential improvements. All too often energy equipment is owned by one person and used by another, for instance the landlord and tenant of a building. The landlord does not want to spend money on the building to reduce fuel bills, because the tenant pays the bills; and the tenant either cannot spend money on the building because it belongs to the landlord, or does not want to because the tenant may soon move elsewhere. So the building remains unimproved. Many households and small businesses cannot spare enough capital to invest in improved efficiency, because other demands are more pressing. People contemplating efficiency investments frequently look for a very rapid payback of the investment – at most a year or two. Those investing, say, in a new power station are content with a significantly longer payback time – that is, a lower real rate of return

---

[43] See, for instance, Michael Grubb, *Energy Policies and the Greenhouse Effect*, vol. 1, Royal Institute of International Affairs/ Dartmouth, 1990; Jose Goldemberg *et al.*, *Energy for a Sustainable World*, Wiley Eastern, 1987; and Thomas B. Johansson *et al.*, *Electricity: Efficient End-use and New Generation Technologies and their Planning Implications*, Lund University Press, 1989.

on the investment. This biases investments towards increasing supply instead of improving end-use efficiency. Many people and many businesses see their fuel and electricity costs as only a small proportion of their outlay, take little interest in them and cannot be bothered to look for efficiency improvements.

These and other barriers continue to impede the progress of efficiency improvements even in OECD countries where politicians routinely proclaim the importance of improved efficiency.[44] In a country such as Romania, where the concept of energy efficiency is as yet familiar only to specialists, and where even specialists have limited knowledge either of the latest technical options or of the most effective measures to promote them, institutional barriers like these are yet more problematical. Institutional barriers, shortage of funds and the lingering distrust of 'energy conservation' centrally imposed, combine to make promoting energy efficiency in Romania a challenging undertaking. Nevertheless a growing number of Romanians are eager to rise to the challenge.


### 5.3 Changing minds

Efforts to promote energy efficiency in Romania must be tailored to the local situation, not only technically but socially and indeed psychologically. Foreign visitors to the countries of central and eastern Europe return with many travellers' tales about the habits of mind instilled in the people under the old communist regimes. 'It's a non-plug culture,' commented one foreign visitor, lamenting the difficulty of stopping water from running wastefully out of bathtubs and sinks. Innovative energy analysts in OECD countries have used precisely this analogy when contrasting the options of increasing energy supply or reducing energy losses: 'If you want to fill the bathtub, do you open the tap wider or put a plug in the drain?' First, however, you have to recognize that you *can* plug the drain – that you don't have to wait for someone else to do it. Changing the mental habits of a lifetime is not easy. If you have been taught to believe that 'the state' owns almost everything, and that you are passively subject to its arbitrary jurisdiction in almost every aspect of your

---

[44] The most comprehensive study to date of these non-technical but crucial aspects of efficiency policy is Lee Schipper and Stephen Meyers, *Energy Efficiency and Human Activity*, Cambridge University Press, 1992.

life, you come to accept that 'the state' will have to put things right – that whatever is wrong is 'someone else's problem'. Romanians are steadily breaking out of this passive mould, taking responsibility for their own affairs and their own lives, as witness the more than 500,000 private enterprises set up since 1990. But the mentality ingrained during four decades of communism still leaves debilitating traces. A potentially crucial aspect of the case for improving energy efficiency in Romania is that almost any Romanian can become actively and personally involved, without waiting for permission or authorization. Because energy efficiency in one context or another impinges on every Romanian at some point – at home, at work, on the farm, in the factory – improving energy efficiency could become an 'enabling' and 'empowering' activity right across Romania, stimulating personal initiative and personal responsibility, reinforcing the social transition. Individual Romanians can take their own measures to increase energy efficiency, and by so doing improve their own living and working conditions, provided they have the necessary information, appropriately presented, and the appropriate impetus – not central direction, but more subtle encouragement.

Some essential elements of a programme are already in place, ready to build on – notably a significant number of technically expert and enthusiastic Romanian energy specialists. The sequence of measures that might be introduced to promote energy efficiency could be based on examples from programmes in OECD countries, and from programmes already under way in other former Comecon countries, suitably modified to the Romanian context. As noted earlier, the key prerequisite is cost-based prices for fuels and electricity. With the removal of subsidies in 1993 Romania has already made a major step in this direction, sending more appropriate price signals to Romanian energy users. The bad news of higher bills, however, should be accompanied by the better news that bills need not be so high. One important starting-point is to raise awareness of the benefits to be reaped from improved efficiency, by taking what OECD specialists lump together as 'no-cost, low-cost' measures. According to Romanian specialists, the first stage might involve preparing and distributing information and advice to the public and to workers, couched in persuasive popular terms, like advertising: 'What energy efficiency can do for YOU, and what YOU can do about it'. The message could be carried by brochures and leaflets, by newspaper and magazine articles, by radio and television. Then would come more specific guidance and encouragement to foster positive attitudes towards 'good housekeeping' in homes, schools, hospitals, public buildings, farms and factories, to minimize wasteful losses of energy. Full-fledged 'energy management' could follow, with energy specialists actively responsible for initiating improvements. Practical examples and demonstrations would help to convince the sceptical that efficiency measures are feasible and beneficial. As broad awareness and experience accumulated, the programme could expand to embrace serious financial commitments in the form of investment in energy efficiency. Subsequent sections of this chapter will consider some aspects of 'no-cost, low-cost' energy efficiency measures in Romania; Chapter 6 will consider investments in efficiency.

## 5.4 Energy education

Technical education for energy is well developed in Romania. A network of industrial *lycées* specializes in energy; when their studies are completed, students gain the qualification of 'specialist worker'. The polytechnic institutes of the principal university centres in the country – Bucureşti, Iaşi, Cluj, Timişoara, Oradea, Craiova and so on – likewise include energy centres. This network meets the requirement for specialists with various qualifications, both for enterprises that supply energy and for those that use it. The current problem is to introduce certain energy themes, including energy efficiency, into the courses of other *lycées* and faculties whose focus is technical or economic.

The current programme of study provides courses in physics or electrotechnology, in which the laws and phenomena are studied at a high level. As a rule, Romanian pupils and students take places in the front rank at international scholastic olympiads. Technical and economic aspects do not, however, receive enough attention. In these circumstances a dialogue between what Romanians call *energeticiens* and technological specialists or managers is sometimes more difficult to establish. In the period of the centralized economy, energy and fuel prices were subsidized; the mechanisms of central planning secured for everyone a quantity of energy that was limited but cheap. Now the subsidies for energy are almost eliminated, and prices aligned with those of the world market. Technologists and managers will probably have to take energy lessons for economic reasons.

Support from institutes of education would nevertheless be necessary. A new education law is before parliament, and may soon be discussed and approved. It gives institutes of higher education substantial autonomy, in respect among other things of their scholastic programmes. Energy and environmental protection could then be given appropriate coverage, at least to the extent of organizing faculty courses on these subjects. RENEL has its own Centre for Professional Training, equipped with good material. At the centre, specialists from all branches of the economy can take courses for information or specialization on various subjects in the energy field for a greatly reduced fee. This centre can also organize, on request, courses in different parts of the country.

However, the problem of organizing publicity and educational activities for the Romanian general public still remains. As noted earlier, in the 1980s Romanian mass media carried intensive energy propaganda, reiterating heavy-handed slogans exhorting personal sacrifice for vague national benefits. Remember the old slogans: 'If you turn out a light for two hours daily, you assure the operation of a lathe for ten minutes'. 'It's true that you are standing in the cold, but don't forget that we have a larger per capita steel production than England'. The Romanian public developed an acute allergy to energy publicity campaigns. Romanian energy specialists know that they need to launch an appropriate publicity campaign, to convince the public that they can get the same or better services and comfort while using less energy, and to tell them how, in practical terms. But devising an effective campaign will require care, thought and sensitivity to overcome the Romanian public's historic distrust of energy propaganda. Discussions with foreign colleagues, from both OECD countries and other former Comecon countries, would undoubtedly be illuminating and instructive as to both successes and failures.

## 5.5 Energy centres

One especially thought-provoking example for Romania is that of the Hungary-EC Energy Centre, established in Budapest with the sponsorship of the European Commission through its PHARE, Thermie and Synergy programmes. The aim of this centre is to promote energy efficiency and energy management in Hungary, with the cooperation of energy specialists from both Hungary and the European Union. The centre publishes a wide range of specialist material about energy-efficiency, including a quarterly technical journal highlighting successful projects, and detailed technical manuals on, for instance, energy-efficient lighting and energy efficiency in hospitals. It also prepares and disseminates popular information, including television advertising. It organizes practical training courses for energy managers in buildings and industry, covering both technical and managerial aspects of improving efficiency. The centre also stages conferences and workshops throughout Hungary, on topics ranging from energy efficiency for municipalities to standards and labelling for appliances and third-party financing for efficiency. The centre is also linked to the network of some forty OPETs – Organizations for Promoting Energy Technologies – across Europe, backed by the European Commission, and can make the expertise and resources of the OPET network available to Hungarian enterprises.

Romanian specialists have been seeking to establish a similar activity in Romania, thus far without success. Officials of the European Commission have hitherto declined to designate an OPET in Romania, to become part of the international network, because of what they consider to be the lingering political instability in the country. To Romanian specialists and the present author the Commission's stance seems both unjustified and unhelpful, and Romanian energy specialists continue to hope that it will change. In the meantime, Romania has made a start on the basis of its own resources. As noted earlier, district energy centres already have a tradition in Romania; the old Energy Inspectorate, with its sixteen regional centres, was already giving industries advice on energy efficiency in the 1960s, but its role in the 1980s became adversarial and repressive, and poisoned the atmosphere between its inspectors and industrial managers. In 1990, the inspectorate was reconstituted as the Romanian Energy Conservation Agency, ARCE. ARCE was founded using the old structure of the Energy Inspectorate, but with totally different attributes. It has both premises and an organizational structure for district energy centres. Its responsibility is to give advice to energy users; if it is to do so effectively, at least two conditions must be met. First, energy users must have confidence in ARCE's advisors – not only technical confidence, but institutional confidence. Because ARCE is a government agency, and because of its earlier history, it met with some reticence in the initial phase; but this is being gradually overcome. Second, ARCE branches must be equipped with suitable material, and have enough qualified personnel. The agency, financed by the government budget, must therefore have access to sufficient funds. ARCE has difficulty recruiting new skilled staff, because its salary levels are too low. To date ARCE's role has focused on working with industry; if it is to expand, as senior ARCE specialists wish, it must be given an appropriate structure and an appropriate brief (see Chapter 8).

Energy suppliers, too, can advise users about improving efficiency; RENEL already has a tradition of doing so. It intends to build on this tradition, by (among other things) offering users direct advice, publishing instructions about the technical operation of end-use installations, and organizing conferences and courses on efficient use of energy. RENEL finances these activities, which constitute the least costly but not the least effective aspect of RENEL's involvement on the user's side of the meter. Since 1992 RENEL's subsidiary ICEMENERG has been developing materials to advise specialists in industry, agriculture, transport and services, both to improve energy efficiency and energy management in their own activities and to inform the public about ways to save electricity and heat, especially since the recent price rises.

During 1992-3 RENEL organized the national phase of UNIPEDE's international energy efficiency competition, known as 'Eta', after the Greek letter symbolizing efficiency in engineering. In 1993 the national jury, made up of representatives of RENEL, ARCE, Bucureşti Polytechnic University and ICEMENERG, were to award two major prizes, one for a firm with up to 100 workers, and one for a firm with more than 100 workers. In the event, only one prize was awarded; but the winners of the national competition took part in the final phase of the international competition, in Birmingham in November 1993. This sort of competition is important not so much for the value of the prizes awarded as for the competitive atmosphere it stimulates.

In general, nevertheless, suppliers still take relatively little interest in energy efficiency, for various understandable reasons. The energy quota system, so long in effect, engendered attitudes not easy to change. Suppliers were not obliged to deliver the amount of energy the user wanted, only the amount of energy the user had been allocated. Moreover, users had an interest in using their entire quota, because otherwise the allocation for the following period would be reduced. In the national electricity and heat supply system a very large installed capacity is now unused (see Chapter 3 above). Some senior RENEL staff believe that efforts to increase the efficiency of energy use would lead to a continuing fall in sales, and would therefore be contrary to the interests of the company – a view also frequently found in utilities in OECD countries. Environmental protection legislation from the previous decade is now considered out of date; new legislation is being drafted for approval. Romania's network to measure and analyze polluting emissions is inadequate, and Romanian suppliers are therefore not yet facing the kind of environmental pressures common in some OECD countries. Without such environmental pressure, and with surplus supply capacity, Romanian suppliers are consequently less inclined to encourage efficiency, much less to get involved in DSM. On the other hand, DSM advocates within RENEL insist that DSM can promote electrical technologies, with the effect of selling more energy. Moreover, some client enterprises of RENEL might have to shut down if they do not become more efficient; and RENEL could offer essential assistance in avoiding this fate. In any case, despite its surplus of nominal generating capacity, RENEL still has to import fuel and find the scarce hard currency to pay for it. Improving the efficiency of using electricity and heat would alleviate this central problem for RENEL.

Starting from the institutional structure already in place, Romania has already made significant headway. But Romanian specialists warn that conflicts of interest could be troublesome, as for instance between ARCE and RENEL, each desiring to extend its field of activities to promote efficiency. To a foreign observer, the potential for improving efficiency in Romania covers such a vast range that such conflicts of interest should be irrelevant; enough potential exists for all interested participants to take part. Indeed, another category of participant may soon also figure in the picture. In OECD countries, non-governmental bodies like the Association for Energy Conservation in the UK, the American Council for an Energy-Efficient Economy in the US and many similar organizations, as well as international environmental organizations like Friends of the Earth and Greenpeace, have long played a prominent role in promoting more efficient and therefore less environmentally detrimental energy use. In Romania, too, non-governmental groups are now emerging, with energy efficiency as part of their campaigning activity. Such grassroots interest could prove crucially important in stimulating public awareness of the opportunities for improving efficiency and of the benefits available. Here too, however, debilitating conflicts could arise between governmental and non-governmental organizations. Mutual trust and a measure of tolerance will have to be established.

### 5.6 Energy performance standards and labelling

One category of efficiency measure of concern to governments in many countries is setting standards for the energy performance of buildings, industrial plant and appliances, and labelling them accordingly, in connection both with manufacturing and with imports and exports of energy-using equipment. In Romania, the Ministry of Industries had by 1992 already laid out a framework programme to introduce systems of energy labelling and minimum permitted standards for energy efficiency. The programme provides both for research and development and for activities to offer information and financial incentives to enterprises. As well as the Ministry of Industries, the Directorate General of Energy, ARCE, the National Standards Commission and relevant institutes including ICEMENERG, the Building Research Institute INCERC and others, are participating in the programme. The first stage aims to set standards for thermal resistance to heat transfer in buildings, for heavy-duty industrial appliances and for refrigerators and household electrical appliances. Financing to develop standards and labelling will come from the government budget. The programme is supported financially by RENEL, for the part dealing with electrical appliances, and by the Ministry of Research and Technology.

The 'energy law' and 'energy conservation law' now being drafted by the MoI, as noted earlier, provide that these standards be applied explicitly, both in domestic manufacturing and in the import of energy installations and appliances. Concern exists that in the current economic climate both people and enterprises would be interested in appliances that are relatively cheap but have a low energy performance – perhaps purchased secondhand from other countries. Market evidence indicates that this is already happening. Establishing and – more important – implementing a programme of standards will be very important to forestall it.

Because the Romanian programme includes standards and labelling for some industrial installations – heat exchangers, electric furnaces for heat treatment, and so on – industrial retooling will be qualitatively better. The fundamental problem, however, is how to finance retooling for manufacturing firms, so that the appliances they manufacture will qualify for the labels. Joint venture agreements and investment of foreign capital could play an important role here (see Chapter 6).

Because Romania hopes to accede to the European Union, Romanian standards will also have to be 'harmonized' with those of the EU.

## 5.7 Financing energy efficiency

Programmes to promote energy efficiency will incur administrative costs even when the measures advocated do not entail investment. Preparing and disseminating information material, training staff, recruiting 'energy managers' and similar activities may be airily described as 'no-cost, low-cost' measures in OECD countries; but in a country such as Romania even these costs may not be easy to meet. Some funds, perhaps best regarded as 'seed money', will undoubtedly have to be provided from the government budget, directly or indirectly, either from the appropriate ministry itself or through organizations like ARCE and RENEL. Some should come from industrial enterprises, particularly to enlist the participation of their own staff in improving efficiency in workplaces. Some may become available from foreign sources, provided that they can be convinced that the funds will be spent effectively in Romania. Thus far, energy efficiency activities in Romania are essentially ad hoc, not part of an overall policy or a coherent strategy. Formulating the above mentioned 'energy conservation law' – possibly better designated an 'energy efficiency law' – could help to shape a national Romanian strategy for improving efficiency. It could establish objectives, options and priorities, and help to assure that finances from whatever sources are directed to the most effective measures. The law could define the role and attributes of ARCE. It could cover the obligations of energy users, for instance to carry out periodic energy audits of energy-using industrial installations, public buildings and dwellings. It could set minimum performance standards for boilers, furnaces and household electrical appliances. It could also establish financial and fiscal incentives for measures to improve energy efficiency. To be credible, an efficiency strategy should make explicit who pays, who benefits and how.

## 5.8 From central planning to the market

As Romania continues its transition from a centrally planned economy to a market economy, most of the major institutions involved in the energy sector – among them the energy suppliers and distributors, ARCE, the energy research institutes, the universities and other educational bodies, plant and equipment manufacturers and key financial sources – are still in one manner or another linked to the government. Privatization of at least some of these organizations, and reform of the economic and legal context within which they operate, will interact strongly with energy policy in general and energy efficiency in particular. Some relevant considerations are outlined below.

### 5.8.1 Privatizing for efficiency: agriculture

Collectivization of agriculture in Romania was completed in 1962. Almost the whole agricultural area of the country was incorporated into the framework of collective agricultural management like the collective farms or *kholkhose* of the Soviet Union, or of state agricultural enterprises. At the beginning of 1991 the 'Law of the Land Fund' was adopted, providing for restitution of the land formerly under collective agricultural management to its previous owners or their heirs. The former state agricultural enterprises were transformed into stock companies, of which previous owners of the land became shareholders. The opposition maintains that this land, too, should be returned to its old owners. In 1993, the private agricultural sector was farming land representing 78.5% of the arable area of the country.

Energy use in agriculture fell by 37% between 1989 and 1992, from 126.2 PJ (4.35 million tonnes of coal equivalent – mtce) to 79.5 PJ (2.74 mtce), and electricity use over the same period fell 47.7%, from 4.17 TWh to 2.18 TWh. (These data do not include personal household consumption.) In the context of the transformations taking place, agricultural production fell 15.3%. The volume of irrigation was much reduced. Energy intensity therefore fell, but on the basis of a fall in total production. On the other hand, the life of the rural population obviously improved; peasants became masters on their land, and prices of agricultural products are now market prices. As modern farm machinery becomes more widely available, and irrigation systems are reconfigured to suit smaller private farms, energy use both by agricultural technology and by rural people in their homes will undoubtedly increase.

Table 5.1 shows the evolution of dwellings completed in rural areas, compared with those in urban areas. Many more households now have electrical appliances. On the other hand, in villages the general level of technical knowledge is lower than in towns. Maintenance and repair services are not developed. Specialized construction firms do not exist, and as a rule dwellings are built by teams of local workers. In the circumstances, Romanian specialists believe that particular measures are required to improve energy efficiency in rural areas. Educational material drafted at a suitable level could be disseminated. Existing radio and television broadcasts for peasant farmers could offer guidelines for energy efficiency. Energy specialists could make periodic tours to advise rural people, especially those building themselves new houses and embarking on other developments; the specialists themselves would have to be suitably trained, to give advice appropriate to the rural context. Studies hitherto do not appear to have differentiated between rural and urban areas concerning energy efficiency.

### 5.8.2 Privatizing for efficiency: industry

The legislative framework to develop the private commercial and industrial sector was created at the beginning of 1990. It permitted investment by physical and legal persons from Romania and abroad, either to build new production facilities or to enlarge or refit existing facilities. The evolution of the number of enterprises between 1989 and 1992, according to the form of ownership, is given in Table 5.2. As the table shows, the number of state-owned enterprises has grown. This is because units have been separated – a single enterprise has been divided into two or even three – and not because new state-owned enterprises have been established. In 1989 the number of privately owned enterprises was zero. At the end of 1992, they represented 11.7% of the total number nationally; yet only 1.5% of the total number of salaried workers in industry work in them. The principal problems at the moment are to develop the private sector in industry by attracting new investment from both inside

**Table 5.1: Housing completed, 1989 and 1992 (units)**

|                                    | 1989   | 1992   |
| ---------------------------------- | ------ | ------ |
| Total in rural areas (villages)    | 7,700  | 11,702 |
| Of which with people's own money   | 4,136  | 11,230 |
| Total in urban areas (cities)      | 52,700 | 15,836 |
| Of which with people's own money   | 1,285  | 2,581  |

**Table 5.2: Number of enterprises and employees, 1989 and 1992**

|                          | 1989    | 1992   |
| ------------------------ | ------- | ------ |
| Total enterprises        | 2,102   | 2,920  |
| Of which                 |         |        |
| state owned              | 1,541   | 1,817  |
| cooperatively owned      | 561     | 727    |
| in mixed ownership       | —       | 35     |
| in private ownership     | —       | 341    |
| Total employees ('000)   | 3,690.2 | 3032.8 |
| Of which in enterprises: |         |        |
| state owned              | 3,325.9 | 2,782.8|
| cooperatively owned      | 364.3   | 174.4  |
| in mixed ownership       | —       | 30.8   |
| in private ownership     | —       | 44.8   |

and outside the country, and to privatize industrial enterprises that at the moment are state-owned.

Change is clearly under way, if gradually; but its effects on energy use and energy efficiency are as yet only conjectural. Examples both from OECD countries and other former Comecon countries indicate that privatization accompanied by competition will give industrial management and personnel a powerful incentive to reduce waste, including energy waste, and to introduce process refinements and efficient technologies, in order to cut production costs and bring down the price at which products can be sold in a free market while returning an acceptable profit. As privatization moves ahead in Romania, valuable statistical information could be gathered about the changes brought about by privatization, including changes in energy performance. Indeed, evidence from early privatizations might usefully be adduced in subsequent phases, to encourage prospective investors as to the potential for improvements in plants to be privatized. Chapter 6 offers some intriguing pointers for specific Romanian industries.

As state-owned industries are privatized, major shake-ups can be anticipated. One of the most obvious and potentially troubling will be reduction of staffing levels. Some industrial sites are reported to be already essentially idle, because of lack of orders and lack of funds; but workers still clock in every day. One measure possibly worth considering would be to take the opportunity to provide on-site training at sites like these, to enable workers facing redundancy to acquire new skills. An obvious area for training would be energy efficiency: workers able to make practical use of the wide range of skills associated with energy efficiency would be valuable not only at the original site but elsewhere in industry or indeed elsewhere in the Romanian economy. If workers could acquire new and marketable skills, shutting down uneconomic operations would be much easier.

What of privatizing the energy supply industries themselves? The energy supply industries – RENEL, ROMGAZ, PETROM, RAH and RAL – were set up as RAs, on the basis that they were strategic industries that should remain state-owned. Nevertheless, as restructuring progresses, some parts of them have already been hived off as SAs, qualifying for privatization; and some foreign specialists, including the World Bank (as already noted) are believed to be advocating privatization even of some of the core energy suppliers themselves. Each has different attributes, prospects and problems, and the issue of privatization of the supply industries is complex, beyond the scope of this study. One point of relevance can, however, be noted. If RENEL or ROMGAZ were to be privatized, competition could be introduced into production of electricity, heat and gas, as is being done in many OECD countries; and some form of market might then determine prices – although as yet this procedure is still taking shape, for instance in England and Wales. As in other productive industries, commercial competition between private producers would undoubtedly foster efficient energy production. However, some regulatory agency would have to be created to set tariffs for the grid-based natural monopoly distribution systems delivering electricity, heat and gas to users. The powers of the regulatory agency would have to be carefully defined – especially its powers to promote energy efficiency. Some regulators, notably in the US, have played a key role in developing DSM, improving the efficiency of end-use of energy, as a major activity for energy and gas suppliers. But any such role for a Romanian regulator would have to be tailored to fit Romanian circumstances.[45]

---

[45] Structures of grid-based industries already vary widely, and are changing rapidly. Even within the EU, for instance, electricity industries exhibit many different structures and trends; see Francis McGowan, *The Struggle for Power in Europe: Competition and Regulation in the EC Electricity Industry*, Royal Institute of International Affairs, 1993.

# Chapter 6

## Investing for Energy Efficiency

### 6.1 Understanding investment

Since 1990 Romanian interest in energy efficiency has tended to assume that improving energy efficiency implies investment, particularly investment in upgrading and replacing technology. In reality, however, as the previous chapter has indicated, investment is neither the most urgent nor the most important measure to improve energy efficiency in Romania. Indeed, premature investment may aggravate problems, by misallocating scarce finances and wasting opportunities for more rapid improvements. In Romania, the most urgent and most important requirement is to develop a broader and fuller understanding of the fundamentals of energy efficiency. Householders, managers, workers, farmers, politicians, bureaucrats and the media all need to become more aware of the concept of energy efficiency, and the benefits it can bring to Romania and Romanians. They need information, education and training, not only about technical options but also about 'good housekeeping' in homes, factories, other workplaces and offices; about energy management; and about the implications of market economics and market prices for fuels and electricity, and other basics, as outlined in the previous chapter. Such general public awareness is far from easy to establish anywhere, as experience in OECD countries has long demonstrated. In a country like Romania it is harder still, because of habits of mind ingrained under four decades of communist dictatorship. Nevertheless, awakening public awareness of this major opportunity to make life better – to exercise personal responsibility and to benefit personally, obtaining better services and better amenities at lower cost – could be a significant factor in Romania's economic and social transition.

Such broader and fuller understanding of the basic concept is also an essential prerequisite for effective investments in energy efficiency. Obvious questions arise. Who is to invest, and who is to decide, on what criteria, and for what purpose? Under the old regime such considerations were swept aside; investment decisions – essentially all investment decisions, other than those by householders – were made centrally, by communist planners with their own agenda. To make effective investments in a democratic market economy, however, the process must be very different. The investor – whether a government body, an enterprise or a householder – should be clear about the purpose of the proposed investment. No investor can ever obtain perfect information; but certain questions have to be asked. Is the proposed investment the best available option, according to appropriate technical and financial criteria? Does it fit into other plans, as part of an overall 'strategy'? Is it top priority, or might alternative investments be more urgent? How risky is it? Will it accomplish its technical objective? Will it accomplish its financial objective? What outlay will be required, and how rapidly will it be paid back? Who will provide the funds, and on what basis? A householder investing his or her own savings probably weighs these questions almost instinctively; a private entrepreneur must do so more explicitly, or risk bankruptcy. Historically, however, government bodies and state-owned enterprises in Romania – and not only in Romania, as OECD experience demonstrates – have been less evidently attentive to such considerations, in the energy sector as in others. In a market economy, companies that make the right decisions prosper; those that do not, do not.

In the context of energy, to make optimum use of available capital, skills and time, options for investing in efficiency should be compared not only with options for investing in supply but also among themselves. Which efficiency investments should receive highest priority? Which offer the most rapid and secure paybacks? To assess alternative options adequately, the decision-makers in government and industry need to have a view of the future development of the Romanian economy and Romanian society. How will the structure of fuel and electricity use evolve? Which sectors of the Romanian economy will grow, and which decline? Into which sectors should most resources and effort be directed? How will Romania's domestic markets and export markets develop, and on what time-scale?

Questions like these are challenging, and do not readily yield adequate answers. The overall track record of governments and enterprises in OECD countries in finding good answers is by no means impressive; and they have much more experience than government and enterprises in the emerging democracy and market economy of Romania. But the questions have to be asked, and Romanians themselves must insist on satisfactory answers. The following sections describe some areas in which investing for energy efficiency could play an important role in rebuilding Romania.

## 6.2 Improving energy efficiency in buildings

Building standards in force until 1985 for insulating, sealing and heat loss were based on the mistaken idea that thermal insulating materials had to be avoided, because manufacturing them used large amounts of energy. This erroneous conception, and poor maintenance services, meant that panel-built blocks of flats erected from the 1970s to the mid-1980s recorded an overall thermal resistance of less than $0.7$ $m^2$-K/W. Buildings built after 1985 were designed for a thermal resistance of $1.15$-$1.25$ $m^2$-K/W; but they often fell short of this standard, and in any case this performance was less than that of an up-to-date energy-efficient structure suited to Romania's climate. For exterior walls, roof, floor and doors and windows, appropriate values are $3.3$, $4.0$, $2.0$ and $0.5$ $m^2$-K/W respectively.

The majority of apartments are connected to district heating (see Section 6.3 below). No meters or thermal controls are installed in apartment blocks; only a few heat delivery points have such devices. Under these conditions a large potential for energy savings exists, as is shown by the measures and associated effects given in Table 6.1. On the premise – crude but plausible in this context – that these measures are additive and do not interact significantly, the potential energy savings would be at least 59% and possibly substantially higher.

According to the census of 1992, Romania has 7,664,000 apartments in individual dwellings or in multi-family buildings. The distribution of dwellings according to the heating system used is given in Table 6.2. Dwellings in rural areas use almost exclusively individual stoves with solid fuel – usually firewood. Many urban areas use centralized heating systems, installed especially after 1970; heat for district heating is produced either in cogeneration plants or in local boiler plants. Neither rooms nor apartments have tempera-

## Table 6.1: Household energy savings

|                                                                | Energy savings % | Payback period (yrs) |
|----------------------------------------------------------------|:---:|:---:|
| Improvement of thermal insulation:                             |     |          |
| additional insulation of doors, windows, etc.                  | 4–10 | below 4.5 |
| ventilation control                                            | 4–9 | below 3 |
| additional insulation                                          | 25–50 | 4–10 |
| Heating control                                                | 8 | below 4 |
| Improved maintenance                                           | 5–7 | below 4.5 |
| Implementation of individual measurement systems               | 13–15 | below 4.5 |

*Source*: ICEMENERG study.

## Table 6.2: Distribution of dwellings by heating system

|                                              | 1970 No. ('000) | 1970 % | 1980 No. ('000) | 1980 % | 1992 No. ('000) | 1992 % |
|----------------------------------------------|:---:|:---:|:---:|:---:|:---:|:---:|
| Urban dwellings                              | 2,355 | 100.0 | 3,632 | 100.0 | 4,079 | 100.0 |
| of which heated by:                          |       |       |       |       |       |       |
| Natural gas-fired stoves                     | 370   | 15.7  | 372   | 10.2  | 271   | 6.7   |
| Solid and liquid-fuelled stoves              | 1,300 | 55.2  | 1,211 | 33.3  | 904   | 22.1  |
| Central heating, cogeneration                |       |       |       |       |       |       |
| or district heating                          | 685   | 29.1  | 2,049 | 56.5  | 2,904 | 71.2  |
| Rural dwellings                              | 3,395 | 100.0 | 3,691 | 100.0 | 3,585 | 100.0 |
| of which heated by:                          |       |       |       |       |       |       |
| Natural gas-fired stoves                     | 70    | 2.1   | 68    | 1.8   | 103   | 2.9   |
| Solid and liquid-fuelled stoves              | 3,325 | 97.9  | 3,602 | 97.6  | 3,422 | 95.4  |
| Thermal plants in the region                 | —     | —     | 21    | 0.6   | 60    | 1.7   |
|                                              |       |       |       |       |       |       |
| Total Romania                                | 5,750 | 100.0 | 7,323 | 100.0 | 7,664 | 100.0 |
| of which heated by:                          |       |       |       |       |       |       |
| Natural gas-fired stoves                     | 440   | 7.6   | 440   | 6.0   | 374   | 4.9   |
| Solid or liquid-fuelled stoves               | 4,652 | 80.6  | 4,853 | 66.3  | 4,326 | 56.4  |
| Central heating, cogeneration or             |       |       |       |       |       |       |
| district heating                             | 685   | 11.8  | 2,030 | 27.7  | 2,964 | 38.7  |

ture regulators. The energy parameters for housing have relatively low values; the thermal resistance standards for exterior walls for multifunctional dwellings built by the state in urban areas were 0.67 $m^2$-K/W until 1984, and 1.25 $m^2$-K/W after 1984. Values in effect in the UK are understood to be 2.24 $m^2$-K/W, although the climatic conditions are milder. An urban apartment requires about 1 toe/year. In the 1980s, as the energy crisis grew more severe, assuring a minimum temperature in dwellings, especially in urban areas connected to district heating, was impossible. Apartments suffered condensation, leading in many cases to deterioration and to increasing loss of heat. As a result, Romania offers very significant potential for energy savings in heating buildings.

Most dwellings in rural areas are single-family dwellings, built by their owners under their own direction. In urban areas, during the period of centralized economy, a great deal of housing was constructed by the state. Until the end of the 1960s these dwellings were state property, rented to citizens by the enterprises or institutes at which they worked. Constructing dwellings as personal property continued in parallel; citizens could obtain loans from the House of Savings and Deposits, a deposit bank for the population. Accordingly, in December 1989, housing in urban areas could be the personal property of the occupant, state property occupied by a tenant for an indefinite duration, or the property of an enterprise, occupied by a tenant while working at that enterprise. Apartments of all three categories could exist in the same building. How they were maintained obviously depended on the relation between the householder and the apartment.

In 1990 parliament passed a law to sell apartments that were state property built after 1950 to their occupants. Some apartments, the property of enterprises, have still not been sold. Buildings constructed before 1949, which were nationalized by the communist regime, likewise remain state property. The parties of the coalition government and the opposition parties agree that the entire housing stock should be privatized. Relatively significant differences of nuance, however, exist. The opposition parties support the immediate restitution of nationalized buildings to their former owners or their heirs. They likewise support immediate sale at reduced prices of apartments that have remained the property of enterprises. The parties of the government coalition support the rights of the tenants in the nationalized buildings – as a rule, others than the former owners. In any case, improving the situation of the existing housing stock must start by resolving the problem of ownership. In the spring of 1994 the Romanian parliament debated and eventually passed a law on housing. It proposed to restore a single dwelling to its initial owners or their heirs, and to pay for the others. Tenants would then be able to buy the apartments in which they live. Needless to say the debate was heated; how the law is to be implemented remains to be seen.

In the housing domain, as elsewhere, the state has proved itself a bad manager. Once this problem has been resolved – and to a considerable extent it already has – two other problems appear: that of finance and that of designing and carrying out remedial work. At present, as economic problems persist, Romanian citizens, including apartment owners, do not have access to enough money to undertake extensive improvement work on dwellings. Banks do not give credit for such operations. Nor has a system been established to provide information about the most efficient measures to reduce heat losses. The old state enterprises for repairs to dwellings had a bad reputation among citizens; the work was expensive and of poor quality. However, small repair firms have begun to appear. Owners of dwellings are already carrying out some improvements – draught-proofing doors, adding supplementary thermal insulation on exterior walls, installing double or triple glazing – either on their own or in collaboration with such small firms.

Until 1 May 1993, the state subsidized the price of energy supplied to the public. On 1 May 1993 the price of electricity increased 4.6 times, and that of heat delivered by district heating 9 times. This will certainly prompt occupants to take firmer action to reduce losses of heat from dwellings. Such activities require support. A publicity campaign of information, aimed at apartment owners, could be mounted. Some typical projects could be undertaken, perhaps with finance from the government budget through ARCE, to demonstrate different technical measures to reduce thermal losses from dwellings, as could other demonstration activities. A first such activity is under way in Bucureşti: supplementary thermal insulation of a block with forty-four apartments on eleven floors is being financed with the help of RENEL and ARCE. The hope is that this will convince occupants' associations to undertake similar activities with their own funds. Small construction firms could be supported, perhaps by financing specimen projects and reducing taxes. Credit could be offered to apartment owners to carry out modernizing work. For new construction, a legislative framework must be laid out to guarantee that corresponding quality parameters will be met from the outset.

In its final years, the communist regime undertook large-scale urban 'systematization', demolishing many dwellings and starting to construct new blocks. After 1989, the construction activities of state enterprises slowed almost to a standstill. The government and the mayors are promoting the idea of selling these unfinished buildings to citizens' associations – future owners – which will take the responsibility for completing them. Very few people have access to sufficient money to acquire buildings either already completed or still incomplete, but the banks do not offer loans to citizens except in very particular cases and under very onerous conditions. Construction of smaller buildings, usually single-family dwellings, built under the direction and on the land of the owners, is developing.

To establish a legislative framework concerning the quality of new construction is absolutely necessary. A law on this matter has already been drawn up and laid before parliament. It provides for the need to construct energy-efficient buildings. New standards for thermal resistance to heat transfer are being worked out; they must be set at values close to those of OECD countries with similar climatic conditions. ARCE is coordinating this activity.

Of the total of 1,314 PJ (45.3 million tce) that represented the final use of energy at the end of 1992 for all sectors of the national economy, use in the residential sector represented about 24%, that is, 315 PJ or 10.8 million tce, delivered in various ways (see Table 6.3). As a very rough estimate, if half the dwellings in Romania use half of this energy, in blocks with the potential for energy savings indicated by the measures listed in Table 6.1 above – at least 59% – applying these measures could save more than 3 million tce per year. The cost of the measures would be paid back in under five years, and the savings would continue for the lifetime of the buildings. Yet more important, however, would be the increase in comfort for the residents.

To illustrate the levels of specific energy use for an average dwelling, and taking account of the fundamental structure of existing dwellings, Table 6.4 gives values for recent years. As can be seen, the availability of energy for household use has improved considerably; whether the energy is used efficiently is, however, another matter. The figures shown confirm that heating

**Table 6.3: Structure of energy supplies to the public by energy carrier, 1990-1992**

| Energy carrier | Units* | Energy supplied | | |
|---|---|---|---|---|
| | | 1990 | 1991 | 1992 |
| Electricity | GWh | 5,353.259 | 6,746.607 | 7,596.000 |
| Heat | 1,000 Gcal | 23,096.846 | 26,195.468 | 28,294.000 |
| Total fuels | 1,000 tce | 5,333.883 | 5,350.352 | 5,790.377 |
| of which: | | | | |
| Gaseous fuels | 1,000 tce | 3,120.166 | 3,551.200 | 3,749.243 |
| | (million m³N) | (2,713.188) | (3,088.000) | (3,247,635) |
| Liquid fuels | 1,000 tce | 581.228 | 499.317 | 640.956 |
| Solid fuels | 1,000 tce | 1,571.667 | 1,279.181 | 1,390.389 |
| Others, new energy sources, secondary energy resources | 1,000 tce | 60.822 | 20.654 | 9.789 |

*Calorific value of natural gas 33.73 GJ/m³N; calorific value of conventional fuel 29.3 GJ/tce.

**Table 6.4: Average specific energy use for dwellings 1990-1992 (kWh/y per dwelling)***

| Type of use | 1990 | 1991 | 1992 |
|---|---|---|---|
| Total | 9,804.0 | 10,603.3 | 11,479.8 |
| Of which: | | | |
| Heating | 7,405.0 | 7,705.4 | 7,134.7 |
| Water heating | 1,049.0 | 1,230.0 | 1,524.5 |
| Lighting | 536.3 | 705.1 | 747.3 |
| Cooking | 813.7 | 962.8 | 2,073.3 |
| No. of dwellings occupied | 7,712,816 | 7,615,845 | 7,632,013 |

*Average useable area per dwelling: 33.6 m²; average number of people per dwelling: 2.92

continues to be the largest category of energy use in dwellings, accounting for 62-75% of total use.

Romania, of course, also has many industrial and public buildings, as well as office buildings that are now beginning to accommodate a growing commercial sector. These buildings, their occupants and their operators, too, would undoubtedly benefit from measures to improve thermal performance, especially in Romanian winters. The first stage would be to carry out energy audits of such buildings, to identify the most appropriate measures to be taken. Buildings for which the government is both landlord and tenant – and such buildings are numerous – are particularly obvious candidates for improvement. Managers of industrial enterprises seeking to improve efficiency might well look first at factory buildings, even before the industrial process plant itself, since space heating often represents a sizeable fraction of total energy use even in industry. 'Good housekeeping' also applies to buildings.

## 6.3 District heating

At present, most residential heating systems in Romania continue to be room heating, based on solid fuels (wood and coal), natural gas, liquid fuels and combinations – solid fuel plus electricity, liquid fuel plus electricity and so on. Such room heating is used in more than 50% of the nearly 8 million dwellings that existed at the end of 1990. Another 10% of residential buildings have central heating systems. The remaining dwellings – about 40% – are heated by district heating, either from local boiler plants or from cogeneration stations that also generate electricity. Dwellings supplied with district heating typically also receive a separate supply of hot water through the same network.

District heating, particularly systems based on cogeneration stations, began to be developed in Romania in 1954-6, under the communist regime. District heating had well-established practical advantages; but it also fitted into the communist philosophy of central planning, central supply and central control. In due course this created serious problems for the public image of district heating in Romania. In the dark days of the 1980s, central control of district heating networks allowed the authorities to redirect scarce heat supplies to industry and away from residential areas. One Romanian specialist recalled ruefully his days as a boiler plant manager, seeing people standing at the plant gate in the winter, shaking their fists at him through the control room window.

Nevertheless, at the moment Romanian specialists still consider district heating to be one of the most technically and economically suitable ways to supply heat to large urban areas. In principle, compared to systems in individual buildings, district heating has major energy and ecological advantages. In cogeneration mode it offers higher efficiency, by producing both electricity and heat together in large stations with automated combustion processes; and it can use low-grade fuel, which is both less costly and more readily available indigenously. At the same time it can reduce pollution, by improving the composition and reducing the quantity of combustion gases discharged from the stack. Moreover, district heating can offer greater possibilities for integration with heat recovery in industries, through possible cooperation between different industrial production units with heat recovery and the main producer of the heat distributed through the centralized system, that is, RENEL. The economic efficiency of large centralized district heating systems depends mostly on the savings of fuel, which can be as much as 30-35% compared with the alternative of decentralized heat production in local boiler plants.

Another significant argument currently favouring district heating as the way to supply heat to dwellings in Romania is the possibility it offers to replace petroleum products and natural gas, used very widely in local heating systems, with solid fuels, particularly lignite, burned in large district heating stations. Forecasts for the evolution of fuel prices have always favoured extending the use of solid fuels; except for occasional periods, the price of fuel oil in Romania has evolved continually upwards. However, the IEA report notes that RENEL appears to pay about the same price per unit of heat energy for coal as it does for fuel oil, weakening the argument for switching to solid fuel.[46] In any case, burning lignite in towns, which the old communist regime also promoted, creates major environmental and transport problems.

The high density of population in certain zones has helped to justify technically and economically continuing to extend district heating in Romania. The fundamental structure of the residential sector, in which most Romanians in urban areas live in communal dwellings, apartments in blocks with many floors, has likewise favoured the adoption of centralized heat supply in general and district heating in particular. Some of the conditions favouring district heating have recently changed significantly: fuel prices have been liberalized, reserves have diminished and large stations need to be refitted.

---

[46] *Energy Policies of Romania*, International Energy Agency, 1993.

Nevertheless, weighing the consequences, as well as the increase in the price of thermal energy, the high cost of transmission and distribution grids for thermal energy, and other factors, Romanian specialists conclude that district heating, and centralized heat supply in general, will remain the most advantageous way to supply heat to the large urban concentrations in Romania at least until the end of this decade.

At the moment, however, district heating systems do not deliver either adequate heat supply for the consumers connected or the designed energy performance. The causes of these shortfalls include a lack of supply capacity, the abolition of system temperature regulation according to external temperature, and the uneconomic operation of the heat-generating equipment. The heat distribution network is often poorly insulated; regulators and meters at thermal points and on heating apparatus are absent, or do not work; and thermal grids and installations at thermal points are in unsatisfactory technical condition. As noted above, many district heating systems also supply hot water for direct use. A foreign visitor staying with Romanian friends in a flat in Cluj found that neither of the hot water taps, in the kitchen and the bathroom, could be turned off. The bathroom tap was pouring out more than five litres of water a minute, at more than 60° Celsius. The Romanian friend, acutely embarrassed, explained that the flat itself had no shut-off valve to enable a plumber to repair the taps, and that the shut-off valve to the block of flats was broken. To fix the taps would require shutting down the local district heating plant itself. As it happened, a midsummer cloudburst a month later flooded the district heating plant and clogged its water intakes; the plant was shut down, and the Romanian friend was able to call a plumber who fixed the taps. The episode demonstrated vividly the problems of the existing infrastructure for supplying heat and hot water.

Measures to restructure district heating systems and restore their design efficiency are clearly urgently needed. They will necessitate significant technical, material and financial efforts in refitting and in undertaking capital repairs on grids and equipment that are obsolete or that have reached the limit of their life. The Bucureşti district heating authority, RADET, held a major seminar in April 1993 to consider the range of options available, and published a series of technical studies on the issue. The measures will have to extend all the way to reconsidering specimen solutions to be applied generally in equipping thermal points and in interior heating installations: increasing thermal insulation; using heating units that are efficient, regulatable and flexible, including adopting low-temperature interior heating systems; meeting peak heating demand with local supplies; and so on. Although some Romanian specialists doubt the feasibility of installing individual meters and controls in dwellings, IEA specialists have insisted that the possibility should be explored. Demonstration projects in Hungary indicate a significant potential for improvement; in one Hungarian city, installing individual meters - with no other modifications, for instance no improvement of insulation – led to a 25% reduction in energy use.[47] All these measures, gradually applied, must first increase the security of supply to the consumers connected, and therefore the internal thermal comfort, within the limits of technical and economic efficiency calculated beforehand. They must also increase the credibility of centralized heat supply systems to potential or actual consumers connected, to obliterate memories of the chilly 1980s.

RENEL, which supplies 40% of the total heat production in Romania, is a major supplier of thermal energy for a good part of the building stock in the residential, industrial and so-called 'tertiary' sectors – offices and public buildings. Ironically, the collapse in electricity demand now sometimes means that RENEL must operate cogeneration plants in order to supply heat in the winter, while having no demand for the electricity output for which the plants were designed. The plants thus sometimes operate in seriously suboptimal mode, inefficiently and expensively. Foreign specialists suggest that RENEL should develop a coherent overall strategy for supplying both electricity and heat, based on system marginal costs, so that electricity dispatching and heat dispatching from the plants on the system are better coordinated. Reducing the heat supply required would help to balance the system better. RENEL thus has an interest in underwriting, technically and materially, measures for improving energy efficiency not only in the distribution systems for electricity and heat but also in customers' premises. Doing so would reduce its own costs and increase its credibility with customers for district heating.

---

[47] Ian Brown, Hungary-EC Energy Centre, private communication. He added that for hot water, the reduction was 60%. One meter was installed over the bath and one over the kitchen sink – 'When you turn on the tap you see it going round.'

## 6.4 Lighting

### 6.4.1 Lighting residences

Residences mostly use classical incandescent lamps of 25, 40, 60, 75 and 100 W. Their luminous efficiency is 7-10 lumen/W, at about 2-3% efficiency of output of luminous flux. A bulb with a lifetime of 800 hours cost from 280 to 450 lei in mid-1994. In Romania the manufacturers are Romlux in Tirgovişte and Steaua Electrica in Fieni. Bathrooms and kitchens sometimes use classical fluorescent lighting. The average electricity use for residential lighting is about 350 kWh/y per family; a classical fluorescent lamp cost from 1,300 to 3,500 lei in mid-1994. Compact fluorescent lamps of 9, 11, 15, 20 and 23 W, with a luminous efficiency of 45-60 lumen/W and a lifetime of 12,000 hours, manufactured abroad, can be found on sale, but at a price of more than 18,000 lei per lamp, which is prohibitive for most Romanians.

### 6.4.2 Lighting offices, educational establishments and hospitals

Offices, educational establishments and hospitals use low-pressure mercury vapour lamps – that is, classical fluorescent lamps – of 14, 20, 40 and 65 W, with a luminous efficiency of 30-55 lumen/W at about 5-8% efficiency of output of luminous flux. A lamp with a lifetime of 6,000 hours cost up to 3,500 lei in mid-1994. In Romania the manufacturers are Romlux in Tirgovişte and Electrofar in Bucureşti.

### 6.4.3 Lighting industrial spaces and roadways

Industrial spaces and roadways use mercury vapour and sodium vapour lamps. The high-pressure mercury vapour lamps with fluorescent envelopes, of 80, 125, 250 and 400 W, have a luminous efficiency of 50-60 lumen/W, at 6-8% efficiency of output of luminous flux. A lamp with a lifetime of 6,000 hours cost from 6,700 to nearly 20,000 lei in mid-1994. In Romania these lamps are manufactured by Romlux in Tirgovişte and Electrofar in Bucureşti. The high-pressure sodium vapour lamps with opal envelopes, of 70, 150, 250 and 400 W, have a luminous efficiency of 66-125 lumen/W, at 12-14% efficiency of output of luminous flux. A lamp with a lifetime of 12,000 hours cost more than 7,000 lei in mid-1994. In Romania these lamps are manufactured by Electrofar in Bucureşti.

As indicated, classical incandescent lamps, low- and high-pressure mercury vapour lamps and high-pressure sodium lamps are manufactured in Romania. The characteristics cited above are those given in the catalogues of the manufacturers. In practice, according to Romanian specialists, the performance of the lamps is below these levels, at least from the point of view of lifetime. Even the performance data given in the catalogues are below the level of performance of lamps manufactured by well-known international firms. The technical level of the installations for lamp manufacture in the Romanian factories mentioned, and by implication of the products, is lower. Collaboration with foreign specialist firms would be useful.

Since a significant proportion of Romanian lighting is in buildings and other facilities that are still state-owned, including street lighting, one possibility worth considering would be a government programme to upgrade this lighting across the country. Government orders for large numbers of high-efficiency lamps could be a springboard for mass production in Romania, to bring down unit costs of manufacture and thus to make the lamps affordable also for private purchasers. A well-designed programme could be financed on the basis of savings in electricity costs, probably within a very few years. The government could seek financial support from international agencies to design and then to implement such a programme, possibly also involving foreign specialist firms in joint ventures with Romanian manufacturers. RENEL, too, could participate; if the programme were structured as a form of DSM, RENEL could even take the lead. Refitting would cover not just lamps themselves but entire illumination facilities, including the so-called *luminaires* or housings, which can have a significant effect on lighting efficiency. Such a programme would also create a substantial range of employment throughout Romania in manufacturing and installing efficient lighting.

## 6.5 Industrial opportunities

In recent years, particularly since December 1989, foreign analysts have tended to appraise Romania's industries and economic performance in terms of 're-dundant industries', 'industries that are uneconomic, with large loss-making enterprises', 'industries with troubled sectors such as metallurgy, chemicals and petrochemicals, machine building, highly capital intensive and having considerable excess capacities', or even more critical expressions. In general, to be sure, assessments like these are supported by macroeconomic statistics – industrial production declined by more than 50% between 1989 and 1992 – and by discussions with people whose information is second-hand. In the view of Romanian specialists, however, such assessments reflect a kind of preconditioned attitude towards the Romanian state of things. The studies that express such judgements, carried out with the assistance of foreign consultants, offer the image of deeply anachronistic and uncompetitive industries. However, they seriously exaggerate the isolation of Romania's economy. Although in the 1980s hard currency shortage severely restricted imports, particularly technology transfers, in the 1960s and 1970s Romania was the recognized champion within central and eastern Europe as regards consistent links with western economies.

The World Bank, the European Commission, the US Agency for International Development, the OECD and other western organizations have supported a number of studies aiming to gain insight into the economic and technological capabilities of the industrial facilities in Romania's energy sector, in the face of the rising requirements of the free market. These studies have been conspicuously oriented towards the supply side of the energy pattern. As far as the energy end-use side is concerned, they have examined only aspects such as the provisions of economic reform; existing regulations, tariffs and taxes; and the interrelations among certain government administrative bodies and enterprises.

Apart from one USAID project (180-0015, May 1992) that surveyed eight industrial plants – covering steel, fertilizers, cement, machine building, soybean oil, milk, and power – the aforementioned studies offer no concrete data about technologies employed, nor comparisons of performance with similar foreign plants. To be relevant, according to Romanian specialists, the features of Romanian industry have to be considered not according to the enterprises but according to the technological framework. The old regime of central planning, with its goal of economic autarchy, and limited technological standards and practices, favoured repetition and replication. A typical example is that of a soybean plant that had to modify certain facilities as a result of changes in local conditions. The central planners thereupon decreed that all soybean processing facilities had to carry out the same modifications, even though they used different technologies.

In the transition period, enterprises have experienced a certain degree of autonomy, many of them being broken up. As described earlier, those to remain under state control, for strategic or similar reasons – including all the energy suppliers – have been made into *regies autonomes* or 'autonomous administrations', designated RA. Those to be privatized have been made into *societates anonimes* or commercial societies, designated SA; at present there are some 660 RAs and 6,280 SAs. The government's goal is to privatize all SAs by the end of the decade. Nevertheless, because of the shortage of resources, only minor technical changes have been possible. The main technological characteristics of Romanian industry can be summed up as follows. The output is remarkably diverse, compared to the country's economic potential. Only a relatively small number of items cannot be manufactured in the existing industrial facilities; the exceptions are generally linked to certain materials and components. The majority of production takes place in sizeable enterprises organized in large-scale integration. A significant share of industrial output has been dedicated to supplying capital plant for the energy sector, primary processing and other industries. As a result of this policy, Romania has many factories that can manufacture a diverse range of capital plant, as later sections of this chapter will describe; see also Appendix 3.

From a technological viewpoint, the so-called energy-intensive industries perform better than the corresponding facilities in other central and east European countries. This is particularly true for steel and laminates, cement, building materials, ammonia and fertilizers, glass, caustic soda, petrochemicals and aluminium – that is, for those technologies responsible for more than 50% of end-use of energy in Romania. The basic facilities of the major energy-using industries in Romania were delivered by, or manufactured under licences purchased from, well-known western international suppliers; and in the 1960s and 1970s economic cooperation with these companies was relatively close. In the 1980s, however, it grew very tenuous. As well as banning the majority of imports, officials of the Ceauşescu government applied an intensive campaign to 'cheapen' capital goods. They frequently interfered with and applied pressure on engineering institutes and advisory bodies to use low-grade materials and neglect the standards then in force.

R&D and engineering services are concentrated in units large by western standards; production plants make only a minor contribution to these activities. In the 1980s, at least, investments in industrial energy efficiency were either non-existent or ill-advised, with respect to generating non-marketable heat as warm water. A few programmes, such as those for regenerative ceramic burners for industrial furnaces, energy measurement systems for industrial users and district heating, lenticular graphite electrodes for electric arc furnaces for electric steel-making, and fluidized-bed boilers for sugar plants, were compromised by the technical drawbacks of immature equipment – in particular unreliability. They were further compromised by the way the programmes were administered, and by the lack of any real incentive for improvement, because of the energy quota system described earlier.

As regards the value of energy intensities, opinions still differ. The differences are reinforced by significant discrepancies between actual 'physical' specific energy use, and 'money-valued' specific energy use – discrepancies found even as real energy prices are gradually harmonized with the world market level. In general, because of the differences in quality standards, the value of output is significantly lower in Romania than in corresponding western technologies. Moreover, methodological differences in calculating energy use complicate matters: in Romania some auxiliary or peripheral services may be included as process operations, as described earlier. The industrial energy intensity in PJ per dollar of GDP has been estimated as being at least three times that of western Europe; however, as will be shown, the specific energy use for the major industrial technologies that account for more than 50% of industrial energy use in Romania are only 15-30% higher than those of corresponding western plants. The proportional influence of the different factors responsible for this low energy efficiency is also poorly understood, although the individual factors have been correctly identified. Some technological processes and/or equipment are obsolescent; past practices – the absence of incentives, lack of metering and control, and the impact of 'energy quotas' on initiative in enterprises – have led to lingering managerial and behaviourial shortcomings; and energy pricing policy has been counterproductive.

Generalizations may nevertheless be misleading. Only detailed audits, site by site, can establish the true status and prospects of individual industrial facilities in Romania. To be sure, the prospects for various industries will also depend on international market considerations; some sectors – for instance refining and steel – already have serious over-capacity internationally, which will impinge on the prospects for Romanian industrial exports and imports. That said, each industry and indeed each industrial plant has to be assessed on its merits. In particular, the potential for improving efficiency has to be evaluated in terms of the market prospects for the particular industry or plant, the technical opportunities, access to efficient technology either within or outside Romania, the capital outlay required and access to this capital, and the estimated real rate of return on proposed investment – that is, the payback time. Managers of enterprises and their staff need to be convinced that efficiency measures are not merely a reintroduction of the old 'energy conservation' directives from the central planners; energy efficiency has to be presented as beneficial to the enterprise itself, and to its personnel, in lowering production costs, improving working conditions and enhancing the quality of output. The point cannot be emphasized too strongly: improving the energy efficiency of industry involves not only implementing technical measures but changing the attitudes and habits of managers and staff. In a democratic market economy such changes cannot be imposed by coercion. They must be brought about by persuasion, information, education and training – not by penalties but by incentives. Only then will the changes be fully effective. Privatization will give enterprise management the opportunity to use its own judgement about investments in general and efficiency investments in particular, to assess the risks and rewards and act accordingly. Funding sources both inside and outside Romania will have to weigh the prospects of different industries or facilities as places to invest; and they can do so effectively only on the basis of specific information, acquired on-site. One factor they would do well to consider will be the potential for improving the efficiency of the operation. The following sections offer some preliminary insights.

## 6.6 Industry-wide efficiency measures

Some measures to improve energy efficiency could be applied essentially throughout Romanian industry – for instance, thermal insulation of industrial buildings and upgrading of industrial lighting. Evidence suggests that 'good housekeeping' – maintenance of boilers, steam lines, pumps, valves and other standard equipment, and avoidance of wasteful practices – is often neglected, yet it is basic and essential. Romanian specialists also suggest two particular technical innovations that could be widely applied: the introduction of variable-speed motor drives and of regenerative ceramic burners for furnaces.

### 6.6.1 Variable-speed motor drives

One measure alone – introducing variable-speed drives for electric motors in industry and public services – could save about 5% of the total end-use electricity in Romania. The main applications would be for pumps, fans and fluid compressors, which together use more than 50% of the electricity supplied to industry. The electric motor driving such a unit is supplied with energy not directly from the grid but through an electronic converter. The motor speed is then correlated automatically with the fluid flow required at a given moment. This avoids fluid bottlenecks at valves, taps, throttles, and so on, and thus avoids an energy loss of 15-40%. For example, a compressed air substation of 5.6 MPa equipped with four centrifugal compressors can save 12.3 GWh – that is, 22% of the present consumption – annually. Implementation of the solution at the water pumping station at SC Doljchim Craiova, equipped with pumps of 1,000 kW each, reduces electricity use by 4.1 GWh/y, or 18%. At the cooling tower fan station of the same enterprise with five 315 kW fans, using variable-speed drives saves 1 GWh/y, or 27% of the electricity. The frequency converters are of various types and powers, depending on the characteristics of the electric motors to which they are coupled.

In OECD economies, variable-speed motor drives are now standard on new facilities; they have also been analysed thoroughly in Romania. Romania has sufficient know-how, and also has converter manufacturers, for instance ICPE-SA, UMEB SA, Electroputere SA and IPA. Converters for special applications or with special reliability may have to be imported. ICEMENERG, which is already engaged in the RENEL DSM programme, can provide the engineering. At the industry level, the 1991 saving potential was as shown in Table 6.5.

Several other applications can also be mentioned, in agriculture (for irrigation), public transport and water supplies. In general the measure pays for itself by energy savings in two to four years.

**Table 6.5: Variable-speed motor drives: potential energy savings in industry**

| Branch | Total end-use energy (GWh) | Energy saving from total end-use (GWh) | (%) |
|---|---|---|---|
| Chemistry | 6,035 | 308 | 5.1 |
| Metallurgy | 9,148 | 183 | 2.0 |
| Wood and building materials | 3,216 | 100 | 3.1 |
| Petrochemistry | 1,853 | 132 | 7.1 |
| Mines | 1,491 | 64 | 4.3 |
| Machine building | 4,732 | 57 | 1.2 |
| Oil | 2,252 | 83 | 3.7 |
| Light industry | 1,118 | 27 | 2.4 |
| Electric engineering industry | 72 | 18 | 2.4 |
| Electric energy industry | 8,342 | 834 | 10.0 |
| Total | 42,431 | 1,806 | 4.2 |

The Ministry of Industries is promoting the introduction of variable-speed electric motor drives throughout the Romanian economy. The programme, under the technical coordination of RENEL's research institute ICEMENERG, includes research and development, demonstration activities, popularizing this technology with enterprises, and various forms of financial support for enterprises that introduce new technologies. The Directorate General of Energy of the MoI, ARCE and other research and design institutes are also taking part in the programme.

*6.6.2 Regenerative ceramic burner systems for metal heating furnaces*
Although Stordy Combustion Engineering Ltd in the UK developed the concept of regenerative ceramic burner systems for metal-heating furnaces in the mid-1980s, it was rapidly implemented by two Romanian enterprises, Fortus in Iaşi and INTEC SA in Bucureşti. A regenerative ceramic burner (RCB) is an all-ceramic burner coupled to a compact regenerator. Installed in pairs, the RCBs are programmed to fire and collect waste gases alternately. As one is in the firing mode, the other is in the exhaust mode, the burner being used

as the waste gas port from the furnace chamber. The RCB saves 30-60% of fuel by improving combustion efficiency. When the process temperature ranges from 1,000 to 1,500° Celsius the final exhaust gas temperature is only 150-200° Celsius.

In Romania, between 1986 and 1989, under the direct supervision of top Communist Party officials, an intensive programme was launched to install RCBs on some 1,500 industrial furnaces, aimed at saving a minimum of 0.5 billion cu m of natural gas. The administrative methods, and problems with the reliability of certain immature equipment components, set back this important energy efficiency programme. Romanian specialists believe it should be resumed.

## 6.7 An industrial shopping list

As already noted, the status and prospects for Romanian industries have to be evaluated industry by industry, and even plant by plant, in the context of an overall economic strategy for the country and against a background of international markets. The following sections offer an introductory overview of the wide range of industries in Romania, presenting the industrial technologies now in place and what they produce. Many of the data cited are from before December 1989, because the majority of audits were done at that time and industry then operated much closer to full capacity. For each technology, the overview describes the existing industrial capacity, its age and suppliers, equipment manufacturers, the main measures that could be taken to improve energy efficiency and local capabilities to participate in a retrofitting programme. The analysis focuses on energy intensity; even in this respect it is not meant to be exhaustive but merely to offer a survey of the existing levels and potentials. Detailed on-site audits to update this information, as a guide to priorities and opportunities, would be invaluable.

The analysis was facilitated by the existence of an energy/technologies database known as BDTEHNO, structured around the main industrial, transportation and agricultural technologies. ICEMENERG, in cooperation with R&D design institutes involved in engineering in the respective branches, created this database in 1987-9, demonstrating perhaps that Romanians were deeply concerned about the energy intensity and energy efficiency of their economy, as it was forced to follow the wrong models. The information, based on extensive audits, makes weak spots evident and identifies the remedial actions needed, the solutions and investments required to improve energy efficiency for about 400 technologies that together represent more than 65% of total energy end-use. Unfortunately, although the database also gives costs, they must now be recalculated because capital costs and energy prices have changed so much.

The comprehensive description of the technologies covers information about industrial process flows and phases, and associated specific energy use; the uses of raw materials and energy carriers; the characteristics of the basic equipment; the impact on energy intensity of various production factors, such as the quality of raw materials or the load factor on the equipment; specific energy use recorded for similar technologies abroad; and the cost-benefit balance for potential measures to improve energy efficiency. Unfortunately, scarcity of funds has slowed down the expansion and updating of the BDTEHNO database and its extension to include information about public services and residential appliances. Assessing its current status and potential for improvement and extension could be an early priority.

### 6.7.1 Ammonia

Using roughly 6 billion cu m of natural gas per year at full capacity, ammonia is by far the largest energy-using industrial technology in Romania. Ammonia is used throughout industry, but the major end-use is for nitrogen fertilizers. Since 1962, eighteen ammonia plants have been commissioned; a further two new units were under construction in 1989. They were erected at the chemical plants sited in Piatra Neamț, Craiova, Targu Magurele, Targu Mureş, Arad, Fagaraş, Bacau and Slobozia, with successive generations of technology: 1962-5 GIAP (Russian); 1967-8 Uhde (German); 1970-3 Sybetra (Belgian); and 1974-5 Kellogg (USA, but only the first two units were original). The total capacity is approximately 4 million tonnes $NH_3$/year, of which the basic facilities – Sybetra and Kellogg, 0.3 million t/y/for each unit – share 80%. In 1991 the load factor was only 30.3%, representing 37.2% of the peak annual production (1986). The average specific energy use in 1989 was 46.4 GJ/t for the Kellogg plant and 51.1 GJ/t and 657 kWh/t for the Sybetra plant; that is 20-5% higher than those of up-to-date world facilities, for instance, Sumatra in Indonesia. Spectacular increases of energy intensity have been recorded in the transition period, because of low load factors and other problems, as shown in Table 6.6.

IPROCHIM SA, the Romanian engineering company in the field, is well aware of the necessary retrofitting solutions – generally highly capital-intensive. The requirements are more active catalysts, advanced heat recovery systems and a new column interior at Sybetra.

## 6.7.2 Electric steel-making

The structure of 1987 steel output in major western producing countries and in Romania is shown in Table 6.7. Graphite iron melting in Romania has a potential capacity of roughly 5.5 million t/y. Electric arc furnaces vary widely with respect to unit capacity and manufacturer. The smaller units, with outputs ranging from 1 to 5 t/load, are common in the steel foundries of mechanical engineering enterprises. Producers of commercial steel laminates, like SIDEX in Galaţi, SIDERURGICA SA in Hunedoara, COST SA in Tirgovişte, Industria Sirmei (Wire Works) in Campia Turzii and Siderca SA in Calaraşi have units of 20, 50, 65 and 100 t/load. The regular energy intensity of these major steel manufacturers is over 700 kWh/t, well above design specifications, mainly because of the low-grade quality of graphite electrodes and refractories, and also improper preparation of the scrap. World state-of-the-art facilities need only 450-500 kWh to melt a tonne of steel.

The basic equipment of the large arc furnaces was manufactured in the former Soviet Union, Poland, Federal Germany, Japan and Romania. It is fairly modern and can be upgraded without serious technical difficulties. IPROMET, the Romanian design company in the field, has carried out projects to modernize the technology and to meet western standards. The solutions employed – computerized control systems, new insulation based on ceramic fibres, oxygen blowing and scrap preheating with the sensible heat of flue gas – can increase energy efficiency substantially, although they have not been implemented on an industrial scale. Using high-grade graphite electrodes and installing ladle metallurgy can save more energy and allow for much higher quality.

**Table 6.6: Ammonia plants**

| Technology | Cumulative specific energy use, projected values (GJ/t) | Manufacturing enterprise | Cumulative specific energy use values obtained (GJ/t) | |
|---|---|---|---|---|
| | | | 1989 | 1990 |
| Kellogg | 44.3 | CIC Craiova | 48.3 | 54.2 |
| | | CIC Tg. Mureş 3 | 44.4 | 44.8 |
| | | CIC Tg. Mureş 4 | 44.3 | 47.3 |
| | | CIC Slobozia | 48.5 | 53.8 |
| | | Mean value* | 46.4 | 550. |
| Sybetra | 43.4 | CIC Craiova 2 | 57.4 | 69.8 |
| | | CIC Slobozia | 62.4 | 67. |
| | | Mean value* | 59.5 | 68.5 |
| Uhde | 50.6 | CIC Tg. Mureş | 53.5 | 56.4 |
| Salzgitter | 56.4 | Azochim P. Neamţ | 73. | 85.6 |
| Giap | 72.3 | CIC Craiova | 78.6 | 79.6 |
| | 64.7 | Azochim P. Neamţ | 65.8 | 74.8 |
| | | Mean value* | 64.7 | 77.2 |
| | | | *Country mean value* | |
| | | | 53.2 | 58.5 |

*Calculated as weighted mean.

**Table 6.7: Structure of steel output (%)**

| | Oxygen converters | Electric | Open hearths |
|---|---|---|---|
| Total world | 56.2 | 26.5 | 17.3 |
| USA | 62.3 | 37.7 | — |
| Federal Germany | 82.5 | 17.5 | — |
| Japan | 70.2 | 29.8 | — |
| France | 74.7 | 25.3 | — |
| Italy | 48.5 | 51.8 | — |
| Romania | 48.0 | 24.0 | 28 |

## 6.7.3 Iron and steel castings

Romania is a major producer of cast metal parts; the car manufacturing industry alone has capacity totalling 260,000 tonnes of cast iron parts and 450,000 tonnes of steel parts. Cast iron is made in electric induction furnaces (63%), in coke cupola furnaces (31%) and in duplex installations (6%). Virtually all the basic equipment of a foundry can be fabricated in Romania. Crucible induction furnaces are manufactured in sizes from 0.1 to 12.5 tonnes (8,000Hz, 2,500Hz, 50Hz) and have a specific electricity use of 520-700 kWh/t. For example, the 12.5t furnace needs 525 kWh/t of liquid steel, compared to 515 kWh/t and 482 kWh/t used by furnaces manufactured by the firms AEG and ASEA respectively.

The following representative examples illustrate the energy-intensive technologies used in Romania. The foundry of the SATURN SA company in Alba Iulia, for cast parts, is equipped with induction furnaces and has a capacity of 50,000t of parts per year. The equipment was manufactured by ROTEC SA in Buzau and MECATIM SA in Timişoara. One tonne of liquid cast iron – preparation of the charge, melting, maintenance and modification – uses on average 780-800 kWh and 18 cu m of natural gas. State-of-the-art technology on the world scale needs between 550 and 650 kWh of electricity for each tonne of liquid cast iron; energy intensity is reduced especially by automatic control of the furnace regime, and superior preparation of furnace loading, including preheating with hot gases.

The UNIO enterprise in Satu Mare has a cast-iron foundry of 17,000 t/y, equipped with cupola furnaces. In 1988 it produced 8,500t of parts, of which 5,000t were of cast iron with nodular graphite. All the equipment was manufactured within the enterprise. The specific use of coke is from 140 to 145 kg/t of liquid cast iron, and of electricity 31 kWh/t of liquid. These levels are comparable to those achieved, for example, in the UK.

The steel foundry of the truck factory in Braşov has a production line with a capacity of 48,600t of parts per year. In 1988 it produced 27,200t of carbon steel parts, slightly alloyed and alloyed. The foundry, equipped with electric arc furnaces of 3t capacity, manufactured in Hungary and Poland in the 1970s, uses 830-900 kWh/t of parts and 130-150MJ/t of parts, compared to 650-750 kWh/t of parts recorded in modern foundries in the USA.

## 6.7.4 Aluminium

Primary aluminium technology was among the biggest energy end-users in Romania before December 1989, using a total of about 4 TWh/y. In 1992 the energy use was only 1.772 TWh. A two-stage aluminium melting plant based on Pechiney technology went into operation in Slatina town in the Olt district in 1963. ALRO SA has 704 (63 kA) and 768 (83 kA) melting pots, the last of them commissioned in 1970. The total capacity of the plant is approximately 240,000 t/y. The project gave specific energy use of 14,000 kWh/t for the first stage and 13,500 kWh/t for the second. The figures were confirmed in operation. At a later time, IMNR, the Romanian co-designer, and the plant engineering team, made several attempts to retrofit the plant with a view to reducing energy intensity, pollution and the consumption of other process materials such as electrodes and cryolite. The improvements – introducing computer process control and covering the pots – were applied only on a small scale in 1987-8 because of the lack of money, although altogether they could reduce the specific energy use by around 350 kWh/t. To judge the energy-saving potential of the technology, the energy efficiency of the most up-to-date Australian and Brazilian melting pots (150-239 kA) is about 12,000 kWh/t. The average results of other west European aluminium companies are between 13,000 and 13,500 kWh/t.

## 6.7.5 Oil refining and petrochemistry

According to the IEA report, 'Refining of indigenous crude oil began, near Ploieşti, in the late 1850s, making the Romanian refining industry the oldest in Europe. Until the second world war, the Romanian industry was among the largest in the world, with extensive foreign participation'.[48] The IEA report goes on to note that at the end of 1992, nominal crude distillation capacity at Romania's ten refineries – Astra, Darmaneşti, Vega, Crişana, Steaua Romana, Arpechem, Petromidia, Petrobrazi, Petroţel and RAFO – was almost 34 million tonnes of petroleum per annum (mtpa), far in excess of current domestic demand of about 12 mtpa. In 1989, 30.6 mt of crude oil were refined. As the IEA survey noted, Romania's oil refining industry is 'by far the largest in central and eastern Europe', and 'the most sophisticated in

---

[48] *Energy Policies of Romania.*

central and eastern Europe and at least as complex as the average western European industry': 'Four of the five large, more modern refineries – Arpechim, Petromidia, Petroţel, and Petrobrazi – have fully-integrated olefin and aromatics plants based on a combination of naphtha and LPG feedstocks from the adjacent refineries'. As far as pipeline connections are concerned, 'Nowhere else in central or eastern Europe is there such an intensive network of pipeline links between refining sites for the transfer of feedstocks'. The IEA report goes on to say: 'By the mid-1980s, Romania had by far the largest petrochemical sector in eastern Europe, capable technically of producing the full range of olefin and aromatic bulk chemicals, as well as an extensive range of lower-volume, speciality derivative products'.

However, as regards the economic and technical performance of the Romanian refining industry, the IEA report declares that 'The sector has been beset by poor operational performance, extended down-time, extensive losses, and disregard for energy conservation and the local environment'. Judging summarily, in the opinion of Romanian specialists, who consider the information general and incomplete without an *in situ* technical audit, the IEA report refers again later to 'the high losses and low energy efficiency of Romanian refineries'.

Romanian specialists view matters in a somewhat different light. Nevertheless, they add that the IEA report is correct to remark that in view of the overcapacity in bulk petrochemicals evident since 1990 throughout Europe, and other factors, 'maximizing output of gasoline for export has been more attractive than operating the downstream cracker and aromatic plants'. Romanian specialists say that this trend was in fact the principal argument for undertaking a programme of refitting at Romanian petrochemical complexes, especially Petrobrazi, with the aim of maximizing extraction of light products – because, for example, in 1985, the output of petroleum refined into feedstocks for petrochemistry was 9.5% compared to only 7% in the US.

Refinery utilization declined sharply to about 45% in 1992, principally as a result of shortfalls of imports from Iraq and former Yugoslavia, and to some extent also as a result of the inappropriate fit between the product structure and the market. The product structure was adjusted in 1992; fuel oil yields from crude declined from 32.8% by weight in 1991 to 28.4% by weight, and gasoline and gasoil yields both increased, to 21.7% and 27.6% respectively.

To picture the energy efficiency in refineries more concretely, take for example a preprocessing line of 3.5 mtpa of crude at Petroţel. This technological system includes the following installations or processes: atmospheric and vacuum distillation (3.5 mtpa); catalytic cracking (1.0 mtpa); catalytic petrol reforming (0.5 mtpa); petrol hydrorefining (0.9 mtpa); delayed coking (0.7 mtpa); petrol-diesel hydrorefining (1.0 mtpa); and separation of paraxylene and isomerization of metaxylene (0.05 mtpa). The technology, corresponding to that of ICERP SA in Ploieşti in 1974, produces LPG, petrol, diesel, vacuum distillate and vacuum resid. The equipment – distillation columns, furnaces, pumps and so on – was supplied by firms from France (Guinard), Spain (MIBSA), the former Soviet Union, the former Czechoslovakia (KBS) and within Romania (Griro Bucureşti, Aversa Bucureşti, and so on).

Table 6.8 shows the specific energy use recorded in 1988, and the corresponding values for a modern 5 mtpa line, achieved according to western standards, for two basic installations. Ploieşti has drafted studies and projects to improve energy efficiency in refineries, with the accent on modifying flowsheets and modernizing furnaces, systems and distillation columns. Through measures such as these, OECD countries have obtained significant reductions in specific energy use. Foreign specialists also suggest that while refinery utilization overall is so low, preference should be given to operating the best units at maximum capacity and maximum efficiency, rather than operating all units well below capacity at low efficiency.

For polymers of large tonnage, the specific energy use in Romania exceeds the peak achievements by 18% for low-density polyethylene; 20% for high-density polyethylene; 8.2% for polyvinyl chloride; and 58.5% for polystyrene. Modernizing the current installations for polyethylene and polyvinyl chloride would reduce current energy use by 8-20%; the installations for polystyrene, however, have to be replaced.

### 6.7.6 Cement

Romania is a major cement producer, and an exporter of technology in the field. In 1987 more than 11.8 million tonnes were manufactured, 82.6% by the 'dry' process. The production facilities are installed in the *combinats* at Alesd, Cimpulung, Deva, Fieni, Medgidia, Tirgu Jiu, and Turda. They include sixteen lines of 300 tonnes of clinker per day and six lines of 800 tonnes

**Table 6.8: Specific energy use in refineries, 1988**

|  | Petroţel line of 3.5 mtpa | Western line of 5 mtpa |
|---|---|---|
| Atmospheric and vacuum distillation |  |  |
| Fuel (MJ/t) | 940 | 756 |
| Steam (MJ/t) | 200 | 355 |
| Electricity (kWL/t) | 4 | 8.4 |
| Recovered energy resources (MJ/t) | 141 | 164 |
| Catalytic cracking |  |  |
| Fuel (MJ/t) | 2,800 | 1,172 |
| Steam (MJ/t) | 492 | 15,588 |
| Electricity (kWh/t) | 50.65 | 43.2 |
| Recovered energy resources | 1528 MJ/t | 34 kWh/t |

of clinker per day by the 'wet' process, and twenty-three lines of 800 tonnes of clinker per day and ten lines of 3,000 tonnes of clinker per day by the 'dry' process, one of them with precalcining. The principal fuel used is natural gas; Medgidia uses fuel oil and petroleum coke. The raw materials are, respectively, limestone, clay and marl or diorate sand, found in abundance and good quality in the local area. ICPILA, the Institute for Research and Design for Binders and Asbestos Cement of Bucureşti, designed the technology. The majority of the equipment was manufactured in Romania, at Progresul in Braila, Independenţa in Sibiu, and Faur and IMGB in Bucureşti. For the 3,000 t/day lines, some components were supplied by Wedag of Germany.

The specific fuel use achieved is between 6.0 and 6.6 GJ/t of clinker for the wet process, and between 3.55 and 3.9 GJ/t of clinker for the dry process. In 1983 the average use in western Europe was 3.93 GJ/t, in the USA 5.76 GJ/t and in the former Czechoslovakia 4.51 GJ/t of clinker; the most efficient furnace to date uses only 3.2 GJ/t.

The principal technological measures to be taken are to replace natural gas with coal; to automate complexes and equip them with information technology; to abandon the wet process; and, eventually, to install precalcining at large-capacity furnaces.

### 6.7.7 Glass products

Glass products are among the main users of energy in Romania, along with chemical lubricants, petrochemical products, aluminium, steel, cement and caustic soda. Specific energy use in 1988 is given in Table 6.9, by principal category of product.

The specific energy use is comparable to good performance at the world level. For example, for household glassware, 1 million products – that is, average items – use about 33,000 GJ and 258 kWh. In the year 1988 the entire production from glassworks, except for windowglass, used 6,100 GJ per 1 million pieces and 69 kWh per 1 million pieces – better than in the former Czechoslovakia (6,410 and 98.6 respectively), the country in which the technology is traditional. ICPTSCF, the Institute for Research and Design for Glass and Fine Ceramics in Bucureşti, developed the technologies; the plant was made in Romania, principally by Nicovala SA in Sighişoara.

Energy use can be reduced further. The programme drawn up by the specialized institute for the 100 operational furnaces was in the course of implementation in 1989. It provided for total reductions of 1,960,000 GJ, principally by improving the system of insulation and the geometry of glass-melting furnaces, controlling combustion and extending automation.

### 6.7.8 Earthenware plates

The technology, dating from 1967 under licence, is used at IMC CESAROM in Bucureşti, SANEX SA in Cluj and MONDIAL SA in Lugoj. It gives double firing in tunnel-type furnaces. The current equipment at these factories is produced in Romania by suppliers including UNIO in Satu Mare, NICOLINA in Iaşi, INDEPENDENŢA in Sibiu, VENTILATOARE and AVERSA in Bucureşti, IM in Buzau, IUPS in Bucureşti and Iaşi, IM in Stei, and so on. The quality of the plates is comparable to that of similar products offered on the international market, and 60-70% of production is exported.

The raw materials – kaolin, clay, sand, dolomite, marble and talc – are found in Romania. The energy efficiency – 8.1 GJ of thermal energy, 125 GJ of natural gas and 3,120 kWh for 1,000 coloured glazed earthenware plates – is however about twice as bad as that achieved in Italy, France and Germany. According to the specialized institute, ICPMC in Bucureşti, the principal technological modernization needed includes introducing roll furnaces

**Table 6.9: Specific energy use for glass products**

|  | Fuel<br>Natural gas<br>(TJ) | Electricity<br>(GWh) |
|---|---|---|
| Total | 21.39 | 272 |
| Of which: |  |  |
| Household glassware | 4.64 | 35 |
| Bottles and jars | 4.98 | 79.7 |
| Drawn plate glass | 5.93 | 34 |
| Household ceramics | 0.40 | 1.1 |

for rapid firing; effecting single firing, in one layer; and using light refractory materials, including ceramic fibres. Applying these measures can make these products fully competitive on the international market, as fuel and electricity prices are liberalized.

Similar comments can be made about porcelain sanitary ware and other fine ceramic products for construction.

### 6.7.9 Natural cotton fibres

In the old regime, spinning mills and textile factories were organized according to a territorial criterion, in 'industrial holdings', for cotton flax-hemp in Bucureşti, Iaşi and Arad, and for linen in Bucureşti. The technologies used, classical or unconventional, produce natural carded type cotton or vicuna yarn, crude or dyed. The equipment of some forty-five large spinning mills – spinning, laminating and reeling machines, and so on – was made especially in the 1970s by local and to some extent foreign suppliers, recognized in the international market. The specific electricity use is on average about 3,400 kWh/t produced, a value that also includes depowdering and ambient conditioning operations, about 500 kWh/t. For comparison, a completely automated technology offered by the Swiss firm of Rieten uses only 2,440 kWh/t.

Rehabilitation is imperatively necessary. To begin with it will have to ensure increased productivity by complete automation and robotization; increased speed of machines, from 11,000 rotations per minute to more than 15,000 rotations per minute; and use of unconventional technologies. Modern energy management systems must be introduced. The technology design institutes, IPIU and ICT in Bucureşti, have drawn up extensive audits that show how these retooling measures will affect energy efficiency.

### 6.7.10 Cotton textiles and flax-hemp

The technologies – classical, with textile machines with cams and rotors, and unconventional, with textile machines with cams – were made at the beginning of the 1960s. The classical technology is used in twenty-six large enterprises (371 million sq m in 1988), while unconventional technology is used in 18 (173 million sq m). The equipment – weaving, warping and reeling machines and so on, is from the manufacturers Schloforst in Germany, Schweiter in Switzerland, Metalul Rosu in Cluj, Technometal in Bucureşti and others. The specific energy use averages 1,800 kWh/t and 16GJ/t for the classical technology, and 3,000 kWh/t and 12.3GJ/t for the unconventional.

Increasing the speed of work is the principal aim of retooling. Using modern machines, the speeds can be multiplied on average threefold, for example from 400 to 1200 m/min on the bobbin machines, and from 300 to 1,000 m/min on the warp machines. Weaving machines with projectiles have speeds of up to 750 rotations/min, compared with the 180 rotations/minute of the machines used in Romania, and moreover permit the elimination of one phase of quilling technology, bringing savings of 500 kWh/t. Altogether, the peak achievements in the field have technological uses of energy less than 50% of those recorded on average in Romania. As well as increasing work-speeds many times, the modern facilities incorporate real-time process control and dyeing operations with energy use reduced to a third.

### 6.7.11 Leather goods and footwear

Romania has about twenty large tanneries, fur plants, footwear and leather goods factories, integrated complexes that prework oxhide, sheepskin, goatskin and pigskin. They use modern technologies, manufactured in the 1980s by IPIU, the Research Institute for Leather Goods and Footwear in Bucureşti, the Leather Goods Enterprise and the Timişoara Fur Plant. The equipment – defleshing, pressing, smoothing and equalizing machines, and so on – is from suppliers in Italy (Gozzini, Aletti), France (Mercier), Germany (TTH), the UK (Turner) and the Czech Republic (Svit); the principal local manufacturer is FIMARO SA (Metalul Rosu) in Cluj. The specific energy use per tonne of product, averaging 63 kWh and 1,400 MJ, corresponds to western standards.

### 6.7.12 Sugar from sugar beets

Technology for making sugar from sugar beets, although used seasonally, that is to say about 100 days a year, represents the principal energy user in the entire Romanian food industry. Most of the production capacity was made in the 1980s, from indigenous designs by ISPCAIA and with plant manufactured in the country by Technofrig in Cluj, UNIO in Satu Mare, IUT in Buzau, INDES SA in Sibiu, IUC in Ploieşti, Nicolina in Iaşi, Metalotehnica in Tirgu Mureş, Timpuri Noi in Bucureşti and so on. Lines of 4,000t of beets per day in Giurgiu, Babadag, Timişoara, Calafat, Zimnicea, Ianca, Urziceni, Tandarei, Arad, Roman and Pascani have a total annual capacity of 572,000t of sugar, and lines of 1,000t of beets per day have a nominal capacity of 130,000t of sugar.

The lignite-fired fluidized-bed combustion boilers installed have proved inadequate, because specific energy use has exceeded design values by 10-15%, for example 1,850 MJ/t of beets preprocessed, compared to 1,625 MJ/t specified in the design. To attain western standards for energy use, the boilers must be rehabilitated, and descending-film evaporators, continuous centrifuges and automatic boiling control must be introduced. The analyses drafted by ISPCAIA show that the costs necessary would be rapidly recovered.

## 6.8 Efficiency activities in progress

In principle, Romania's energy supply companies, and RENEL in particular, could play a major role in increasing the efficiency of energy use, by initiating and carrying out DSM programmes. RENEL made a start in 1993, by investing 2 billion lei in its customers' facilities. Half of this is to modernize enterprises, beginning by introducing variable-speed electric motor drives and modern energy management systems at the Petroţel and Petrobrazi refineries and the Bucureşti municipal water supply enterprise. RENEL is responsible for these investments; it administers the funds, does most of the work and has to deliver 'turnkey' installations. The other 1 billion lei is to modernize a portion of the Bucureşti municipal district heating grid. The Institute for

Energy Studies and Projects (ISPE), attached to RENEL, is responsible for this investment. However, in the absence of an appropriate regulatory arrangement, this version of DSM does not allow RENEL to recover a return on its investment, except arbitrarily; nor has the investment necessarily been shown to meet the 'least-cost' criteria that would be stipulated for DSM investments as practised in OECD countries. RENEL's intentions are clearly laudable, and the experience undoubtedly valuable; but introducing DSM as a significant contribution to rebuilding Romania's economy will require coherent preparations to establish appropriate legal, financial and regulatory structures. If DSM is to have maximum beneficial effect it should be developed in the context of a Romanian national strategy to promote energy efficiency that establishes clear objectives and priorities.[49]

In this connection, Romania could draw on the example of Poland. At the request of the Polish government, and with the support of USAID, the US consultancy RCG/Hagler, Bailly in cooperation with Polish colleagues drafted a lengthy report on the potential for DSM in Poland. Based on detailed information about the structure of Polish industry, the report identified a wide range of technical options that DSM might promote.[50] The Romanian government has already discussed the possibility of assistance from USAID to carry out a similar study in Romania. Such information would be a valuable guide for future development of DSM in Romania.

ARCE was set up to promote activities to increase energy efficiency (see Chapter 3). In 1991 ARCE, with enterprises, analyzed 562 possible projects for modernization, recovery of secondary energy resources, substitution for hydrocarbons, and utilization of new sources of energy, with the potential to save 1.5 mtce of fuel and 1,100 GWh of electricity. Of these fifty-eight were selected for technical and economic studies, and twenty-six projects were finally chosen. The total capital investment to carry out these 26 projects was

---

[49] A useful reference is Tim Woolf and Craig Mickle, *Integrated Resource Planning: Making Electricity Efficiency Work in Europe*, Association for the Conservation of Energy for Greenpeace International, London, 1992. See also Walt Patterson, 'Demand-Side Management: from West to East?', paper presented to Inaugural Seminar for UNESCO Chair in Energy and Environment, Polytechnic University of Bucuresti, October 1993; published in English and Romanian in *Revista Energetica*, Anul 42 seria B, May-June 1994.

[50] *Demand-Side Management in Poland: Assessment and Pilot Programme*, RCG/Hagler, Bailly for USAID, June 1993.

**Table 6.10: Efficiency projects with ARCE support**

| Sector | No. | Total investment (000 lei) | ARCE support (000 lei) | Estimated savings (tce/y) |
|---|---|---|---|---|
| Industry | 23 | 139,425.7 | 29,550.6 | 20,636 |
| Of which: | | | | |
| Metallurgy | 4 | 20,250.7 | 5,169.7 | 8,865 |
| Chemicals | 2 | 4,370 | 5,169.7 | 8,865 |
| Machine building | 9 | 61,453 | 13,607.2 | 4,343 |
| Electrotechnology | 2 | 11,064 | 2,150 | 1,927 |
| Paper | 1 | 13,630 | 1,300 | 1,472 |
| Glassworks | 1 | 5,000 | 1,000 | 83 |
| Building materials | 1 | 6,000 | 1,200 | 264 |
| Food industry | 2 | 7,258 | 1,646.7 | 219 |
| Electricity | 1 | 10,400 | 2,600 | 3,011 |
| Agriculture | 2 | 4,292 | 1,517 | 65 |
| Local authorities | 1 | 41,704 | 13,581 | 2,326 |
| Total | 26 | 185,421.7 | 446,48.6 | 23,027 |

195.4 million lei (in 1991 prices), of which the enterprises contributed 140.8 million lei (76%); the rest came from the government budget, through ARCE. The documentation shows that these investments save 23,027 tce of energy annually, paying back the capital invested in 2.1 years. The projects, classified according to activity sector, are shown in Table 6.10.

Work also began in 1991 on twenty-eight of the projects completed in 1992; 938.3 million lei was spent in 1991 and the remaining 699.6 million lei in 1992. ARCE provided 33.3 million lei in 1991 and 130 million lei in 1992 in subsidies from the government budget for these projects. According to the feasibility studies, the calculated savings were 81,502 tce/year. Some Romanian specialists nevertheless suggest that ARCE would make a more persuasive argument in favour of efficiency investments by supporting some highly visible demonstration projects, whose costs, payback time and practical results could be displayed to visitors, politicians and the media. They would like ARCE to be more explicit about its criteria for choosing particular projects to support, to explain the analysis it uses to assign priorities for funding, its requirements for investment and return on capital, and its expectations for the future prospects of particular industrial facilities. In so doing, ARCE would reinforce its role in disseminating information and training about efficiency, and strengthen its case for expanding its role into sectors other than industry. It would also offer valuable guidance to other individuals and organizations in Romania seeking to apply limited funds in the most effective ways. Investing in efficiency also implies investing efficiently.

# Chapter 7

## International Cooperation

### 7.1 Rebuilding relations

*7.1.1 Initial context*

Between 1965 and 1980, Romania was more open than other countries with centralized economies. From the early 1980s until December 1989, however, Romania followed a policy of restraint in international relations, with many restrictions arising from artificial criteria and/or shortage of hard currency, a direct consequence of ill-conceived forms of external commerce. This opacity in international relations also affected energy, even though dependence on imports of primary resources and the low efficiency of energy use would have indicated the contrary. Somehow, exceptionally, during this period, Romania's foreign contacts within the CMEA (Comecon) were more systematic. Of the many activities in this framework, those relevant for energy included exchanges and commerce in goods, including energy resources and equipment; standard-setting, covering also the energy performance of industrial equipment; economic and energy forecasting; and technical and scientific cooperation in different fields, including new energy sources, district heating and cogeneration, the use of low-grade fuels, and reducing energy use in industrial processes.

In the final decade of Comecon's existence, Romania's position differed somewhat from those of the other members, because at the level of national representatives it refused to take part in integration that would have emphasized the differences between partners to gain the benefits of cooperation. Romania also embraced the alternative of cooperating outside the framework of Comecon, with developing countries and indeed with OECD countries; this stance was reflected at all levels and throughout all sectors of organization. Before December 1989, Romania had a number of relationships with countries with market economies, some of which centred on energy. It imported petroleum, particularly from Iran and Arab countries. It imported high-power energy equipment such as steam boilers for lignite, 330 MW turbo-alternator sets and hydroelectric sets, and also acquired licences to manufacture them. It imported technology and acquired manufacturing licences to design and construct the Cernavoda nuclear power station, with CANDU reactors and 770 MWe sets. It took part in the initial projects of the UN Economic Commission for Europe – the international seminar for use of secondary energy resources, the Balkan interconnection, and so on. It took part in the ENCONET programme and network, in the framework of the UN Industrial Development Organization. It also took part in the activities of international organizations and associations such as the World Energy Council, CIGRE, the International Conference on Industrial Energy, VGB and so on. It pursued exploratory contacts with potential collaborative partners – most of which, however, remained at the proposal stage. Sometimes it arranged training for Romanian specialists, on the basis of finances from specialized foundations, such as Humboldt, Duisburg and ACTIM, or by convening activities with foreign firms such as EdF and AECL.

## 7.1.2 The early transition

In the initial stage (1990-92) of the period of transition to a market economy, two kinds of economic transformation took place in Romania. Some transformations linked to ownership of the capital stock were slow and timid, with difficulties arising particularly from the shortage of capital resources, internal or external, available in the economic structure strictly speaking; the proportion of private social capital is only 2%. Some transformations, however, were more radical, namely those in the framework of organization, that is, the system of relationships, awards of qualifications and the freedom of activities, including renouncing centralized 'guardianship'. They were achieved by abolishing and demolishing centralized organizations, and attempting to introduce relationships specific to a market economy.

These transformations have also affected international relations, including those concerning energy. Artificial restrictions and limits – often political – have disappeared. Competence for initiatives and decisions about external partners and how to cooperate with them has been decentralized. The Comecon system has been abolished, and cooperation with former socialist countries has consequently drastically diminished. For example, Romanian imports of petroleum from the former Soviet Union fell about 40% in 1990. The centre of attention has shifted towards relations with OECD countries; this shift has been reinforced by the activities and programmes of such countries to support the transition in the countries of eastern Europe. However, the diminution of production and of the buying power of the populace, as well as the slow progress of privatization, still makes the Romanian market less economically attractive to foreign investment. The stubborn financial crisis limits the possibility for Romanian partners to engage in external collaborative activities.

Logically enough, the difficult economic situation and the relatively cautious rhythm of introduction of private ownership, as well as the legislative framework, which in some respects is still anachronistic, bring about a certain political and social instability. In turn this instability causes reluctance to integrate or co-opt Romania into the circuits and systems of international relations. Romanian specialists nevertheless consider that on the whole, and taking account of developments to date, the trends since December 1989, although slow and with many moments of impasse, are positive.

## 7.2 International relations today
Even if they have not expanded as much as was once expected, international relations in the energy field are already very diverse.

### 7.2.1 Trade relations
The anticipated decline in Romania's internal primary energy resources, now confirmed, means that high priority must be given to efforts to secure imports of energy resources. If RENEL seeks to use its available capacity to produce electricity for export, the resulting international relationships will become more complex and various.

Trade in energy equipment and apparatus now includes imports from Canada and Italy of equipment for the Cernavoda nuclear power station; imports of mechanical, electrical and electronic components for rehabilitating power stations; and exports of equipment manufactured in Romania, for example to the People's Republic of China. Import activities suffer badly from shortage of finance. International banks, such as the World Bank, the International Bank for Reconstruction and Development, the European Bank for Reconstruction and Development, and intergovernmental agreements offer external financial support through lines of credit, currently at different stages of finalization; but most of these are too small to compensate for the internal financial deficit.

### 7.2.2 Technical assistance programmes

Romania is currently participating in many projects and programmes of assistance initiated and supported financially by different international institutions and organizations, including the UNECE, the UNDP, UNIDO, the OECD, the EU and so on, as well as by national institutions and agencies – USAID, ADEME and the Institut Français de l'Energie of France, and so on. The World Bank and the EBRD are also very much involved, although as lending institutions they offer financial support on the basis that Romania will in due course repay it with interest – a point sometimes overlooked. The World Bank has provided US$266,000 for 'Project Energy Advisor', for feasibility studies on modernizing and rehabilitating the energy sector. The EU has provided US$640,000 for technical assistance to competent Romanian organizations, including ARCE, the Ministry of Industries and RENEL, to help develop strategies to increase the efficiency of energy use. 'Energy Efficiency 2000' is a vast project initiated by the UNECE, that helps specialists to take part in technical and scientific symposia and benefit from transfer of information, and encourages the identification of possibilities to develop commerce and cooperation on efficient techniques and management of energy. In the framework of this project an 'energy efficiency zone' is being established in the locality of Deva, in Transilvania.

More recently, the World Bank has announced agreement on a loan of US$175.6 million to Romania, to improve the petroleum and gas sectors. The loan is to offset the fall in production that would have continued until 1995, by developing local capacities. Negotiations are under way with the World Bank about financing refitting work at ten or more power stations, according to RENEL's medium-term R&D programme. The project is based on a feasibility study prepared by Merz & McLellan of the UK, who won the contract after competitive bidding. The district heating system in Bucureşti is being modernized and its capacity extended. The firm of Bechtel assisted ICEMENERG in drawing up a feasibility study for the system.

In 1994/5 the PHARE programme of the EU is to make Ecu 5 million available for PHARE national programmes in the energy field, covering studies for electricity, gas, oil and energy conservation; Romania is the coordinator of the regional PHARE Programmes for Energy, with a budget of Ecu 13 million, covering all the eleven PHARE beneficiary countries. The Synergy Programme of Directorate General XVII of the European Commission has seconded an energy advisor to Romania's MoI, to support the process of drafting new energy laws.

### 7.2.3 Technical and scientific cooperation

Romania's participation in international scientific and technical cooperation is steadily increasing. Topics include energy and environmental conservation; interconnecting Romania's national electricity system with the UCPTE; new sources of energy; rehabilitating and refitting power stations and electricity networks; advanced systems to produce, transmit and distribute electricity and heat; training and instruction of personnel; development of informatic and information systems for process, administration and operation; and the Cernavoda nuclear power station.

ICEMENERG has been given approval by the European Commission to take part in five energy R&D projects under the JOULE II programme; by mid-1994 contracts had been concluded for three of them.

Electricité de France, with its Division of Studies and Research, has been carrying out a study of load regulation on Romania's national electricity system, in connection with interconnecting the system to the UCPTE. In 1992 the Society of Engineering Technology (SOCETEC) of France signed a protocol of cooperation for a study on feasibility and transfer of technology, and to organize a seminar on saving electricity. In 1993 ICEMENERG transmitted the necessary documents on the subjects in the protocol. Activities now under way cover technical equipment for research and experimentation; a complex informatic system to operate power stations; variable-speed motor drives; and desulphurization of flue gases from power stations. In 1994, in accordance with the cooperation protocol, ICEMENERG received confirmation that French sources would finance a study for installing pilot variable-speed equipment on a 3,150 kW motor at the Ploieşti refinery.

In 1992 TRACTEBEL of Belgium exchanged proposals with Romania for cooperation, and activities are continuing. Collaboration with the G+E Company of Belgium in the field of load management for industrial users has been developing since 1992. In collaboration with Energies Nouvelles et Environnement SA of Belgium, a demonstration project for photovoltaic electrification is to be carried out in a Romanian village during 1994-5.

In 1992 ENTUV of Essen agreed a protocol of cooperation for exchange of experience, technical expertise, training personnel and consultancy in problems of refitting, supervision and determining the remaining life of components of steam boilers. However, this cooperative activity depends on financing for the project from the German government. A cooperation agreement was signed in 1993 between ICEMENERG and TUV Bayern Sachsen in Germany, according to which ICEMENERG carries out consulting activities for design and implementation of the quality system at the request of the Germany company.

In 1992 KEMA of the Netherlands discussed and exchanged thirteen specific proposals for cooperation, and signed an agreement to submit three study proposals to SEP, the Dutch electricity company. The three proposals covered applying the concept of DSM; development of RENEL's thermal power stations to 2005, bringing them up to emission standards; and cogeneration policy. In June 1994 KEMA and ICEMENERG agreed to cooperate on energy, the environment and other fields of mutual interest; the agreement was to be signed by both participants in September 1994.

In 1992 ETSU of the UK held discussions with Romanian colleagues about initiating cooperation on energy efficiency, on condition that funds could be obtained from the EU PHARE programme. An application for funds was submitted in 1993. In 1992 the Electricity Association of the UK sent proposals to ICEMENERG to initiate cooperation on salary structures; centralization/decentralization/privatization; and technological research and engineering. In 1993 the groups agreed to draw up a feasibility study about defining the direction of research and development in the energy sector in Romania. Doing the study depends on finding sources of finance.

In 1993 ICEMENERG and L'Ecole Polytechnique Fédérale in Lausanne, Switzerland, signed a cooperation agreement for a joint project on 'digital simulation of a district heating network in Romania', with the approval and support of the Swiss National Fund.

Beginning in 1992, Boston Edison of the US has been holding discussions with RENEL about modes of technical and documentary assistance, with the backing of the Utilities Partnership Program of the US Energy Association, the US national committee of the World Energy Council.

Although the range of international cooperative activities in the energy sector is thus already extensive, the emphasis to date has been on fuel and electricity supply. As described in earlier chapters, opportunities for improving end-use efficiency are also substantial, and international cooperation here, too, would be invaluable.

## 7.3 Expanding the circle

Restructuring and reform of the energy sector in Romania involves a high degree of international cooperation. Romanian specialists hope that such cooperation will bring a number of benefits. They are looking for comprehensive information about the current level of technological progress, and the short-and long-term prospects of advanced techniques; and about the content of international R&D and demonstration projects and opportunities for Romanian scientific and engineering organizations to take part in these projects. They hope for effective transfer of advanced technologies and of the related know-how, and for international financial aid on favourable terms. They seek opportunities to offer Romanian engineering and scientific services on the international market, in fields in which Romanian achievements are advanced. They want to improve the financial balance sheets of the energy utilities, now in bad shape because of the depressed energy market, by supplementing sales of energy. They hope that foreign investments to rehabilitate and extend capacity in the energy sector will increase.

As noted above, some international cooperation has already started or is almost finalized. To expand international cooperation in line with requirements and opportunities, a great deal needs to be done in Romania, at different levels and in different sectors of activity.

### 7.3.1 Improving the information base

As discussed in Chapter 5, information about energy efficiency – opportunities, methods, costs, payback time and other benefits – needs to be developed and disseminated to the Romanian public, including politicians, civil servants and the media. This important measure will be explored further in Chapter 8. As a starting-point, Romania can call on its nucleus of skilled energy scientists and engineers; but they, too, will need to expand their access to relevant information, for example about energy-efficient design, through better access to foreign experience and know-how. Romanian specialists suggest, for example, that Romanian research and engineering organizations, enterprises and universities need to be connected to international technical information networks. Romania could contribute the necessary hardware, but would need software and free access to the energy sections of European data banks. The area over which information about European energy projects is disseminated should be extended. Information should be provided not only about project content and objectives, but also about procedures and/or conditions for admittance as a project participant, or access to results obtained. Romanian specialists say that the Romanian authorities, which at the moment are the correspondents of international organizations, should see to this; but so should international organizations, by expanding their connections in Romania to include private or state-owned energy organizations. They would also like to have a list published of new manufacturing and engineering companies, created by joint ventures or other forms of cooperation in central and east European countries with the participation of organizations and companies from advanced countries. Because some conditions are already favourable for cooperation in this area, such a list could encourage transfer of advanced technologies.

### 7.3.2 Improving supply links

Romanian specialists say that to strengthen Romania's links with western Europe, and to optimize international opportunities in electricity supply, the Romanian power system should be interconnected to the UCPTE system, by using in the first stage the existing 400 kV Rosori-Mukacevo-Lemesani link, and in the second stage a new 400 kV interconnector that Romania and Hungary agreed to include in regional studies being undertaken within the PHARE programme. Analyses of the economic opportunity to use surplus Romanian capacity for electricity generation and export should continue. How economically competitive would Romanian electricity exports be, considering the price of imported fuel, conversion efficiency and internal costs? How large is the potential market? What needs to be done technically to create the necessary conditions, for instance for the reliability of generation and the transmission facilities?

Romanian specialists likewise say that the possibility of connecting the Romanian gas supply system to existing and/or projected gas supply networks in the region should be explored, including integrating Romanian gas storage capacity. They would like to see agreements with foreign oil companies extended, to upgrade and use the significant available capacity of Romanian refineries and petrochemical enterprises.

## 7.4 Regional cooperation

After the break-up of Comecon, countries in central and eastern Europe, freed from the yoke of an international association imposed externally, all looked to the west for international contacts, in energy as in other activities. Contacts among former Comecon countries themselves subsided to a very low level. In 1993, the World Energy Council (WEC), the largest international non-governmental organization of energy specialists in the world, set up an East-West Cooperation Programme under the directorship of Klaus Brendow. Brendow had recently retired from the UNECE, where he had been running the UNECE programme called 'Energy Efficiency 2000'. At Brendow's instigation, WEC member committees from many central and eastern European countries agreed to take part in a two-day Regional Forum in June 1994. The Romanian national member committee of WEC served as hosts for the forum, which took place at the resort of Neptun south of Constanţa on the Black Sea coast. The discussions were cordial but somewhat tentative, as might have been expected; participants from different former Comecon countries were reluctant to subordinate their new-found national independence to international joint activities, even at the level of research and development.

Nevertheless, the fact that the WEC Regional Forum took place at all, with voluntary participation from so many countries in the region, suggested that as the lingering traces of the Comecon coercion dissipate, the former Comecon countries may come to realize that they still have a lot in common, including energy problems and energy opportunities, and that free dialogue and cooperation among the countries of the region may be mutually beneficial.

# Chapter 8

## Energy, Efficiency and Policy

### 8.1 Completing reform

In Romania these days commentators frequently remark that in a real market economy government intervention in the economy must be minimal. After a period of excessive centralization, a risk exists that any attempt at government intervention may be interpreted as a tendency to return to old habits. On the other hand, in Romania the mechanisms of a real market economy are not yet fully functioning. Moreover, even in a country with a traditional market economy the government has to intervene in certain problems of major importance; and the problem of energy in general and of efficient energy use in particular has an importance that no longer needs to be demonstrated. Accordingly, Romanian specialists consider certain government measures necessary. Among them are measures of general economic policy not directly related to energy but having a direct influence on it. These measures can be summed up as 'completing economic reform', including macroeconomic stabilization, price reform, and restructuring and privatizing industry.

Price reform is already in progress. Subsidies on tariffs for household users have been ended; but the IEA report notes that cross-subsidies are still occurring, especially between industries and households and between electricity and heat, so that ascertaining who is paying how much for fuels is less transparent than it should be.[51] As noted earlier, the Romanian government announced in mid-1994 that some 3,000 state-owned SAs would be privatized in the following twelve months. Privatizing industries would undoubtedly foster more efficient use of energy. A proverb widely quoted under the old

---

[51] *Energy Polices of Romania*, International Energy Agency, 1993.

regime says that 'collective property is nobody's property'. In many instances, replacing collective 'property' with genuinely private property would be clearly beneficial. Accelerating the privatization of enterprises that manufacture household appliances and measuring and control equipment, service firms and other energy-related firms would be particularly relevant. Restructuring the RAs for fuel and electricity supplies, and possibly even privatizing some or all of them, would take longer; but studies have targeted major restructuring by the year 2000. Liberalizing the exchange rate of the leu would ensure that economically efficient firms have access to hard currency, and by implication access to energy resources of the quantity and quality desired, as well as to imported plant and equipment. Such a measure should also encourage foreign investors, which are still concerned that they may not be able to repatriate their profits. Completing the legal framework for economic activities will likewise assist in achieving real economic efficiency.

## 8.2 Laws and regulations

The government and parliament also need to lay down the appropriate legal and regulatory groundrules for the energy sector itself. As described earlier, the MoI is drafting an 'energy law' and an 'energy conservation law'. Depending on their final wording, and on how they are implemented, these laws could help to define a national strategy for energy efficiency. Setting standards for thermal insulation of buildings, setting performance standards for appliances and reorganizing the system of energy statistics in Romania, all discussed earlier, will require drafting, issuing and implementing official regulations. The most important and perhaps most difficult stage will be effective implementation.

Another potentially important law is that on environmental protection. In all developed countries, legislation on protection of the environment has led also to increased efficiency of energy use, because the two problems are correlated. In Romania the Ministry of Environment, Water and Forest has issued decrees setting certain standards; but such decrees cannot take the place of corresponding legislation, consonant as far as possible with the legislation of other countries and with international standards. On the other hand, approving a law on environmental protection would have to be followed by verifying its application, which implies the existence of some measurement centres, perhaps mobile teams, suitably equipped and adequately staffed – much more than exist at present. The section on sanctions would have to be a distinct chapter of the law. The penalties paid by enterprises that offend could be used to finance pollution-control activities and to increase energy efficiency. Furthermore, such a law would increase the interest of energy companies, including RENEL, in DSM.

A proposal for an 'environment law' has been presented to parliament, and returned by the specialist committee to the Ministry of Environment, Water and Forest for revision. It is expected to be completed by incorporating PHARE programme study proposals for 'integrated monitoring' in Romania. This will entail activities and material measures involving not only the Ministry of Environment but also those of Industries, Health, Agriculture and Public Works, as well as the specialized research institutes, called 'focal points', and the laboratories within larger enterprises, called 'base laboratories'. The new 'environment law' lays down clear responsibilities and creates the necessary institutional background. It also sets limit values for emissions that are in general more stringent than those of the EU and Romania's neighbouring countries. The law provides for the creation of several 'special protection zones' where ecological demands are more exacting, and for which two categories of measures are foreseen: 'reduction of pollution' and 'application of measures for ecological recovery', the latter described in detail. Whether applying the recommended measures for 'ecological recovery' will help to meet the higher demands of the 'special protection zones', or ecological reserves, is not yet clear; the category of measures to reduce pollution should come first, but no details for this category are given, and those in charge will have to establish measures and apply them. In the meantime the present legal position is based on Law 9/1973, which is still in force. This law sets limits on the basis of health effects, but does not stipulate how such limits are to be met.

In the interim, the provisions of this 'former' law of 1973 have been augmented by order 462/1993, 'Technical Conditions Concerning the Protection of the Atmosphere', promulgated in July 1993 by the Ministry of Environment, which introduced – for the first time in Romania – standards to limit polluting emissions from combustion installations, including RENEL energy boilers. More recently, order 619/1994 from the Ministry of Environment refers to the obligation to carry out an 'impact analysis' for every existing industrial, commercial, public interest or similar objective, and an 'impact study' for any new objective. In early May 1994, through Law 24/1994, Romania ratified the Framework Convention on Climate Change signed at the UN Conference on Environment and Development in Rio in June 1992; accordingly, Romania has undertaken to fulfil its commitments under the Convention.[52]

The environmental standards of the EU are growing steadily more stringent and more widely applied; Romanian specialists insist that Romanian standards must be brought into line with them. The Merz & McLellan PHARE study of refitting eleven Romanian power stations makes clear that the admissible concentrations of pollutants in Romania are too high, compared to those of the EU. Romanian specialists suggest that an environmental fund should be set up, resourced from charges on polluting emissions. The absence of environmental legislation is compounded by the need to inform and stimulate public attitudes, to change mindsets and persuade people to deliver products and services only with clean technologies. Polluters should pay, through charges that could establish a fund to be spent appropriately and rationally on environmental improvement.

Foreign specialists, however, warn that Romania should not set standards so high that it cannot enforce them, or that inflict unnecessarily severe economic penalties. Apart from pollution 'black spots' near major industries and in some city areas, much of Romania has suffered surprisingly little serious environmental damage. Indeed, recent experience suggests that potentially the most difficult environmental problem to manage may soon arise not from industry but from the burgeoning population of private cars.

---

[52] *Greenhouse Gas Emissions: Initial Inventory and Implications*, a study for the government of Romania by Touche Ross, May 1992, found that 'Romania is unlikely to have to take constraining actions to comply with targets for the year 2000,' but went on to say that 'Continued economic growth after 2000 is likely to result in increasing emissions. Actions will be needed in Romania to constrain carbon dioxide emissions in the long term if targets are to be achieved. Such actions might promote improved efficiency of energy use and conversion, encourage the use of less carbon intensive fuels, such as hydro and nuclear power, and ensure sufficient forestation to help to absorb carbon dioxide'.

## 8.3 Information, education and advice

Beyond the purely technical problems, the key problem of efficient energy use is that of creating awareness, of informing and educating. This applies both to general public opinion and to workers. From this viewpoint the situation in Romania is comparatively sensitive. As noted earlier, in the 1980s the public was subjected to intense propaganda to cut household energy use, to preserve supplies to industry. Such propaganda was reinforced by administrative measures – making energy more expensive, disconnecting towns and villages from the grid, reducing the temperature of hot water in district heating grids. The propaganda was exhorting people to do without even the minimum level of comfort they still had, to keep industry functioning. Yet the salaries of workers were also conditional on fulfilling norms for energy use. In the 1990s, if energy propaganda is introduced thoughtlessly, it risks provoking an adverse public reaction, starting with comments like 'Right – energy is going to get more expensive,' 'They are going to start disconnecting the electricity again,' and provoking ironic counterattacks in the press. Factory workers are a slightly different case, because for decades they were taught that what was essential was to achieve and exceed the production plan. They at least are familiar with the problems of economic efficiency and energy efficiency. In the circumstances, nevertheless, producing effective propaganda to promote efficiency will be difficult, and its content must be different. The old motivation, 'For the good of the country and for the future of our children', must be replaced with explicit personal motivation. Advice on energy saving must be replaced with concrete advice about how to get the same or better services – comfort, illumination and so on – with less fuel and electricity.

Romanian specialists favour establishing local energy efficiency advice centres, free to the public, in principal Romanian cities and towns, perhaps one per county, and publishing and distributing free brochures, as is now common in OECD countries; ARCE's regional branches might be adapted to fill this role. Introducing specialized energy themes into the scholastic programmes of *lycées* and institutions of higher education would also help. In schools, at various stages, lessons on electricity or mechanics are given at a high theoretical level; however, concepts like energy efficiency are so far missing.

Strategy for public information and education, its conception, dissemination and financing, needs to be thought through carefully. Suitable publicity material to enhance public understanding must be prepared; it must be well founded technically and economically, and visually pleasing. Authors and sources of finance must be identified, and sociological surveys done to assess the impact of the material on the public. National publicity could be broadcast on radio and television, with programmes and competitions. Small-scale and large-scale demonstrations of energy efficiency for all categories of use – industrial, household and services – could be set up. Schools and the army could offer educational programmes worked out together, for instance, with RENEL and ARCE, about the components of social behaviour that foster efficient use of energy. Expanding the role of ARCE in publicizing energy efficiency will depend on its strategy and finances. ARCE could cooperate more closely with other bodies. It could also assess the level of popular understanding, for instance by polling.

Courses of schooling could be organized at the local level or centrally, as could district or national centres of professional preparation and consulting or advisory centres for household users and small industrial users. The strategy for courses of schooling would have to be clear beforehand, including the level, periodicity, place, lecturers, sources of finance and final scope. Training manuals or books could be prepared, giving specifications for energy efficiency – once again with careful attention to the treatment level, authors, evaluation level, and testing. Regional centres for professional preparation for energy specialists could be organized, for instance for the personnel of RENEL and other bodies. Preliminary work would entail considering feasibility studies, investments, endowment of primary material, the framework and the budget. Within the framework of electricity branch offices, consulting/counselling centres could be set up for household users and small industrial users, again requiring basic material, technical personnel specializing in electricity and thermal energy, publicity for these centres and sources of finance. The effectiveness of the centres should be evaluated continually, and adjusted accordingly.

Themes about efficient use of energy could be introduced into the scholastic programmes of middle- and upper-level educational institutions, with technical and economic specialization. RENEL specialists and other energy professionals active in education could take part in preparing appropriate material, by identifying topics necessary for training future specialists, including aspects of energy efficiency. Energy professionals could also help to prepare scholastic manuals and university courses, taking account of sources of finance, level, organizational framework and so on. Exchanging experience within and outside Romania – about themes, organizational framework, sources of finance, evaluation level and results, applications and so on – would help to develop concepts for instruction in schools and universities for future specialists, through modern advanced methods.

In this connection one especially encouraging development was the establishment of a professorial chair in energy and environment at the Polytechnic University of Bucureşti, with the support of UNESCO. The UNESCO Chair, Programme Energy-Environment, was inaugurated in October 1993; its first incumbent is Professor Aureliu Leca, president of RENEL from 1990 to 1993. Under his direction the UNESCO Chair is mounting a wide-ranging programme embracing not only academic instruction in the Polytechnic itself but also briefings and other activities reaching out into the Romanian business and political community, and indeed internationally.

As the role of ARCE evolves and its standing improves, professional associations concerned with energy efficiency could cooperate with ARCE, which could keep a register of their aims and statutes and share information about activities of common interest, including training in energy efficiency activities through announcements and sponsorship. Such activities might include taking part in Romanian and international symposia, on the basis of sources of finance and sponsorship that do not affect the independence of the organizations; training personnel of the organizations and associations; and disseminating the results of efficiency activities – perhaps with the assistance of ARCE, or indeed through an association specifically linking non-governmental organizations involved in efficiency activities. Periodic meetings about activities undertaken by non-governmental organizations could be arranged and the results obtained – significant or not, successful or not – described and discussed. These meetings could also include links with other national and international professional organizations in Romania.

Within ICEMENERG, a strong institutional framework could be created for research and development projects for technologies and methods to train personnel both within and outside RENEL in the spirit of energy efficiency – to promote quality systems, to motivate and stimulate active and creative participation by employees in the manufacturing process and in selecting professions, according to professional criteria and their own aptitudes.

## 8.4 The view from ARCE

'A Strategy for Energy Conservation in Romania', a study carried out by ADEME of France with ARCE, with the support of the EU PHARE programme, recommended a series of measures to reinforce ARCE. It said that ARCE's authority should be increased, by placing it under the Economic Council for Strategy and Reform, or directly under the prime minister. It should be internally reorganized and its finances should be doubled: from the government budget to cover the cost of its own operations; from the income obtained by performing consulting services, from donations, or from the international programme of technical assistance, to mount programmes of ARCE's own activities. The autonomy of ARCE's central office should be gradually increased, by presenting an annual programme approved by the administrative council that becomes the work plan for the current year, and by reporting on activities at the end of the budgetary year. At the same time the autonomy and decentralization of the activities of the territorial branches should also be gradually increased, by establishing an annual or semi-annual work programme for each.

ARCE specialists have suggested creating an 'energy efficiency fund', by instituting a tax of 1% on final energy use, to finance programmes of energy efficiency including demonstration operations, research studies, feasibility studies, training, promotional campaigns and so on. They propose setting up a system of bank credit, with preferential interest rates, for investments to increase the efficiency of energy use throughout the Romanian economy, and especially to reduce the use of imported fuel.

## 8.5 Something for everyone

An economic and social transition does not happen by itself. People make it happen. Romanians have been doing so for five years, and their achievements to date are substantial. The Romanian government, the Romanian parliament, mayors and local authorities, civil servants, managers, workers, entrepreneurs, farmers, teachers, students, doctors, scientists, engineers, bankers, lawyers, householders, indeed all Romanians are involved in the transition; all can contribute and all can benefit. One potentially significant aspect of the transition to which all can contribute and from which all can benefit is improving Romania's energy efficiency. To be sure, the Romanian government, with the support of parliament, needs to establish the appropriate framework, a coherent set of policies, laws and regulations that can be implemented and enforced. Either implicitly or explicitly this framework could include a practical manifestation of a national strategy for energy efficiency. But the government's role in this strategy should be clearly limited. In a democratic market economy, energy efficiency is everyone's business, not that of government alone, or even predominantly.

To a foreign specialist this is perhaps the most important message to convey. With access to the necessary information, and the freedom to act on it as they see fit, Romanians themselves can decide what measures to take and how to take them. They can ask for help; but they do not have to ask for permission, or wait for 'someone else' to do it. Energy efficiency offers ideal opportunities to develop this healthy attitude. The simplest energy efficiency measures – plugging leaks and draughts, turning off lights and machines when they are not in use, taking personal responsibility for basic 'good housekeeping' – are available to everyone. These measures can start reducing waste and cutting costs immediately, while making people more aware of how fuels, electricity and heat are being used, and how they might be used better. In households, schools, hospitals, public buildings, offices, farms, factories and other workplaces, noticing the potential for improvement is the first essential step. Deciding how best to go about it may entail more specialized help, to evaluate the technical and economic options and to put them into effect; but everyone can notice the potential. The key principle to keep in mind is that energy efficiency, properly implemented, does not reduce services: indeed, it can enhance them, while lowering costs and alleviating environmental impacts.

To a foreign specialist, energy efficiency appears to offer Romania and Romanians an abundance of opportunities for constructive initiatives at every level from the governmental to the personal. However, if the concept is to be truly effective, the impetus towards it must come from Romanians themselves; and it is already doing so. In June 1994 Romanian energy specialists staged Romania's second National Energy Conference of the 1990s, at the resort of Neptun on the Black Sea coast. The theme of the 1994 Conference was 'Towards Sustainable Energy Efficiency for Romania'. Nearly 1,500 delegates attended, and more than 300 papers were presented, on every conceivable aspect of energy and energy efficiency. The concept of energy efficiency has already fired the imagination of Romanian specialists. Some of the policy proposals they are putting forward are itemized concisely in Appendix 1.

In an OECD country, participants in a 'energy' conference in the 1990s tend to be economists and accountants. Participants in the 1994 Romanian conference were still predominantly scientists and engineers; but the 1994 conference included more economists than the precursor conference in 1992, reflecting the growing understanding in Romania that energy issues are not purely technical. In a market economy, costs and prices play a central role in energy policy, as a basis for comparing alternative options. As economic reform in Romania proceeds and markets are liberalized, energy prices should deliver realistic signals to decision-makers at every level, from ministry to household. Only in such a context can energy efficiency become a valid, consistent and coherent aspect of energy policy and economic policy overall.

As Romanians themselves get to grips with improving their country's energy systems and energy efficiency, the international dimension also becomes more prominent. The 1994 conference involved many more foreign participants, from more countries, than the 1992 conference. On the opening day of the conference the author of the present study gave the final keynote address, outlining the basis of the study and stressing the importance of international dialogue and international cooperation on energy and efficiency. For many months, analysts both inside and outside Romania have been preoccupied with financial problems arising from the need for new investment to modernize Romania. In the energy field, however, many of the most useful immediate measures would actually incur comparatively modest costs. In most instances they follow directly from 'comparing notes', as Romanians and non-Romanians describe to each other how their energy systems work – not just the physical, technological systems but also the institutions, organizations, laws, regulations, education and so on. This is a two-way process. OECD countries, too, are now deeply embroiled in vigorous rethinking of their entire energy policies, to deal with changed circumstances worldwide – low oil prices, increased environmental pressures, technical innovations, privatizing and restructuring supply industries, and many other factors. Energy issues are taking OECD countries, too, into novel and unfamiliar territory.

Consider, for instance, energy statistics. No one can make satisfactory plans for the future without knowing what the situation is now. Romania's system of collecting and analyzing energy statistics is very different from systems long established in OECD countries. However, even in OECD countries these traditional systems of statistics do not reveal enough about how fuels and electricity are actually used, about the services they provide, and about how end-use hardware – buildings, lighting, electric motors, household appliances and so on – actually performs in practice. International cooperation on reorganizing energy statistics would be immediately and probably mutually valuable, and not very costly.

Another example is legislation, regulation and standards. Both inside and outside Romania, laws, regulations and standards relating to energy are being steadily revised and refined, to restructure the framework of energy activities and make it more appropriate for the new shapes of energy future that seem to be emerging. Expanding international cooperation in this area, devising and drafting suitable instruments, would likewise be beneficial and comparatively inexpensive.

Energy forecasting, developing of projections and scenarios for possible futures, also offers scope for international cooperation. Techniques and methodologies that can cope with the ever vaster range of possible futures, and give plausible guidance, are by no means reliably available anywhere yet; the track record of forecasting for more than two decades, nationally and in international bodies, has been frankly embarrassing. Here again countries can learn from each other, not least about past mistakes.

One particularly intriguing area is that of detailed energy auditing of existing facilities. Romania has a remarkably broad range of different types of industrial plant, and many different manufacturing capabilities. Some, to be sure, are probably too inefficient or obsolescent to warrant further expenditure; others, however, may well be comparable with those in OECD countries, and some may actually be better than facilities elsewhere in central Europe. The only way to find out is to carry out detailed on-site examinations and assessments of the individual facilities. Here again, the cost of finding out would not be prohibitive; and it would provide essential information for both Romanian and non-Romanian businesspeople, to identify the best ways to utilize scarce capital.

International cooperation of this kind is valuable and comparatively easy. By enhancing mutual understanding, it can lay the foundations for broader and more substantive joint activities. In the 1990s, the rebuilding that matters most is not the material reconstruction of power stations, refineries, factories, residential blocks and so on. What need to be rebuilt above all, and indeed first of all, are attitudes of mind, individually and communally, both inside and outside Romania. Romania's energy offers a wealth of opportunities for fresh insights and fresh initiatives, for Romanians themselves and for their foreign partners. All can take part, and all can benefit. The potential is there, and the process is under way.

# Appendix 1

## Concise Energy Policy Proposals

Listed here are policy proposals put forward by Romanian specialists from ICEMENERG and ARCE in the course of the present study. They are offered for consideration by Romanian policy-makers, as policy options worth considering.

### Energy statistics

1. Gathering and processing energy statistics in Romania should be reorganized into a system better suited to the requirements of a democratic market economy. This measure should receive high priority; it is essential to support other energy policy measures, it should be comparatively low in cost and it could benefit significantly from international cooperation. The reorganization should establish a system of energy statistics fulfilling three essential functions. The statistical system should assist the government to form, to implement and to manage energy policy; it should meet statutory and other requirements to bring it into line with obligations and recommendations laid down by international bodies; and above all it should provide the public, including commercial and industrial planners and decision-makers, with ready access to relevant, reliable and timely information about Romania's energy use and supply.

2. Statistics about the supply of fuels and electricity should be distinguished from statistics about the use of fuels and electricity. To take optimal advantage of opportunities to improve Romania's energy systems, much better statistical information about the end-uses of different fuels and electricity in Romania is urgently needed. A coherent and comprehensive system to gather

and process statistics on end use should be designed and implemented as soon as possible.

3. The National Statistics Commission gathers and presents general energy statistics on a national basis; the authorities and companies responsible for individual sectors – oil, coal, gas, electricity and so on – should also gather and present sectoral statistics.

4. Gathering and processing of local and regional statistics, at the levels of cities and counties should be encouraged, to allow both international and internal comparisons.

5. A special programme should be devoted to end-use statistics: the terminology, the system approach and experimental applications in all specific end-use sectors. In Romania such information is essentially non-existent (although, in fairness, it is also far from complete elsewhere).

6. End-use surveys should utilize sampling methods and ad hoc occasional activities to learn the state of the art on specific issues.

7. Because cogeneration, combined heat and power and district heating play such a prominent role in Romania, and because improving the systems will entail major capital expenditure, the sector deserves continuing particular attention. The Romanian experience, supported by relevant, pertinent and reliable statistical data, could be an asset of value to other countries, including industrial countries that are only now beginning to expand their use of cogeneration and district heating.

8. Romanian national efforts and international assistance should promote private agencies to gather and process energy statistics, especially demand-side and end-use statistics.

9. Volunteers could also participate in sampling and collecting statistical data.

10. Research and academic institutes must play an active role in the field of energy statistics. One institute – possibly ICEMENERG – should become the focal point for the programme to reform Romania's energy statistics.

**Institutions and organizations**

1. A high priority should be given to increasing the autonomy of the managements of energy RAs in their day-to-day activities. The quota system for allocating fuel, electricity and heat supplies should be replaced with appropriate commercial contracts between suppliers and users. For those parts of the Romanian energy system that are natural monopolies, a regulatory body separate from the MoI should be established, with appropriate regulatory powers. International cooperation could assist in devising the appropriate institutional structures and drafting the necessary legislation. Where possible, sub-units of RAs should be freed for privatization, and their relationships with former parent organizations put on a contractual basis.

2. The Romanian Energy Conservation Agency, ARCE, should be restructured and reorganized in line with studies carried out together with ADEME of France. Its autonomy should be increased and its activities extended.

3. Fuel, electricity and heat suppliers should be involved in activities to improve the efficient end-use of energy, applying the concept of demand-side management.

4. Research institutes with different specialisms in energy and technology should establish a network of collaboration to improve efficiency across the whole range of extraction, conversion and utilization of different forms of energy.

5. Professional organizations and associations in the energy field should develop activities to improve the knowledge and cultivate the interest of the general public about energy efficiency.

6. Themes relating to efficient use of energy should be introduced into the scholastic programmes of secondary schools, institutes of higher education with a technical and economic focus, and centres for professional training and qualifications.

**Laws, regulations and financial framework**

1. High priority should be given to complete the drafting and passage of an energy law, an environmental protection law and possibly a separate law specifically concerning energy efficiency. International cooperation and assistance in drafting these laws would be beneficial, and the measures – at least in themselves – would be comparatively low in cost, although they might lead to consequent costs both to the government, for monitoring and enforcement, and to enterprises, for compliance. The Synergy programme of the EU is already providing relevant support for drafting laws on energy and on energy efficiency.

2. Legal regulations concerning the quality of building construction, and obligations to be met by new buildings, should be introduced.

3. Standards for the energy performance of those types of household appliance and industrial equipment that use large amounts of energy should be established. Household appliances and industrial plant should carry labels describing their energy performance.

4. District energy centres, to advise energy users about problems of efficient use of energy should be set up. These centres should be subsidized from the government budget and/or by the fuel and electricity suppliers.

5. The government budget should give financial support to model installations to demonstrate energy efficiency.

6. Householders who modernize old buildings should receive financial assistance from the government budget, and advantageous credit terms.

7. A system of taxes and fiscal measures should be established to promote official policy in the energy field, including substitution between different fuels in end-uses, and efficient use of energy.

8. The prices of energy carriers should be aligned with those of the global market, and where possible set by market forces. The systems of tariffs for electrical and thermal energy should be refined, as should systems of measurement.

## Energy forecasting and planning

1. Energy projections and strategies, from primary resources to techological designs to final uses, should be developed, taking into consideration problems of environmental conservation and efficient use of energy. International cooperation on methodologies, data management and collection and other aspects would be beneficial and comparatively low in cost.

2. Projections from ICEMENERG and other Romanian bodies should be analyzed critically in comparison, for example, with those from the World Bank and the IEA for the countries of central Europe.

## Relevant technical and industrial experience and capabilities

1. A high priority should be given to detailed assessment of Romania's existing industrial structure, its current performance, capabilities, economic status and potential, to identify priorities for improvement at one extreme or closure at the other. Generalizations are misleading; ideally, on-site inspections and discussions, perhaps with foreign counterparts, would be desirable. Such assessments themselves would be comparatively low in cost, and would clarify the much larger potential sums that might be needed for refitting and upgrading to fulfil market requirements, and give potential investors, financial supporters and customers a basis on which to reach decisions.

2. New technologies and improvements of existing technologies that could be applied on a large scale in Romania, and for which Romania has – at least in part – a basis of engineering and equipment manufacture, include the following:

- variable-speed motor drives;
- regenerative burner tip systems for industrial plant with flames;
- drying, firing and baking with microwaves – forms and cores in metal foundries, textile products and food;
- burning coal instead of natural gas in cement plants;
- partial replacement of coke by powdered coal in iron smelters;
- recovering waste heat with vaporization cooling systems in heating plant and metal foundries;

- equipping industrial plant with burner control systems; automatic control of operation of metal foundries;
- refitting the Slatina aluminium factory with new smelting pots and automation of operations for aluminium fabrication;
- refitting the electrolytic caustic soda factories at Rimnicul Valcea and Borzeşti with titanium electrodes and membrane technology;
- modernizing glass foundries – geometry, burner control, insulation – and carbide and ferroalloy plants;
- improving existing technologies for manufacturing refractory and insulating material;
- abandoning some technologies that are heavy users of energy in extractive industries, including subterranean combustion of petroleum, deep seams of lignite, deep mining of coal;
- applying new and unconventional technologies in machine-building, for example electroerosion, vibration stress relief, brick finishing with coke, replacement of rotating converters in induction heating furnaces;
- applying technologies for painting and enamelling with lower energy use;
- refitting RENEL power stations burning fuel oil or natural gas into gas and steam combined cycle plant;
- improving technology for fabricating graphite electrodes for steel making, with significant effects on energy use in the steel industry;
- rehabilitating some 100 irrigation systems, with areas of up to 200,000 ha, 3.1 million ha in total, that now have open canals and an efficiency below 70% for transfer of water.

3. Modern measuring systems should be introduced, including:

- energy management systems (EMS), based on Romanian engineering and software with some imported hardware components, for industrial enterprises and sectors, public institutions, agricultural organizations, and public transport;
- heat meters in district heating grids and for end-users; accurate meters for natural gas and liquid fuels;
- modern tariff and billing systems for electricity;
- modern temperature-measuring systems for furnaces.

4. Financial backing should be found to create a network of private services for improving energy efficiency, including:

- consultancy,
- auditing and expertise,
- engineering,
- fabrication of equipment and components,
- commercialization,
- doing the work;

for which the necessary technical capability already exists. Likewise, support should be found to create some regional 'energy centres', for meetings, expositions, demonstrations and training.

5. A high priority should be given to updating and expanding databases on energy efficiency in industrial, agricultural and transport technology, both Romanian and foreign. The cost would be comparatively low, and international cooperation would be beneficial.

**International opportunities for cooperation**

1. Romanian energy specialists should be extensively informed about the possibilities and methodologies to use opportunities created by international plans, for example those of the EU, the UN and other bodies. Means should include:

- special columns in publications;
- brochures and leaflets.

2. Condensed initial information should be available about business opportunities in the energy field in Romania, including:

- institutions;
- legal framework;
- partners;
- characteristics of the market.

3. Information should be disseminated in Romania about international offers of second-hand equipment and reusable plant of appropriate quality.

4. International connections between Romanian professional associations and international associations and federations should be extended.

5. Bilateral agreements of association or partnership between organizations and companies in Romania and similar bodies outside Romania should be encouraged, including:

- institutes;
- companies;
- research and development organizations;
- local authorities and municipalities.

6. Forms of collaboration between institutions of university education should be diversified, including:

- international networks of documentary information;
- refining programmes of education;
- teaching exchanges;
- study excursions;
- stages of doctorates;
- cooperation on interdisciplinary themes.

# Appendix 2

## Organizations in the Energy Field

### Academia Romana (Romanian Academy)

The Romanian Academy is the supreme scientific forum, comprising specialists in different fields of culture, arts, technology and spirituality. The Academy has an energy section, currently led by Academician Gleb Dragan, professor at Bucureşti Polytechnic University. The energy section promotes technical and scientific progress in energy, and disseminates information in turn to specialists. It is not concerned with fundamental research.

### Energy Research and Modernizing Institute (ICEMENERG)

ICEMENERG does applied technological research and development, technological engineering, consultancy and manufacture of prototypes in the fields of electricity, heat, nuclear energy and unconventional energy. It is the specialized energy technology research and development institute of RENEL, of which it is a subordinate and within which it is organized like a research institute. Its headquarters are in Bucureşti.

### Nuclear Research Institute (ICN)

ICN does applied technical and technological research and development and technological engineering in the field of nuclear energy, and manufactures the nuclear fuel for the Cernavoda nuclear power station. Its headquarters are in Piteşti, about 100 km from Bucureşti, and it is a subordinate of RENEL.

## Institute for Research, Technological Engineering and Mining Design for Lignite (ICITPML)

ICITPML specializes in research activities, engineering technology and design for underground and opencast mining, and also works on technologies for lignite processing, to grade it and thus to improve it as a fuel. The energy characteristics of lignite also have been and are studied outside ICITPML, in particular at ICEMENERG and in the Faculty of Industrial Chemistry of Bucureşti Polytechnic University. The headquarters of ICITPML are in Craiova, 250 km from Bucureşti, and ICITPML is a subordinate of RAL.

## Centre for Research for Hard Coal (CCH)

CCH specializes in research activities and engineering technology for underground mining, and also works on technologies to process the hard coal extracted, to separate the brown coal to obtain coke and semicoke. For energy, it can take part in grading of coal fines and washery rejects destined to be burned in the Mintea power station. The energy characteristics of fuel destined for combustion in thermal power stations are well known, and have been determined by ICEMENERG; CCH is involved only in research in the field of preparation and grading of coal, technologies that have implications for the energy performance of fuel for thermal power stations. The headquarters of CCH are in Petroşani, the centre of the Jiu Valley coalfield, located about 400 km from Bucureşti; CCH is a subordinate of RAH.

## Institute for Research and Design for Petroleum and Gas (ICPPG)

ICPPG specializes in research activities, engineering technology and design for the extractive industry for petroleum and associated gas. Its headquarters are in Cimpina, about 100 km north of Bucureşti, and it is a subordinate of PETROM.

## Centre for Research and Design for Natural Gas (CCPGM)

CCPGM specializes in research activities and design for the natural gas extraction industry, for transport and conditioning of natural gas. Its headquarters are in Mediaş, in the centre of the Transilvania gasfield, about 450 km from Bucureşti. It is a specialized subsidiary of ICPPG in Cimpina, for natural gas.

**Institute for Energy Studies and Design (ISPE)**

ISPE specializes in drawing up studies and designs in the fields of electricity, heat and nuclear energy. Its headquarters are in Bucureşti, and it is a subordinate of RENEL.

**Institute for Hydroelectricity Studies and Research (ISPH)**

ISPH specializes in drawing up studies and designs in the field of hydroelectric power plants and other hydro works. Its headquarters are in Bucureşti, and it is a subordinate of RENEL.

**Institute for Research and Design for Thermoelectric Equipment (ICPET SA)**

ICPET SA specializes in research activities, engineering technology and design for thermoelectric equipment of large and small capacity. It also works in advanced fields like magnetohydrodynamics (MHD) and fluidized-bed combustion. Its headquarters are in Bucureşti, and it is a subordinate of the Ministry of Industries.

**Institute for Research and Design for Electrotechnical Equipment (ICPE)**

ICPE specializes in research and design for electrical equipment and apparatus. It also works on renewable energy research, including solar and wind. Its headquarters are in Bucureşti, and it is a subordinate of the Ministry of Industries.

**Centre for Research for Machine Building Plant (CC-UCM)**

CC-UCM specializes in research activities for hydroelectric equipment – hydroelectric turbines, hydrogenerators and auxiliary hydraulic installations.

Because of industrial restructuring, the centre, which operated autonomously before 1989, is now integrated with the Machine Building Plant. It is located in the city of Reşiţa, in southwestern Romania, about 500 km from Bucureşti.

## University Energy Research Centres and Groups

The research activities of some university institutions of higher education have links with the Romanian energy industry; for instance, faculties of energy and mechanics conduct studies and research and give specialized training for personnel from the energy sector, through postuniversity courses and doctorates. Some universities also carry out fundamental energy research.

### Polytechnic University of Bucureşti

The faculty of energetics does work on thermal, electrical, hydro and nuclear energetics, and energy conservation. The faculty of mechanical engineering does work on steam generators, steam and gas turbines, and nuclear engineering.

### Technical University of Timişoara

The faculty of electrotechnics and energetics does work on steam generators, electroenergetic equipment and systems, and aerogenerator equipment.

### Gheorge Asachi Technical University of Iaşi

The faculty of electrotechnics and energetics does work on electroenergetic equipment, and on the operation and reliability of electrical systems.

### Other Romanian energy organizations

Some other organizations operating with a legal statute, in general non-governmental, declare, practise and promote activities in the energy field, and express a professional interest for energy specialists. Private firms that offer consulting services and draw up studies are rapidly increasing in number in Romania, but they are not itemized here.

## Romanian Technical Association for Energy Efficiency (ATEER)

ATEER promotes energy efficiency in all sectors of the national economy, and expresses the professional interests of all people working to increase energy efficiency, regardless of the level of their professional qualifications. Its headquarters are in Bucureşti, at ICEMENERG.

## Society for Optimizing Energy Use (SOCER)

SOCER promotes the energy efficiency of industrial processes through modern techniques and technologies, emphasizing energy conservation by consumers. Its headquarters are in Craiova, and it publishes an interesting and useful quarterly.

## Romanian Solar Energy Society (SORES)

The direct purpose of SORES is to carry out scientific research on capturing, converting and using solar energy in all its forms. It does research, provides information and documentation, consulting and educational activities, and organizes scientific demonstrations in Romania. Its headquarters are in Bucureşti, at ICPE, and it has branches in seven large cities in Romania.

## Romanian Wind Energy Association (ROWEA)

ROWEA proposes to support and encourage the promotion of wind energy in Romania, to exchange technical and economic information about wind energy applications, to hold a national registration day with documentation about ROWEA, to counsel the Romanian government for wind energy and to draw up annual programmes and perspectives in the field. Its headquarters are in Bucureşti, at ICEMENERG, and it has branches in many large cities in Romania.

# Romanian Society of Energy Engineers (SIER)

SIER aims to increase the role and the efficiency of the activity of energy engineers from the viewpoint of the development of Romanian energetics and the national economy. It aims to do specialized research, to protect the title of the profession of energy engineer and to exercise it effectively, to recognize and defend the respect of the dignity and social prestige of engineers, to promote modern and efficient energy legislation, and to collaborate with other specialists. The headquarters of SIER are in Bucureşti, at ISPE.

# General Association of Engineers of Romania (AGIR): Energy Section

The Energy Section of AGIR promotes the general interests of the energy community in all government bodies and in specialized institutes working in the energy field. It supports the recognition and defends the professional interests of engineers in general, and of energy specialists in particular. AGIR organizes technical debates on important problems of society, and recommends to the government or government bodies the promotion of fundamental objectives and opinions of the professionals, in light of the aims and policies of national economic programmes.

# Thermal Power Engineers Society (SIT)

SIT promotes the professional interests of engineers specializing in thermo-energetics, in accord with the general interest of Romanian society, aiming to use the abilities of these specialists for the economic progress of the country. The headquarters of SIT are in Bucureşti, in the energy faculty at the Polytechnic University, and also at ISPE for cogeneration and district heating engineers. SIT, founded in 1972, is the oldest society for energy professionals in Romania.

# Appendix 3

## Romanian Institutions and Organizations in the Energy Field: Contacts

**Official bodies**

Ministerul Industriilor – Directia Generala a Energie (Ministry of Industries – Directorate General for Energy)
Calea Victoriei 152, sector 1, Bucureşti
Tel.: 6505020
Fax: 3120513

Agenţia Romana pentru Conservarea Energiei (ARCE) (Romanian Agency for Energy Conservation)
Str. Splaiul Independentei nr. 202 A, sector 6, Bucureşti
Tel.: 6376374
Fax: 3123197

Comisia Nationala de Statistica (National Statistics Commission)
Str. Stavropoleos nr. 6, sector 3, Bucureşti
Tel.: 6158200
Fax: 3145560

Federaţia Patronala de Electricitate, Petrol şi Gaze (ELPEGA) (Electricity, Petroleum and Gas Employers' Federation)
Str. Biserica Amzei nr. 23, sector 1, Bucureşti
Tel./fax: 3128416

**Regies autonomes (autonomous administrations)**

Regia Autonoma de Electricitate (RENEL) (Romanian Electricity
Authority)
Bd. Magheru nr. 33, sector 1, Bucureşti
Tel.: 6596000, 6507220
Fax: 3120290

Regia Autonoma a Petrolului (PETROM) (Romanian Petroleum
Authority)
Calea Victoriei nr. 109, sector 1, Bucureşti
Tel.: 6502345
Fax: 3129635

Regia Autonoma a Gazului (ROMGAZ) (Romanian Gas Authority)
Piata Trandafirilor, Targu-Mureş
Tel.: 065 437601

Regia Autonoma a Huilei (RAH) (Romanian Hard Coal Authority)
Str. Timisoarei nr.1, Petroşani
Tel.: 054 541315

Regia Autonoma a Lignitului (RAL) (Romanian Lignite Authority)
Calea Bucureşti nr.75, Targu Jiu
Tel.: 053 913031

Regia Autonoma a Minelor (RAM) (Romanian Mines Authority)
Str. Mendeleev nr.34-36, sector 1, Bucureşti
Tel.: 6597045

Regia Autonoma de Distributie a Energiei Termice (RADET) – Bucureşti
(Bucureşti District Heating Authority)
Str. Cavafii Vechi nr. 15, sector 3, Bucureşti
Tel.: 6147600
Fax: 3155874

**Research and design institutes**

Institutul de Cercetari şi Modernizari Energetice (ICEMENERG) (Central
Energy Research and Modernizing Institute)
Bd. Energeticienilor nr. 8, sector 3, Bucureşti
Tel.: 3216966/3213241
Fax: 3211010
(RENEL subsidiary)

Institutul de Studii şi Proiectari Energetice (ISPE) (Energy Study and
Design Institute)
Bd. Lacul Tei nr. 1, sector 2, Bucureşti
Tel.: 2107080
Fax: 3123620
(RENEL subsidiary)

Institutul de Studii şi Proiectari Hidroenergetice (ISPH) (Hydroenergy
Study and Design Institute)
Bd. Carol nr. 29, sector 2, Bucureşti
Tel.: 6147270
(RENEL subsidiary)

Institutul de Studii Geofizice şi Geotehnice (GEOTEC) (Geophysical and
Geotechnical Study Institute)
Str. Gala i nr. 5-7, sector 2, Bucureşti
Tel.: 6148550

Institutul de Cercetari Nucleare – Piteşti (ICN) (Nuclear Research
Institute)
PO BOX 78 Piteşti
Tel.: 048 612610
Fax: 048 612449
(RENEL subsidiary)

Institutul de Cercetare şi Proiectare pentru Electrotehnica (ICPE SA)
(Electrotechnical Research and Design Institute)
Splaiul Unirii nr. 313, sector 3, Bucureşti
Tel.: 3222813
Fax: 3213769

Institutul de Cercetare şi Proiectare pentru Masini Electrice,
Transformatoare, Echipamente Electrice şi Tractiune (ICMET) (Research
Institute for Electrical Machines, Transformers, Electrical Plant and
Traction)
Calea Bucureşti nr. 144, Craiova
Tel.: 051 143795
Fax: 051 163210

Institutul de Cercetare şi Proiectare pentru Echipamente Termoenergetice
(ICPET) (Research and Design Institute for Thermoenergetic Plant)
Sos. Berceni nr. 104, sector 4, Bucureşti
Tel.: 6833825
Fax: 3832747

Institutul de Cercetari pentru Constructii (INCERC) (Building Research
Institute)
Sos. Pantelimon nr. 266, sector 3, Bucureşti
Tel.: 6274085
Fax: 3218062

**Producers of energy plant and appliances ('Commercial Societies' SC)**
SC EL-CO SA
Str. Fabricii nr 9, Targu Secuiesc, jud. Covasna
Tel.: 067 362520
Fax: 092 151458
(Low-voltage electrical equipment)

SC Aparate Electrice de Masura 'AEM' SA
Calea Buziasului nr.26, Timişoara
Tel.: 056 162010
Fax: 056 190928
(Electrical and electronic measurement and control equipment)

SC ELECTROAPARATAJ SA
Bd. Pierre de Coubertin nr. 3-5, sector 2, Bucureşti
Tel.: 6535430
Fax: 3127840
(Low-voltage electrical equipment)

SC ELECTROMAGNETICA SA
Calea Rahovei nr. 266-268, sector 5, Bucureşti
Tel.: 7802020
Fax: 3123210
(Voltmeters, relays, AC/DC rectifiers)

SC ELECTROMETAL SA
Str. Circumvala iunii nr. l, Timişoara
Tel.: 056 145074
Fax: 056 145369
(Electrotechnical household products)

SC ELECTROMOTOR SA
Bd. Republicii nr. 21, Timişoara
Tel.: 056 192004
Fax: 056 192003
(Single-phase and three-phase electric motors (0.25/2, 2kW))

SC ELECTROPRECIZIA SA
Str. Parcului nr. 18, Sacele, jud. Braşov
Tel.: 068 270783
Fax: 068 271998
(Electrical equipment for motor vehicles)

SC ELECTROTURRIS SA
Str. Portului nr. 7, Turnu Magurele, jud. Teleorman
Tel.: 047 414725
Fax: 047 413529
(Asynchronous three-phase motors)

ARCTIC SA
Str. 13 Decembrie nr. 210, Gaeşti, jud. Damboviţa
Tel.: 045 710565

GRIRO
Calea Griviţei nr. 355-357, Bucureşti
Tel.: 6654090
Fax: 3128742
(Technical equipment for energy industry)

IMEP SA
Soşeaua Bucureşti nr. 112, Piteşti
Tel.: 048 635050
Fax: 048 636452
(Asynchronous single-phase and three-phase motors for household
electrical appliances)

ACUMULATORUL SA
Bd. Biruinţei nr. 98, sector 2, Bucureşti
Tel.: 6272080
Fax: 3128123
(Lead batteries)

APARATAJ ELECTRIC SA
Str. Garii nr. 79, Titu, jud. Damboviţa
Tel.: 6147968
Fax: 045 650412
(Low-voltage electrical apparatus)

**AUTOMATICA SA**
Calea Floreasca nr. 159, sector 1, Bucureşti
Tel.: 6795394
Fax: 6333941
(Programmable robots)

**CASIROM SA**
Str. 22 Decembrie nr. 35, Turda, jud. Cluj
Tel.: 064 316250
Fax: 064 312804
(Refractory materials)

**ELECTROTEHNICA SA**
Str. Lujerului nr. 42, sector 6, Bucureşti
Tel.: 7453610
Fax: 7453610
(Electrotechnical and automation apparatus)

**CONECT SA**
Bd. Dimitrie Pompei nr. 10, sector 2, Bucureşti
Tel.: 6885040
Fax: 3128810
(Connectors, circuit-breakers, commutators)

**ELCARO SA**
Str. Draganeşti, km. 4 Slatina, jud. Olt
Tel.: 049 415699
Fax: 049 415099
(Electrical cables)

**ELECTROARGES SA**
Str. Albeşti nr. 12, Curtea de Argeş, jud. Arge
Tel.: 048 711705
Fax: 048 713552
(Household and industrial electrical equipment)

**ELECTROFAR**
Str. Parang nr. 76, sector 1, Bucureşti
Tel.: 6672040
Fax: 3128615
(Lighting assemblies)

**ELECTROMURES SA**
Str. Calaraşilor nr. 112-114, Targu Mureş
Tel.: 065 417817
Fax: 065 417100
(Household and industrial electrical equipment)

**ELECTRONICA SA**
Bd. Prof. Dimitrie Pompei nr. 5-7, sector 2, Bucureşti
Tel.: 6882080
Fax: 3122260
(Audiovisual products)

**ELECTROTEL SA**
Str. Dunarii nr. 279, Alexandria, jud. Teleorman
Tel.: 047 312008
Fax: 047 315471
(Electrical automation apparatus)

**FRIGOCOM SA**
Bd. Timişoara nr. 58, sector 6, Bucureşti
Tel.: 7451895
Fax: 7453745
(Commercial refrigeration plant)

**PRECIZIA SA**
Str. Teodosie Rudeanu nr. 12-14, sector 1, Bucureşti
Tel.: 6172539
Fax: 3128254
(Water and heat meters)

**ROMLUX SA**
Str. Campulung nr. 121, Targovişte
Tel.: 045 611616
Fax: 045 615778
(Electric lamps and luminaires)

**UZINELE ELECTROPUTERE SA**
Calea Bucureşti nr. 144, Craiova
Tel.: 051 142077
Fax: 051 142077
(Electric locomotives, high-power high-voltage electrical plant, motors, etc.)

**VULCAN SA**
Str. Sebastian nr. 88, sector 5, Bucureşti
Tel.: 7815388
Fax: 3120185
(Boilers)

**STEAUA ELECTRICA SA**
Str. Garii nr. 2, Fieni, jud. Damboviţa
Tel.: 045 774270
Fax: 045 774259
(Electric lamps)

**UMEB SA**
Str. Gen.Vasile Milea nr. 4, sector 6, Bucureşti
Tel.: 7312501
Fax: 7317554
(Electric motors for all uses, generating sets, etc.)

**Professional associations**

Asociaţia Tehnica de Eficienţa Energetice din Romania (ATEER)
(Romanian Technical Association for Energy Efficiency)
Bd. Energeticienilor nr. 8, sector 3, Bucureşti
Tel.: 3216966
Fax: 3129315

Societatea Inginerilor Energeticieni din Romania (SIER) (Romanian
Society of Energy Engineers)
Bd. Lacul Tei nr. 1, sector 2, Bucureşti
Tel.: 2107080

Societatea pentru Optimizarea Consumurilor Energetice din Romania
(SOCER) (Romanian Society for Optimizing Energy Use)
Str. Brestei nr. 2, Craiova, jud. Dolj
Tel.: 051 118378

Comitetul Roman pentru Electrotermie (CRE) (Romanian Electrothermal
Committee)
Splaiul Independentei nr. 313,
Fac. Energetica, Universitatea Politehnica, Bucureşti
Tel.: 6314010

Societatea Inginerilor Termoenergeticieni (SIT) (Thermal Power Engineers
Society)
Bd. Lacul Tei nr. 1, sector 2, Bucureşti
Tel.: 2107080

Societatea Romana a Termotehnicienilor (Romanian Society of Thermal
Technologists)
Bd. Carol I, nr. 176, sector 2, Bucureşti
Tel.: 6424200/int.139

Societatea pentru Promovarea Energiilor Regenerabile Inepuizabile şi Noi (SPERIN) (Society for Promoting Renewable, Regenerable and New Energies)
Splaiul Independentei nr. 313, sector 6, Bucureşti
Tel.: 6314010

Asociaţia Romana pentru Energia Vantului (ROWEA) (Romanian Wind Energy Association)
Bd. Energeticienilor nr. 8, sector 3, Bucureşti
Tel.: 3216966
Fax: 3129315

Asociaţia Generala a Inginerilor din Romania (AGIR) (Romanian General Association of Engineers)
Calea Victoriei 118, sector 1, Bucureşti
Tel.: 3125531

# Index